Liberty's Triumph Through the Lens of Dutch Brazil

J.M. WALSH

Liberty's Triumph Through the Lens of Dutch Brazil

Including a revised and abridged translation of

Friar Manuel Calado's

O Valoroso Lucideno e Triunfo da Liberdade

(Lisbon, 1648)

Inspired Ink : LOS ANGELES

Published by
Inspired Ink
Los Angeles

Direct inquiries to:

J.M. Walsh
2060-D E. Avenida de Los Arboles #270
Thousand Oaks, CA 91362 USA

Liberty's Triumph Through the Lens of Dutch Brazil
ISBN: 978-0-578-66030-1

To the *orixás* that guide us.

Also by the author:

Dial In: Soka Buddhism on the Religious Spectrum (2018)

Your Enlightened Mind Wants to Know (2012)

Available through Amazon in print and e-book editions

CONTENTS

Part One

Dutch Brazil and Liberty's Triumph

Liberty is a grand ideal. It's often fused in our minds with *freedom* and *equality*. Much has been sacrificed to obtain what these three words represent. Each resonates in its own way. Most of us want freedom: to stand unbowed before any authority, as independent agents and masters of our destinies. Unbounded, though, some among us will trample the liberties of others, whose rights deserve equal protection, not the crushing boot of an oppressor.

Liberty, freedom, and equality are enduring topics for scholars and pundits alike. Thinkers debate their significance or opine about their origins. For instance, did America give birth to liberty's modern incarnation, or is Britain or perhaps France its progenitor? Venerable documents are at times trotted out—such as the Declaration of Independence (USA), the Declaration of the Rights of Man and of the Citizen (France), or the Magna Carta (England)—to support one stance or another.

Most English speakers have been taught that liberty came from Britain. The view is so ingrained that it passes without comment. One recent example among thousands comes from the respected periodical *The Economist*. An editorial states that belief in freedom is a British notion, which spread throughout the world.[1] Is that true? As of 1685, Great Britain's monarch ruled by divine right with few limits. The Church of England, which he headed, was the homeland's state religion; other faiths were stifled. A newly ascended ruler plotted to return the realm to Roman Catholicism. Equality was the pipedream of rebels. The same year, France's Sun King Louis XIV revoked tolerance for Protestants, who thereafter suffered vicious persecution. Often overlooked is the fact that as of 1685 the Netherlands had been a republic for a century. Its province of Holland had the freest press in the world. Freedom of conscience was a guiding principle for the Dutch.

Contrary to the inclinations of anglophiles, therefore, an honest review points to the Dutch Republic as being central to the emergence of liberty as we know it today. We can access evidence for

---

[1] 1 February 2020, North America edition, page 10.

the republic's part by peering through the lens of Dutch Brazil. The former outpost is a little-known blip dating from the middle of the seventeenth century. Its story—told in this book—casts into high relief a monumental shift in attitudes. Within the historical narrative lies an enduring message about liberty that still reverberates.

We begin in Part One with a brief history of events. Why did the Dutch challenge the once-mighty Portuguese for control of their biggest colony? In Part Two we enter the turbulent world of Dutch Brazil. We do so through the unique perspective of one who straddled the Dutch and Portuguese realms. His account holds elements both familiar and alien. The contrast highlights the changes taking place during a key juncture in liberty's expansion. We end in Part Three by considering the spread of a new paradigm for knowledge that pushed notions of liberty in novel directions. The embrace of liberty required our forbearers to revise how they thought about other people. Part Three is, in a sense, the history of a very big idea.

Liberty In Context. What do we mean by liberty? I find especially relevant the following words spoken by one of America's most revered jurists, Judge Learned Hand:[2]

> Liberty lies in the hearts of men and women; when it dies there, no constitution, no law, no court can save it(.) What is this liberty that must lie in the hearts of men and women? It is not the ruthless, the unbridled will; it is not the freedom to do as one likes. That is the denial of liberty and leads straight to its overthrow. A society in which men recognize no check on their freedom soon becomes a society where freedom is the possession of only a savage few, as we have learned to our sorrow. What then is the spirit of liberty? I cannot define it; I can only tell you my own faith. *The spirit of liberty is the spirit which is not too sure that it is right;* the spirit of liberty is the spirit which seeks to understand the minds of other men and women; the spirit of liberty is the

---

[2] *The Spirit of Liberty*, speech delivered in Central Park, New York City, 21 May 1944; emphasis added.

spirit which weighs their interests alongside its own without bias(.)

He uttered these sentiments near the end of an epic war against genocidal fascism. The quotation expresses an insight that lies at the heart of this book. Whatever we might believe, shouldn't we be willing to pull back from it—even if but slightly—to acknowledge that others, rightly from their points of view, can think differently? Isn't liberty found in that small space we accord to one another? Societies dominated by those who won't yield an inch are in the grip of Hand's "savage few."

His observation calls to mind the musings of Vladimir Putin, Russia's resurrected czar and longstanding president. He said that a bear needs to roam freely over the taiga, or northern forests. The metaphor, of course, is that Russia—more precisely its upper crust of oligarchs and senior apparatchiks—must dominate everything and everyone within its historical sphere of influence. The bear enjoys its freedom at the expense of lesser beasts. They certainly aren't the bear's equals.

In ordinary usage, liberty and freedom overlap. Equality is related to both but is also to some extent in conflict with them. Notions of liberty or freedom—although conceived of differently—existed in both Portugal and the Netherlands during the days of Dutch Brazil. Early inklings of equality could be found in the Netherlands, while the concept was anathema for the Portuguese.

Equality is typically distinguished between equality of rights and equality of outcomes. The former was once the more salient of the two. Nobles of various degrees had concomitant privileges that were prohibited to the lower orders. Slaves were treated as subhuman. For reasons to be described, nobles as a class were somewhat less dominant in the Netherlands than in Portugal. Chattel slavery existed in Portugal itself; it appears not to have been widely permitted in the Netherlands proper. Its colonies were a different matter. Revolutions in the eighteenth century resulted in titles of nobility being barred in America, and in the mass beheading of nobles in France. Slavery was in large part outlawed during the nineteenth century. Today, rights equality is widely accepted in theory, although more limited in practice.

Equality of outcomes has moved to the forefront. Our political discourse now swirls with proposals for remedying inequalities of wealth, income, healthcare access, career or educational opportunities, and other such social goods. Activists denounce injustices committed along the lines of socio-economic class, race or ethnicity, gender, and so on. However, full equality of outcomes is probably unattainable. It would require a nearly total curtailment of liberty. Largescale experiments with outcome equality have failed. The most successful surviving communist regimes, in China and Vietnam, have thrown in the towel on outcome equality. Socialist states that remain doctrinaire—North Korea comes to mind—have kleptocratic elites and an equality of misery for the masses, which isn't an appealing combination. Healthy societies seem to require some blend of rights equality, outcome equality, and liberty.

The natural tension between liberty and equality is what largely drives politics in modern democracies. In the United States, for instance, in broad strokes Republicans claim the banner of liberty, while Democrats advocate most strongly for equality. Similar orientations, although more typically with pairings of multiple parties, are common in parliamentary democracies.

Liberty or freedom, as noted, had differing connotations for the Portuguese and Dutch. In Portuguese, the word *Liberdade,* from Latin *Libertas,* generally covers most senses of both "freedom" and "liberty" in English. Dutch is a Germanic language; the word *Vrijheid,* etymologically related to "freedom," likewise corresponds to both words. "Freedom" is considered to be the broader of the two terms, whereas "liberty" connotes rights that are conditional in some way. In the ancient world, to be free meant one wasn't a slave, subject to a master. Roman law granted certain liberties to free citizens, such as the right to travel. The unfree had no liberties.

The distinction remained in force from Roman times until well into the European Middle Ages. Nobles and yeomen, as free subjects, retained certain customary liberties, such as the rights to carry weapons or assemble. The mass of peasantry, in contrast, had few if any rights. Peasants were often bonded or effectively enslaved as serfs. Serfs weren't bought and sold like chattel slaves. Rather, they were part of the land, like a pond or shed. Serfs were subjects of the feudal lord in possession of the land to which they were bound. The lord would change from time to time but the condition of serfdom did not.

Nowadays, Portugal and the Netherlands jointly subscribe to democratic norms and regulated capitalism as coequal comembers of supranational organizations such as the European Union and NATO. Back in the seventeenth century the Dutch embraced a relatively expansive take on individual freedom. The Portuguese, in contrast, remained largely mired in medievalism. Strangely enough, at present the Netherlands is a constitutional monarchy, not a republic, while Portugal deposed its king and became a republic in 1910. Democracy came much later.

A blurred line divided the two societies in the days of Dutch Brazil. Both domains were—as they remain—western European states with deep Roman roots. Latin was their shared elite literary language. Their once common Roman Catholic faith had been fractured by the Reformation barely a century beforehand. Ancient Rome's partial absorption of the early inhabitants of both Portugal and the Netherlands loomed large in the respective popular imaginations. The Portuguese considered themselves to be descendants of Lusitanians, an Ibero-Celtic tribal agglomeration. Rome subdued the Lusitanians in the second century BCE. Nations such as Brazil and Angola that share Portugal's cultural-linguistic heritage are still referred to as Lusophone, from Lusitania.

The republican Dutch, who fought against Iberian domination for decades, cobbled together a Roman-linked identity as Batavians. It served to rally the citizens of squabbling provinces in a common struggle for liberation. The Batavians were a Germanic tribe resident in the general vicinity of the modern Netherlands. Roman sources between the first century BCE and fourth century CE mention them sporadically. It appears that they were accorded some freedoms by the Romans, such as exemption from taxes, in return for providing soldiers and other military support. In the late eighteenth century the Dutch Republic was renamed the Batavian Republic. The colonial headquarters of the Dutch East India Company on the island of Java was called Batavia. It's now Jakarta, Indonesia's capital and largest city. From these examples, we can see that the Batavian legend was significant for the Dutch.

Despite their cultural affinities, public attitudes in the Netherlands and Portugal differed markedly. The respective treatment of Jews in the two lands provides an example of their conflicting conceptions of liberty. On the one hand, Portuguese liberty in the seventeenth century meant that members of the dominant class were free to persecute unconverted or secretly-practicing Jews. The presence of Jews was considered to be an affront to the obligatory Roman Catholic faith. No Portuguese subject was free to deny the Christ or sacraments of the official Church. The Dutch, on the other hand, scandalized the Portuguese by not prohibiting synagogues or the open practice of Judaism. A religion that denies Christ's divinity wasn't viewed as a threat to those who believe otherwise. Differing Dutch and Portuguese attitudes produced real-world consequences.

Dutch-style freedom is now embraced to some extent in many parts of the world. The Portuguese have in this respect become much more like the Dutch, rather than vice-versa. As evidence for this statement, consider a memorial erected in Lisbon for the quincentennial of an atrocity committed in 1506. Composed of a granite hemisphere affixed to a slab in a public square in the city's Rossio district, it bears the following inscription—here in translation—framed by the Star of David:

1506-2006
IN MEMORY OF
THE THOUSANDS OF
JEWS WHO WERE VICTIMS OF
INTOLERANCE AND RELIGIOUS FANATICISM
MURDERED IN THE MASSACRE
THAT BEGAN APRIL 19, 1506
IN THIS PLAZA
5266-5766

In 1497, the Jews of Portugal were ordered to convert to Christianity or else depart. At the time Jews made up an estimated twenty percent of the country's population. Many had only recently settled there as refugees from Spain. The Spanish Inquisition—first proclaimed in 1478—intensified in 1492; Jews were expelled from Spain that year. Sephardic Jewish culture had once flourished on the Iberian Peninsula. Roman Catholic Inquisitors employed asset forfeiture, torture, and painful death to root out Jews, Muslims, and the holders of heretical views. The poorest Jews had few places to go. Doors elsewhere in Europe were closed to them. Even those who converted, albeit under duress, remained tarred as former devotees of a hated creed.

On Easter Sunday 1506, with plague and famine ravaging Lisbon's desperate populace, worshippers in a Rossio cathedral beheld a vision of Jesus Christ. A former Jew pointed out that the image was an illusion. Incensed, two priests incited anti-Jewish fervor among the congregants. They killed the man who spoke out and then flooded a nearby neighborhood of Jewish converts to Catholicism. The enraged mob began to butcher the so-called "New Christians" by hand. The rampage went on for days.

How did two marginal countries situated on western Europe's outer fringes end up with such differing views of liberty? How is it that both had enviable runs as the most powerful maritime trading nations on earth: Portugal in the sixteenth century and the

Netherlands in the seventeenth? We'll first examine Portugal's rise and, thereafter, that of the Netherlands.

Portugal. The western Roman empire collapsed in the fifth century CE. Christianity had been its official religion. The territory making up Portugal and Spain was overrun by invading Germanic tribes including Vandals and Visigoths. The population gradually re-Christianized, with Roman Catholicism being reinstated in 550. Muslim armies from North Africa entered the Iberian peninsula in 711. They rapidly conquered most of it. Christian Visigoth rulers in northern Iberia managed to regroup and form a cluster of small kingdoms. Northwestern Iberia revolted against Muslim rule and became the Kingdom of Leon, which covered the Galicia region of Spain and a sliver of northern Portugal.

In 1128 a Christian count won a power struggle for control of the Portuguese sliver, known as the County of Portugal. He began raids into territory to the south controlled by Moroccan Muslims, often referred to as Moors. After a major victory in 1139 he proclaimed himself King of Portugal. He was recognized as such by the Pope in 1179. Portugal kept expanding until 1249, when it reached its approximate modern borders. The country allied with England in 1373. In 1383 the Portuguese won a major battle against the neighboring Spanish kingdom of Castile.

Iberia's former Moorish and Arab rulers had largely tolerated the faiths of their Christian and Jewish subjects. Many Spaniards and Portuguese converted to Islam. Portuguese customs regarding the seclusion of women—evident even as of the seventeenth century—resembled those of Muslims and Sephardic Jews. Christian monarchs extended toleration to Muslims and Jews during the time of their reconquest of Iberia. This was done only as an expediency. Spanish toleration was revoked after the surrender of Granada, Iberia's final Moorish outpost, in 1492.

Religious intolerance was common, circa 1500, in lands ruled by Europe's Catholic nobles. Its opposite, tolerance, was viewed as potentially sinful. Toleration opened the door to the devil. Those he seduced faced eternal damnation. Intolerance was an act of mercy, which protected those susceptible to demonic wheedling. At the time, most non-European lands were more accommodating to diverse beliefs. European tolerance, when it existed, was a royal concession that could be revoked. Those who rejected the ruler's religion—absent his or her grant of tolerance—were in effect committing treason. They could be subjected to severe punishments. Authentic toleration as an irrevocable state only became widespread in Europe following the Enlightenment. We might think of genuine tolerance as the embrace of freedom of conscience and acceptance of religious diversity, including nonbelief. In fact, the broad diffusion of such attitudes is probably necessary for liberty to take root. We see precursors of this attitudinal shift among the Dutch of the sixteenth and seventeenth centuries.

The Portuguese began their overseas conquests in 1415 by capturing Ceuta, a once-prosperous trade depot on the north African coast. At present, the town is held by Spain. Driven by both greed and religious zeal, the impoverished Portuguese began to dream of reaching the sources of the African gold and Asian goods that they'd plundered in Ceuta. Portugal went on to set up outposts in Morocco—which they couldn't hold for long—and from there established bases along coastal west Africa. Shipwrights developed a type of inexpensive, speedy, and lightly armed merchant ship known as the caravel, which was based on Arabic designs and rigging. Portuguese mariners discovered the uninhabited Atlantic islands of Cape Verde, Madeira, and the Azores, all of which were soon settled.

Previously, during the eighth century when Iberia was ruled by Muslims, caliphs based in Damascus in modern Syria brought sugar cultivation and refining techniques from India to Mesopotamia. From there, the know-how eventually reached Iberia. The caliphs sponsored learning and what we now call science. Muslim lands were home to the world's leading scientists up through the mid-thirteenth century. Among them were those who perfected the apparatus for distilling alcohol.

The English word alcohol comes from Arabic, as does its Portuguese equivalent. To distill in Portuguese is *alambicar*; a still is an *alambique.* Both terms were borrowed from Arabic, which was widely spoken in Iberia. The artisanal version of a popular Brazilian cane sugar liquor, *cachaça*, continues to be produced using centuries-old methods. I've translated a term that appears in Part Two—for what was probably cachaça—as rum, which is likewise derived from cane sugar. Rum requires more complex processing of sugar derivatives, such as molasses. During the latter part of the fifteenth century, the Portuguese introduced sugarcane cultivation, sugar refining, and alcohol distilling to Madeira and the Azores. From these outposts, the crop and techniques later reached Brazil.

Slavery was, from the outset, part of Brazil's sugar-based economy. From Roman times, slaves were used in fields, mines, and workshops, and wherever else hard labor was required, such as rowing ships and domestic service. Sexual exploitation of slaves was common. Slavery continued in Iberia under Germanic tribes and later the Moors. Except for convicts, Christians in theory couldn't enslave their coreligionists, although it happened. Italian maritime cities, including Venice and Genoa, traded in European slaves and shipped many of them to Muslim lands. They also intermediated commerce with Arabs for Asian goods such as spices, silk, and gemstones. Portuguese nobles coveted the wealth accrued by Italians from such activities.

Portuguese forces launched slave raids from their west African coastal outposts. West Africans of the time embraced local cults or Islam, making them targets for Christian slavers. By the mid-fifteenth century the Portuguese had established slave depots in the Gulf of Guinea, such as the notorious Elmina. The Cape Verde Islands served as a transshipment base. The Portuguese eventually found that it was more efficient to barter goods for slaves, rather than take the risks involved in directly seizing captives. Weapons and other merchandise were exchanged for both gold and slaves. Thousands of African slaves were kept in Portugal itself, while others were shipped to Madeira and the Azores. Lusitanian slaveholding had ancient Roman, Germanic, and Moorish roots. The Dutch, in contrast, from

Renaissance times onward seem not to have routinely permitted slavery in their homeland.

Portuguese navigators became intimately acquainted with the nuances of the Atlantic Ocean. They were convinced they could reach Asia by sailing around the southern tip of Africa. A ship's captain from Genoa, known in English as Christopher Columbus, pitched to Portugal's monarch the idea of a western sea route to Asia. On the advice of experts, the king turned him down. The world was rightly believed to be much larger than Columbus claimed it to be. Incidentally, educated people of the time knew that the world is a sphere; this wasn't something dreamed up by Columbus. He persuaded the monarchs of the newly united Spanish kingdoms of Castile and Aragon to embrace his wild notion of a short westerly sea route to China and India. The Spanish crown financed Columbus' 1492 voyage, during which he accidentally encountered the Americas. The archipelago of the West Indies is misnamed as a result. To his dying day Columbus thought he'd reached Asia.

Alarmed that Spain was potentially intruding on lands that it wished to claim, in 1494 Portugal negotiated—with the Pope's blessing—the Treaty of Tordesillas, which divided the world outside of Europe between the two nations. Four years later, the Portuguese boldly exploited the wind patterns of the south Atlantic and at last found a way to reach the Indian Ocean. They discovered Brazil in 1500. It was on their side of the Tordesillas demarcation.

Although gunpowder-based weapons—originally invented in China—were known to Arabs and Indians, those carried on Portuguese ships had much more firepower than did Asian versions. Portugal blasted its way into centuries-old Indian Ocean trading networks. Thousands were murdered indiscriminately in the process. The Portuguese sank civilian ships carrying women and other non-combatants out of anti-Islamic malice. By 1520, the Portuguese had secured much of the Asian spice trade for themselves. They managed to seize key ports and depots in the Spice Islands—modern Indonesia—as well as in India, Yemen, Africa, Sri Lanka, and Malaysia. The elites of tiny Portugal became wealthy almost overnight. Italian merchants were stupefied by their losses as Portuguese-freighted goods flooded Europe. Levies on gold, slaves, ivory, pepper, nutmeg, sugar, silk, cotton cloth, gemstones, and countless other luxuries financed the expanding Portuguese empire.

Portugal lacked the manpower necessary to establish itself firmly in the vastness of Brazil. Instead, the monarchy decided to turn over nation-sized swaths of land, known as Captaincies, to well-connected nobles and loyalists. Some Captaincies failed but many took root. Initially, Portuguese traders obtained valuable dyewoods and exotic timber from indigenous Brazilians. Their pre-contact way of life— using stone tools with a mix of basic agriculture, hunting, and gathering—was violent but largely free. Owners of Captaincies soon realized that Brazil's land and climate are perfect for growing sugarcane. They attempted to enslave Native Brazilians as plantation laborers. Their brutal efforts largely failed. Many indigenous Brazilians preferred death, through starvation, punishment, or attempted escape, to life as slaves. Most, however, died from Eurasian diseases. During the sixteenth and seventeenth centuries perhaps ninety percent of the original inhabitants of North and South America were decimated by illnesses such as measles and smallpox, against which they had no immunities.

The people of west Africa, in contrast, lived in kingdoms, with organized landownership, iron tools, livestock husbandry, sophisticated agriculture, and classes of servitude, including slavery. Africa's domestic slavery was largely tribal, not racial, and wasn't typically a permanent status for oneself or one's descendants. Africans had partial immunity to Eurasian diseases due to a degree of ongoing contact. They also had some resistance to the tropical diseases that emerged in the New World. The lifestyle of west African commoners differed little from that of contemporary European serfs or peasants. This fact is often overlooked. The dogma of white racial supremacy, which didn't exist among the Romans, was drummed up to justify the monstrous mistreatment of Africans by Europeans, most of whom were peasants themselves.

Portuguese and New World landowners found that African slaves could do the work they required of field hands and servants. Most African slaves were seized by other Africans. People submitted to captivity as something temporary without realizing that it would result in early death, either at sea or else in distant lands. The captives were shackled, chained, marched off to coastal depots, and ferried out to Portuguese ships, which transported them in the millions. Fully half of enslaved Africans shipped to the Americas ended up in Brazil. Those who survived the voyage could expect to live on average for no more than seven years. Due to Brazil's proximity to Africa, Portuguese slaveholders found it more efficient to import new slaves and work them to death, rather than rely on the reproduction of slave children, which was a practice common in North America.

The indigenous Brazilians who survived initial contact with the Portuguese either retreated more deeply into Brazil's backlands or else became settled under the supervision of Catholic clergy, especially Jesuits. As they learned Portuguese, they became the first people referred to by Europeans as Brazilians. Those in Brazil of European descent remained Portuguese. People of mixed Portuguese and African descent were called *mulatos*. Africans were called blacks, creoles, or any number of other terms. The meanings of such terms shifted over time; because they're often offensive, I avoid using them where possible in Part Two.

Many slaves escaped servitude by fleeing to primitive communities tucked away in remote forests. This brought them temporary relief but no security. Bounty hunters remained a constant threat. Slaves were branded with hot irons, like cattle, so that escapees could be returned to their nominal owners. The Portuguese employed implements of torture and the techniques of terror to enforce submission. For centuries, they trafficked slaves to Spain's American colonies. Portuguese methods for dominating slaves were introduced throughout the Americas, including to the future United States.

In 1580 Portugal found itself without a king or an heir to the throne. King Sebastian had been killed while fighting Muslims in

Morocco. Shortly after his death, King Phillip II of Spain claimed the Portuguese crown under a dual monarchy. His mother was a Portuguese noblewoman. Spain's monarch, as a high noble within the Holy Roman Empire, had sovereignty claims throughout Europe, including the northern and southern Netherlands. By harnessing Portugal and its vast empire to Spain's imperial ambitions, the stage was set for Portugal's eighty years of intermittent warfare with the Dutch. Portugal and the United Provinces of the Netherlands remained technically at war until 1663. Portugal's forced connection to Spain also damaged its longstanding good relationship with England.

In 1588 Spain sent a fleet—its so-called Armada—to the southern Netherlands to board Spanish and Italian troops for an invasion of England. Spain's monarch planned to overthrow Queen Elizabeth in order to put a stop to the island nation's slide into Protestantism, and to halt its sponsorship of anti-Spanish piracy. On its return trip the fleet was to anchor in Lisbon, seize the Portuguese crown, and reduce Portugal to the status of a Spanish province. It would have become like Catalonia, which continues to strain against Spanish rule. Combined action by the Dutch and English stymied the Spanish invasion. Dutch harassment hindered the boarding of Spanish soldiers. English naval attacks and fortuitous storms eventually led to Spain's retreat, which followed the loss of about a third of the Armada's ships. The plan to snatch Portugal's crown on the return voyage was shelved.

Portugal's imperial weakness and its connection to the hated Spanish put its colonial holdings in Dutch crosshairs. A century after the Portuguese rampage through the Indian Ocean, the Dutch East India Company—well-funded and heavily armed—was in control of many former Portuguese possessions in Asia. It was only a matter of time before the newly founded Dutch West India Company launched its assault on the colony of Brazil.

The United Provinces of the Netherlands. Portugal's opponent was a relative newcomer to the world stage. While Portugal proper differs little from its boundaries of 1249, the United Provinces cohered as a sovereign state only in 1585. How it reached that point tells us much about the chaotic developments that helped shape today's world.

First a note about names. The nation—Nederland in Dutch—is now denominated the Kingdom of the Netherlands. Netherlands means "lowlands" or "Low Countries," the latter term also being used for the combined nations of the Netherlands, Belgium, and Luxembourg. These countries are situated along the lower reaches and estuaries of several major rivers. They're low in the senses of being at low elevation and flat. Over half the land in the Netherlands is at or below sea level. The United Provinces began to take shape in 1579 with a formal union between Holland and two other Dutch provinces. By 1585, the first three provinces had united with adjacent northern ones; however, those in the south were left outside the United Provinces. The northern provinces had been part of the Austrian-Spanish Netherlands, which also included provinces in the southern regions of Flanders and Brabant. During the time of Dutch Brazil, the Spanish Netherlands comprised only the southern provinces, which eventually became the nations of Belgium and Luxembourg. Dutch is the Netherlands' primary language. It's also one of Belgium's official languages, along with French, although the dialect is known as Flemish. Holland has been the dominant province of the northern Netherlands since well before its independence.

The mix of terms is relevant for the narrative contained in Part Two. In it, the Dutch are described as the heretics from the land of Holland who invaded Brazil. However, Dutch-speakers from the so-called "obedient provinces" of the south—who had remained loyal to the Spanish monarchy—are generally called Flemings, meaning people of Flanders. The United Provinces and the Dutch Republic are synonymous for our purposes. The nation wasn't the constitutional monarchy that it is today. As a republic, it had no king. However, it wasn't a democracy. Government was in the hands of councils and boards. It tended toward being an oligarchy of wealthy merchants and prominent nobles. Members of the governing councils are referred to as regents. Nevertheless, public opinion had an impact, especially at the municipal level. Regents could ignore the general populace only at their peril.

The history of the Low Countries, like that of Portugal, begins with the fall of the western Roman empire. The Germanic Franks established a kingdom in the southern Netherlands in 481. By the ninth century, the Frankish kingdom had expanded to include much of France and northern Italy. The region by then was largely Christianized. The Frankish language evolved into Old Dutch, while Franks in areas that spoke Latin derivatives—such as early dialects of French and Italian—adopted the local languages. The dividing line between regions speaking Dutch and French began at this time. Frisian is a secondary language spoken along the northern coast of the modern Netherlands. It's the language most closely related to English. The Germanic dialects of the Angles and Saxons were once prevalent in the region. Many of their speakers migrated to England, where they became the Anglo-Saxons of pre-Norman times.

The Low Countries began to prosper in the eleventh century, especially in the south. Swampy areas were drained, yielding new lands for agriculture. Towns and specialized trades flourished. In the thirteenth century local committees were formed to manage the building of dikes and the excavation of waterways and drainage systems. Later, towns began to collaborate in water management, with cooperation facilitated by the aristocracy. By 1300, Holland and its neighboring northern provinces had become virtually a new country, clawed out of the sea and mud. The southern provinces at the time were one of the most urbanized regions in all of Europe. Only northern Italy came close.

The rivers that flowed through the Low Countries created a natural barrier between the northern provinces and those of the south. As Holland's agriculture and commercial activity began to prosper, the south and north commenced their long-term separation. The Black Death of the mid-fourteenth century killed millions throughout Eurasia but was of lesser impact in the Netherlands than elsewhere. During the latter part of the century Holland succeeded in expanding its maritime trade in the Baltic region and its North Sea fisheries off the coast of Norway.

By the early fifteenth century, around the time the Portuguese raided Ceuta in north Africa, the northern Dutch were launching fully rigged ships that could sail the high seas. They specialized in the transport of lower-margin goods such as grain, timber, and fish. As a result, although huge numbers were employed in shipping and related support industries, no large or wealthy mercantile elite emerged. It was a land of craftsmen, sailors, farmers, and laborers. The Dutch became the lowest cost marine shippers in Europe.

These early developments had an impact on later attitudes commonly found among the Dutch. The newness of the land meant that it wasn't encumbered with centuries-old feudal rights. What's known as "fee simple" ownership in common law countries was almost nonexistent in most of medieval Europe. Nearly all land was entailed with often conflicting rights and burdens of various noble estates and ecclesiastical jurisdictions.

For some sense of perspective, consider present-day ownership of a plot of land. It's usually infringed upon by restrictions such as road and utility easements, claims to sub-surface minerals, water drawing rights, zoning restrictions, bond levies, and so forth. Multiply burdens along such lines a hundredfold and eliminate modern property registers; you'll have some idea of the complexity of medieval landholding. Rights to use, income, remainder, transit, or possession often had to be secured by force of arms, on the basis of ancient documents or customary practices spanning generations. Imagine a neighboring lord asserting a right to graze sheep on your land during harvest season. Adversarial nobles pressing their claims posed a constant threat.

For the northern Dutch, however, land was an asset that could be leased, bought, or sold. By the early sixteenth century nearly half the populace was part of a family that owned land. Very few were serfs. Coupled with the flourishing of trades, guilds, water boards, and security militias, along with widespread literacy, the northern Netherlands developed a civic atmosphere notably different from elsewhere in Europe. Foreign observers commented with surprise that nobles and commoners would travel together in the same boat cabins of the canal-based transportation system. Women could appear in public without being molested. They walked alongside their husbands, who would often help supervise their children. Activities that now seem normal to us were quite unusual elsewhere in Europe at the time.

High levels of Dutch literacy were stimulated by the "Modern Devotion" movement. It began in the late fourteenth century as a campaign for educational and religious betterment. Modern Devotion encouraged the spread of schools and libraries. It was connected to both monasteries and civic institutions. The movement avoided disputes about dogma or Church organization, which spared it from being condemned by religious authorities. The main thrust of Modern Devotion was to cultivate the inner life of the individual—in emulation of Christ's humility—in place of devotion directed outwardly toward icons, sacraments, pilgrimages, and processions. Later supporters of the movement influenced the Protestant reformer Martin Luther (1483–1546). They were suspected of heresy.

Modern Devotion took a leap forward in the fifteenth century with the invention of moveable type presses. Adherents undertook the study of Latin, Greek, and scripture. Some major proponents spent time in Italy, where they were exposed to humanist scholarship. The movement came to fuse humanism with Christian spirituality. In this form, it became known as Christian Humanism. From the 1490s on, its followers rejected scholasticism—characterized by the overworked logic of Christianized Aristotelianism—which dominated European academia. Piety and moralism were prized. The "True Christianity" of Christian Humanists was distinguished from "false religion," the latter being associated with most contemporary religious practices, such as pilgrimage and devotion to icons. The movement penetrated nearly all strata of urban society in the Low Countries.

On the political front during this era, in 1428 Duke Philip the Good of Burgundy became the high lord of the Low Countries. The counts of Nassau, who were minor German princes with landholdings in Brabant, became important nobles. Through intermarriage with the Burgundian House of Orange, the lineage became the House of Orange-Nassau. William the Silent, who provided leadership to the Dutch anti-Spanish rebellion, was of this lineage. It continues to provide the monarchs of the Kingdom of the Netherlands. The House of Orange-Nassau is relevant for several reasons. First, its members served as the major Stadtholders or Governor-Generals of the United Provinces. Second, the principal Governor of Dutch Brazil, Johan Maurits Count of Nassau, came from it. Third, it illustrates something of the extreme overlap of claims that characterized Europe's nobility.

The high nobles of Europe formed their own caste. They intermarried across national borders without impediment. Marriages were arranged for political ends. Claims of sovereignty that lay dormant for centuries continued to be asserted in noble titles. In the late seventeenth century, for instance, the Dutch Stadtholder of the House of Orange-Nassau, whose wife Mary was an English princess, succeeded in being crowned King William III of England, Scotland, and Ireland. The current Dutch monarch claims the following noble titles: King of the Netherlands; King of England, Scotland, and Ireland; Sovereign Prince of the Netherlands; Grand Duke of Luxembourg; Duke of Limburg; Prince of Orange; Furst of Nassau-Orange; Furst of Nassau-Orange-Fulda; Princely Count of Nassau-Dietz; Count of Nassau-Dillenburg; and, Stadtholder in the Netherlands.

Through a marriage alliance with the dominant Habsburg dynasty of Austria, the Burgundian Low Countries passed in 1482 to the regency of Maximillian, son of the Holy Roman Emperor Frederick III. The region became known as the Austrian Netherlands. Christian Humanism began to emerge strongly around the same time.

The noted Dutch scholar Erasmus (1466–1536) was a Christian Humanist. He had a powerful impact on religious and intellectual developments in Europe. Erasmus feared Church schism but did much to highlight the institutional failings of Roman Catholicism. He advocated studies in what we now call the humanities, especially of classical literature and Latin, Greek, and Hebrew. Erasmus corresponded with and was initially supportive of the reformer Martin Luther. However, Erasmus grew increasingly concerned that Luther's vehement attacks on Catholicism would lead to the repression of humanistic studies. Erasmus came to be criticized for not denouncing Luther. Under intense pressure, he fled the Low Countries for republican Switzerland in 1521. He finally broke with Luther in 1524, over the latter's ballooning dogmatism.

Luther won the support of many German princes. Germany at the time wasn't a unified country. It was a linguistic-cultural region composed of numerous principalities. Due to princely support, Luther's version of Protestantism—which became the Lutheran Church—survived a ferocious frontal attack by the Roman Church and its supporters. The Austrian nobility, unlike the reformist German princes, remained staunchly Catholic. The Austrians succeeded for the most part in suppressing any outward manifestation of the Protestant Reformation in the Low Countries. The Reformation couldn't gain traction there in an institutionalized form. Nevertheless, the works of Erasmus and other Christian Humanists, as well as of Luther and other reformers, were translated into colloquial Dutch and circulated clandestinely.

The Roman Church in the northern Netherlands had been poorly organized and was riddled with institutional weaknesses. Clerics had a reputation for worldliness; many kept mistresses and neglected their duties. Even as early as 1525 they were widely disrespected. In the eyes of many of the Dutch, the mandatory tithes extracted by the Church were misused. The Dutch Inquisition began its work at Austrian instigation in 1522, initially by burning Luther's books. Two Augustinian friars who supported Luther were burned alive in 1523. They were the first Protestant martyrs. A few years later a Protestant woman was burned at the stake, to become the first female martyr. The Dutch, imbued with the spirit of humanism, were appalled by these acts and came to despise the Church and its clergy. The Dutch elites, who had much to lose, were intimidated by official oppression.

Unlike the case in many German principalities, no prominent figures in the Netherlands stood up to defend the Protestant movement.

Therefore, while firm confessional and theological lines were being drawn in German lands with Luther and in Switzerland with Ulrich Zwingli (1484–1531) and later John Calvin (1509–1564), the proto-Protestantism of the Netherlands remained fluid in practice and doctrine. It was so diverse that it could neither gel nor fragment. People went through the motions of attending official Catholic services but inwardly abandoned the Church's dogmas and sacraments. In the 1530s a Protestant splinter group, the Anabaptists, asserted itself with great fervor. It remained a tiny minority in Dutch society. However, from 1530 to 1560, Anabaptists stood at the vanguard of the Reformation in the Low Countries. As a consequence, they attracted violent official persecution.

In 1545 the Holy Roman Emperor Charles V decided that the Dutch Inquisition's results had been inadequate. He ordered the establishment of regional Inquisition tribunals, along Spanish lines. Thereafter, in 1548 the seventeen provinces of the Austrian Netherlands were unified into a national entity, recognized as such within the Holy Roman Empire. Charles V attempted to use the bureaucratic powers of the reconstituted Austrian Netherlands to stamp out any traces of the Reformation. However, it was already too late. The hearts of the populace had turned against the Church. It was perhaps the first time in history that the vast majority of common people—of their own volition, without the direction of overlords—abandoned their ancestral religion.

A 1550 edict decreed death to all heretics and those who circulated heretical literature, together with confiscation of their goods. Men who confessed to heresy were beheaded; women were buried alive. Those who refused to confess were burned at the stake. Dutch officials were very reluctant to enforce such decrees. Nevertheless, thousands were killed pursuant to the 1550 edict. The decrees were so unpopular that crowds at times attacked Inquisition officials and helped the condemned to escape.

As of 1560 the official Church had been thoroughly abandoned by the Dutch populace. They stopped attending services or confessing unless compelled to do so. Many Dutch Protestant refugees in London and Germany had already adopted Calvinism. The Calvinists had a well-developed institutional framework and theology that could in a sense provide structure to the diffuse strands of Dutch proto-Protestantism. Many who had become Calvinists abroad returned to the Low Countries as preachers and began establishing secret assemblies known as conventicles.

A new noble, Philip II of Spain, became the lord of the seventeen provinces of the Low Countries in 1555. He was the son of Emperor Charles V and Queen Isabella of Portugal. Philip married an English noblewoman, Queen Mary, in 1554. He became king of Spain in 1556 and of Portugal in 1581. The entirety of the Low Countries for a time was known as the Spanish Netherlands. Later, the term was applied only to the southern Netherlands, with the northern Netherlands becoming the Dutch Republic. In 1557, Philip's forces scored a major victory against France. Spain, enriched by New World gold and silver, towered as the most powerful nation in Europe. William the Silent of the House of Orange-Nassau was Philip's right-hand man. Following William's distinguished service in the war against France, he was named Stadtholder for most of the Spanish Netherlands.

The ambitious William strongly supported both royal policy and his own interests. However, he seems to have been genuinely committed to freedom of conscience and religious compromise, in true Dutch fashion. He and other Dutch nobles became increasingly resistant to Philip's fanaticism in prosecuting the anti-heresy campaign. Resentment by the Dutch populace finally exploded. Evading the official churches, an open-air preaching movement ignited among them in 1566. The movement then morphed into outrage against the iconic symbols of Catholicism. Churches throughout the northern Netherlands—and some in the south—were raided and sacked. Holy images were defaced and demolished. The teachings of Erasmus about "false religion" no doubt provided justification for the iconoclastic outburst.

The Dutch were ready to rebel. William and other nobles were with them. However, they weren't yet strong enough to take on mighty Spain. Philip sent 10,000 crack Spanish and Italian Neapolitan troops to the Low Countries. He wanted a quick and decisive victory to minimize the cost of the campaign. In 1567 William retreated to one of his estates in Germany. He gathered other exiled nobles and raised substantial sums. William began a war of attrition the following year on the borders of the Low Countries. Spain oppressed the residents of the Low Countries through high taxation, forcing them to pay for the occupying Spanish troops. They had to billet soldiers, provide conscripts and supplies, and suffer the myriad indignities of foreign occupation. The culminating Dutch revolt, led in the north by Holland, broke out in 1572. Dutch forces began to gain and hold territory. Spanish troops massacred the holdouts of several besieged cities when they fell, such as Haarlem. Atrocities of this type further intensified Dutch hatred of the Spanish.

Holland and two other provinces united under the Treaty of Utrecht in 1579. Others joined and formed the initial Dutch Republic in 1581. Between 1579 and 1585 the Spanish retook all of the southern Netherlands, which had remained heavily Catholic and loyalist. William was assassinated in 1584 but his leadership had already opened the path for northern independence. Facing the power of Spain, though, Dutch factions led by nobles sought foreign assistance by offering sovereignty over the Netherlands first to King Henri III of France and then to Queen Elizabeth of England. Both declined, not wishing to antagonize the all-powerful Philip II.

Antwerp in the southern Netherlands, which had been Europe's leading commercial city, capitulated following a Spanish siege in 1585. Protestants who refused to convert to Catholicism were ordered to leave. Over the next four years about half of Antwerp's population relocated to the northern Netherlands. Many leading industrialists, craftsmen, bankers, and merchants were Protestant. They brought to Amsterdam and other northern cities their skills, equipment, and financial assets. The influx was an important contributor to the flourishing Dutch Golden Age of the following century.

England's Queen Elizabeth didn't want the whole of the Netherlands to fall back into the hands of Catholic Spain. She decided to send thousands of troops and provide financial support to the northern Netherlands. She required the appointment of an English Governor-General, who directed defenses and some aspects of government from 1585 to 1587. During this time, she supported the party of aristocrats, monarchists, and the advocates of a state church against Holland's republican regents.

In 1588 Spain launched its Armada against England. Elizabeth decided to stop opposing the Holland regents. Spain's Armada failed to reach its objectives due to English and Dutch military collaboration and fortuitous storms. Under Holland's leadership, the United Provinces consolidated the republic's governance structure between 1588 and 1590. The regents prevailed over the competing aristocratic party. In 1590 Philip II decided to focus on his conflict with France, thereby effectively halting his battle to subdue the Dutch.

Between 1590 and 1609 the Dutch Republic became a great power. Spanish prestige collapsed in the northern Netherlands. By 1597 the Dutch had the most proficient army in Europe, second in size only to that of the Spanish. They developed new military transport and siege methods. Their battle tactics were later copied throughout Europe. The Republic's navy became world-class. The Dutch introduced a military code of conduct in part to protect civilian populations from the depredations of unprofessional soldiers. The reforms are considered to be a turning point in world military history.

With the influx from Antwerp and elsewhere—combined with domestic talent—Dutch artists, scholars, bankers, merchants, and inventors fueled the Republic's stunning growth. Officials and investors launched the Dutch East India Company in 1602. As a joint-stock company, many consider it to be the forerunner of the modern commercial corporation. It was empowered to seize colonies, maintain fleets of warships, recruit and field armies, and commit piracy, as well as to carry out normal trade and commercial operations. The company dislodged the Portuguese in key locations throughout Asia and generated spectacular profits.

The Spanish and Portuguese, under a joint crown, entered into a twelve-year truce with the Dutch between 1609 and 1621. During this time, proposals for organizing a West India Company began to circulate in the Netherlands. The Dutch saw opportunities in Brazil's sugar trade, the African slave trade, and raids on the Spanish silver fleet. The company was chartered in 1621. It had an early failure in an abortive attack on Brazil's Bahia in 1624. Success came with the capture of the heavily armed Spanish-American silver fleet in 1628. The company paid dividends of fifty percent of invested capital relative to that year. The Dutch invasion of Brazil—although tinged with political-imperial significance—was in reality a commercial venture.

An Eyewitness Account. Dutch Brazil is one of history's intriguing "what ifs." Following their failed attempt in 1624 to seize Salvador da Bahia—colonial Brazil's capital—the Dutch captured the northeastern cities of Recife and Olinda in the state of Pernambuco. They went on to subdue all of Pernambuco plus Brazil's adjacent and northerly states, from Alagoas to Maranhão near the mouth of the Amazon River.

Few outside of Brazil, Portugal, or the Netherlands are aware that Dutch Brazil ever existed. I first learned of it in 1990 while vacationing in Brazil's northeast with my wife and youngest daughter. At the time, I was employed as a legal translator in the megapolis of São Paulo. The story piqued my curiosity. In 1991, I departed Brazil to return to my hometown of Seattle for graduate school. There, I located the classic English-language study of the period, C.R. Boxer's *The Dutch In Brazil 1624–1654.*

Boxer's book contains multiple references to and a few translated passages from an intriguing source. It's the account of an eyewitness to the Dutch invasion. The original work—authored by Friar Manuel

25

Calado (1584–1654) and published in Lisbon in 1648—is titled *O Valoroso Lucideno e Triunfo da Liberdade*. This can be rendered as "The Valiant/Worthy Lusitanian/Portuguese and Triumph of Liberty," or more concisely, "The Valiant Portuguese and Liberty's Triumph." I've abbreviated its title even further as *Liberty's Triumph*, which is likewise part of this book's title. The narrative in Part Two is a revised and abridged translation of Calado's tome.

The shortened title *Liberty's Triumph* also suggests the sweeping events underlying Calado's narrative. As noted, something like our present-day understanding of liberty began to emerge in Europe during the seventeenth century. Calado's tale illustrates the shift from a medieval to modern mindset. His view of liberty resembles that of the ancient Romans. For the Portuguese of the seventeenth century—and as used by Calado—liberty meant the right and power of free Catholic males to dominate others, while under the rule of a Portuguese king and with deference to social and religious superiors. Much of the world has now moved from such an authoritarian and feudalistic view of liberty to one that's more in tune with our relatively open, individualistic, and pluralistic times.

It was clear to me that Calado had a unique perspective. He lived in occupied Recife and befriended its Dutch governor. All the while, he continued to collaborate secretly with pro-Portuguese guerillas and officials in other parts of Brazil. The Pope named him head of the Church in Brazilian lands under Dutch control, bypassing the Bishop of Brazil.

Most researchers who write of Dutch Brazil cite Calado. However, only parts of his book seem to have been translated into English. In preparing this volume, I strove to bring Calado's narrative to life. His story isn't simply a string of events. It provides insight into a worldview in transition. Although Calado was a fierce partisan for the Portuguese cause—and a dutiful servant of the Catholic Church—he at times expresses envy of and even sneaking admiration for the Dutch.

Calado's book begins with the fall of Recife in 1631; it closes with the author's escape to Portugal in 1646. It therefore ends before

Dutch Brazil was forever erased from the map. The Dutch invasion was motivated largely by a desire to gain control of Portugal's lucrative sugar trade. However, the story of Dutch Brazil extends beyond one of simple greed. The Dutch and Portuguese of the time, as has been described, were pursuing their own distinct paths into the early modern era. Calado's book is best understood in context, with consideration of the preceding social, religious, and political developments that shaped the two nations. The preceding sections of Part One, I hope, have imparted the necessary background.

Portugal's final victory in 1654 was gained by a guerilla army cobbled together from freed and enslaved Africans and African-Brazilians, Native Brazilians, men of mixed race, Portuguese, and a smattering of northern European mercenaries. Nearly all of the non-Portuguese are nameless to us. Brazil's forgotten black and indigenous heroes were the theme of the samba school Mangueira's winning entry in the 2019 Rio de Janeiro Carnival.

The guerilla army, which included black and indigenous officers as well as frontline troops, certainly deserves to be remembered. Without them and their string of improbable successes, Portugal—nearly bankrupt—would likely have ended up as a province of Spain, much like Catalonia is today. Northeastern Brazil might resemble Suriname, the former Dutch colony situated to the north of Brazil.

Brazil's unsung heroes marched into and assumed control of Recife, the final Dutch stronghold, on 28 January 1654. The terms of surrender had been negotiated two days beforehand. The triumphant soldiers were highly disciplined and loyal to the Portuguese king. Following the handover, enemy combatants and residents were treated in a humane manner that was exemplary for the era. The defeat of the Netherlands—at the time a major power—by such a makeshift opponent astonished those of all classes in Europe.

I've placed most of Calado's narrative in chronological order. However, a few of his retrospective accounts have been left where they occur in his book. For instance, he provides background on his own education in Portugal and relationship to the nobility. He describes events in other parts of Brazil and Angola of which he had no firsthand knowledge, although he seems to have been well informed.

The story begins with Calado's denunciation of Olinda's rampant sin. Olinda is adjacent to Recife; it was a residential area, while Recife served mostly as a port. Readers might scoff at Calado's preachiness. Holding assets, engaging in banking or trade, feasting on good food, and so on, are part of normal life. We largely consider such things to be desirable, not sinful.

In truth, Calado had no reservations about the wealth or festivities of nobles. He resented instead the riches accrued by merchants. This was a common refrain at his time. Europeans struggled with transitioning from the supremacy of landed nobility to the ascendance of commerce. The eternal and divinely sanctioned Great Chain of Being—at the pinnacle God, then the angels, descending to God's earthly representative the Pope, followed by the king, high clergy, nobles, middle clergy, yeomen and free artisans, low clergy, peasants, serfs, slaves, animals, and so on down the chain—remained a potent image. Movement between levels was thought to violate divine order. Merchants belonged well down the hierarchy in the traditional view.

An undercurrent in Calado's writing is his periodic defense of his monastic order. Martin Luther, like Calado, was an Augustinian monk. Luther's highly intellectualized revolt against Catholicism stained the Augustinian order with the blush of heresy. Calado, perhaps to compensate, repeatedly emphasizes both his intellectual prowess and his obedience to the Church.

An Editor's Note appears at the beginning of each chapter in Part Two. The notes are meant to highlight aspects of Calado's text that connect to the theme of liberty. The chapter headings are my own. You'll find there are no unsullied heroes in Calado's account. You might be so appalled by Dutch brutality that you end up sympathizing with Brazil's defenders. Bear in mind that Calado's book was pro-Portuguese propaganda, published in the midst of conflict in 1648, well before the Dutch capitulation of 1654. Each side committed barbarous acts against the other and elsewhere in the world. What we see in Part Two is flickering images of the conditions prevailing in the Dutch and Portuguese homelands. Unique developments were unfolding in the Netherlands. I call some of them out in the Editor's Notes. The changes were often subtle, which is to be expected during the early stages of any transitional period.

For those not inclined to enter Calado's domain, the Editor's Notes can be read as a synopsis of each chapter. I suggest, however, perusing at least a few of Calado's lines. By listening to his voice we can experience a strange and yet not entirely foreign world. Looking at events through his eyes can shed light on our own inner images, implanted by childhood fables or the imprint of language, education, or social norms. Either way, the tale of Dutch Brazil wraps up in Part Three, with some parting thoughts on the ideas that have come to shape us.

We're now ready to set sail for the distant shores of seventeenth century Brazil.

Part Two

Liberty's Triumph

Content Warning

Part Two of this book contains an abridged and revised translation of *O Valoroso Lucideno e Triunfo da Liberdade*, which dates from the seventeenth century. It includes scenes of war, rape, theft, homicide, assault, bondage, torture, forced religious conversion, supernatural intervention, clerical and secular corruption, demonic possession, visions, and other disturbing imagery. The author of the original passages openly advocated for or condoned slavery, violence, racism, discrimination, classism, misogynism, imperialism, anti-Semitism, and various forms of religious bigotry. Please do not read Part Two in the event that such content might cause you distress or discomfort to any degree or in any form.

1 SIN ENTERS

Editor's Note: Both the Dutch and Portuguese commonly believed that misfortune and disasters are God's punishment for sin. Recognition that the universe is orderly and governed by natural laws—like gravity—only began to spread among Europeans during the seventeenth century. Prior to that, all sorts of supernatural interventions were thought to cause the ordinary events of the world. In Calado's text, we revert to a time in which God directly controls human affairs. He rewards and punishes as He sees fit. Calado reaches the conclusion that Olinda's sins led to the ignominious defeat of God's chosen people, the Portuguese, at the hands of Dutch heretics.

Belief in divine purposes no doubt motivates or gives courage to many combatants in wartime. Even the atheistic Soviets—during World War II—called on the persecuted Russian Orthodox clergy to embolden the populace in the fight against invading Germans. Calado and others he quotes exploit such sentiments repeatedly to arouse a fighting spirit among those facing the gruesome realities of war.

The idea that disasters reflect supernatural punishment isn't exclusively Catholic or Protestant. We find it in the books of the Hebrew prophets and the Koran. Outside of the Abrahamic faiths, Confucianism attributes calamitous events to misconduct or ethical lapses, especially those of the ruler. Hindus and Buddhists tend to view disasters as karmic retribution for transgressions. Following the events of September 11, 2001, some Christian leaders in the United States asserted that God decreed the attack to punish America for its sins.[3]

---

[3] As of the first date of this book's publication, the world is in the early stages of what might become a pandemic of a coronavirus known as Covid-19. Calamities are a fact of life and will occur again with certainty.

Don't we often have a nagging suspicion—even in our scientific era—that calamities are caused by something? It might not be sin in its religious sense but we still look for the reasons why misfortune occurs. We gain no satisfaction from the notion that disasters stem from random events. Calado claims that God's wrath finds concrete expression in the Dutch invasion of Brazil.

* * *

Esteemed reader, this is my account of the events surrounding the Dutch invasion of Brazil, which I personally witnessed. The Holy Inquisition seated in Lisbon issued a license to publish it on 8 October 1647. All other necessary authorizations have been obtained.

Our sacred scriptures, saintly commentators, Church authorities, and ancient philosophers all tell us that calamities such as invasion by foreigners have a cause: sin. To understand the cause of this invasion, that is, the sins that were committed, we must consider the conduct of the people of Olinda, the principal town in the Captaincy of Pernambuco, and of those who resided elsewhere in northeastern Brazil.

Before the Dutch arrived, this was the richest and most prosperous land within the Kingdom of Portugal, truly the jewel in the royal crown. It produced gold and silver without limit, and so much sugar that there weren't enough boats to carry it all. The ostentatious luxury of the households was so great that it impelled those who were less fortunate to consider themselves to be miserable if they lacked silver tableware.

The women went about in such elegant and costly clothing that it wasn't enough to wear silk and velvet. Their outfits included the finest textiles and brocade-work. They were adorned with so many jewels that it appeared their heads were sprinkled with raindrops. About their necks were pearls, rubies, emeralds, and diamonds. At home, the wealthy had all the latest implements and decorations for their daily banquets; they had wine cellars and enjoyed equestrian games; for every party they gave, everything was so delicious that it was like heaven on earth.

In all of this abundance, sin entered. The people of Olinda forgot about God and gave themselves over to vice. They were comparable to the people killed by the flood in the time of Noah, or to those of Sodom and Gomorrah who were burned by the fire of divine wrath. The land became stained by impudence.

Usury, the lending of money at compounding interest, and illegal profiteering became the norm. Open cohabitation occurred without public correction because payoffs were made to suspend punishment. There were swindles and brazen robberies; each day had fights, with people being injured and killed. Rape and adultery became commonplace. No one paid attention to the swearing of false oaths.

Former Jews who had become Christians continued to practice Judaism in secret, and encouraged others to do the same. This sin was demonstrated by the fact that when the Dutch came the so-called New Christians began to practice Judaism openly, declaring themselves to be Jews.

The judicial authorities would beat wrongdoers with very flimsy rods if bribed with four boxes of sugar, an amount that was later doubled to eight boxes. This is how justice was administered among cronies. In direct defiance of God and the prophets, lawyers and the judicial authorities abused widows, who often ended up worse off after seeking legal assistance.

When a man of honor had been treated unjustly, he cried out against the abuse and claimed that justice had died. Hearing of this complaint, the local magistrate ordered his arrest and punishment. Things had become so bad that a visiting priest of the Holy Inquisition rose to the pulpit and said: "The difference between the names Olinda and Olanda [Holanda; Holland] is no more than changing the letter *i* to the letter *a*. This town of Olinda is going to be taken by Holland, and the Dutch will burn it down before long. Because of the lack of justice on earth, this town will need to beg heaven for assistance." And as the priest threatened, it soon came to pass.

2 RECIFE FALLS

Editor's Note: The Dutch invasion isn't unexpected. The Portuguese have advance word that a massive fleet has been sighted. However, the need to display loyalty and deference through celebrating the birth of a Spanish prince interferes with defensive preparations. Once the Dutch land, attention to the needs of the privileged—who demand the evacuation of their families and goods—takes precedence over military action. In addition to criticizing the cowardice of the wealthy, Calado also faults them for being collaborators. Dutch hatred of Roman Catholicism and its symbols is evident. However, out of pragmatism and in accord with freedom of conscience, Catholics serve in the Dutch military, even as officers. Calado lays the blame for the invasion squarely on Pernambuco's New Christians, who wish to avoid persecution by the Inquisition. The chapter's events span a year or more following the invasion. During this time, the Dutch forces reach the town of Porto de Calvo, in which Calado resides. The era is one marked by brutality.

* * *

The Portuguese received intelligence that a massive invasion force, an armada, was assembling in Holland with the objective of seizing the Captaincy of Pernambuco. Some defensive preparations were made, mostly in the Captaincy of Bahia. A new militia commander—Matias de Albuquerque—arrived in Pernambuco from Portugal. He received further intelligence from the governor of the Cape Verde Islands that the huge armada was already en route to Brazil.

However, at the same time, Matias de Albuquerque also received notice of the birth of a new prince of Spain and Portugal, which were under a dual crown. He decided to put on a large party to celebrate the prince's birth. Some in Olinda were agitated about the pending arrival of the Dutch but few preparations were made. The party was in full swing, with the discharge of guns and cannons in celebration, when the Dutch armada appeared on the horizon.

The New Christians were delighted to see the Dutch ships arrive. They had contracted with the Dutch West India Company and financed the expenses of the invasion. They did this to free themselves from the Holy Inquisition, which they had heard was going to set up a Tribunal in Pernambuco.

The Dutch began to bombard the port town of Recife. The locals rose up and went to their defensive stations. Those in nearby Olinda, however, thought the artillery was from the party for the newborn prince. They didn't respond as quickly as they should have. Recife surrendered and was occupied.

Matias de Albuquerque went out from Olinda with a contingent of soldiers to fight the Dutch. However, along with him came some of the wealthy, who had grown fat from overindulgence and were unaccustomed to facing death. They began to clamor for the removal of their wives, children, and valuables from the town of Olinda. The commander was pressured to attend to their demands. Only afterward could he send troops to Recife to fight.

After a difficult night the refugees from Olinda continued their evacuation in terror, crying to the heavens. The Dutch kept making progress, discharging fighters at various locations. The New Christians arranged for local guides to assist the Dutch. By 16 February 1631 the Dutch had taken Olinda, Recife, and several forts. They began looting Olinda and made off with all of the valuables that had been left behind.

The Dutch entered the churches. After they stole the precious implements and ornaments, they shattered the images of Christ, the Virgin Mary, and the other Saints. They trampled the images with brashness and impudence, as though they were trying to stamp out the Roman Catholic faith. Continuing with their plunder, soon they found bottles of wine. The Dutch drank so much that they staggered around drunk. They began to set fire to the ornate buildings and convents.

Thereafter, the Dutch continued to make advances along the coastline. The Portuguese retreated inland. The privations and skirmishes went on for many months. A number of the locals began to collaborate with the Dutch. One strong young man of mixed Native Brazilian and Portuguese descent, named Domingos Calabar, joined the Dutch. He did so in part because of his fear of being punished by a Portuguese landowner for various crimes he'd committed. He learned the Dutch language quickly and became friendly with the Dutch commander, Sigismundo Vandscope. Vandscope even made Calabar the godparent of the child he had with his indigenous Brazilian mistress.

The Portuguese soldiers and refugees set up a camp near the town of Porto de Calvo, which is where I resided. Matias de Albuquerque left with most of the soldiers. When the remaining soldiers and many of the refugees departed, the Dutch moved in. At first they promised leniency.

The Dutch sent for me as I was preparing to hide out in the forest, where I planned to await Matias de Albuquerque's return. The Dutch commander in charge, Admiral Lichtart, treated me with courtesy. He subsequently told me that he was Roman Catholic, in service to the Dutch. He hoped to return home soon and seek the Pope's pardon for his sins. Lichtart knew the Portuguese language well, having lived in Lisbon for some time. For the two months he was in charge at Porto de Calvo, he treated the people well and exercised strong discipline over his soldiers.

However, once the Portuguese surrendered their last major fort in Pernambuco, and the soldiers were disarmed, the Dutch broke all of their promises. They took those held as prisoners back to Recife, including many wealthy citizens, and required them to pay ransoms for their freedom. Although the Dutch controlled the coastal areas, the Portuguese men continued fighting a guerilla campaign inland. Many Portuguese civilians, including women and children, remained with the fighters in their defensive redoubts.

The Dutch left Porto de Calvo poorly defended and the Portuguese moved back in, killing many of the defenders. The remaining Dutch troops surrendered and became our prisoners. Matias de Albuquerque accepted their surrender with dignity but imprisoned Domingos Calabar, the friend of Vandscope, as a particularly notorious criminal and traitor.

I received Calabar's confession of his many sins. Shedding tears of remorse, he pleaded for forgiveness. He asked me to promise to arrange for the settlement of various debts and other affairs of his through his mother, a promise I later fulfilled.

That afternoon, a magistrate and a scribe came to question him about other traitors of whom he might have had knowledge. It turned out that those guilty of treason were mostly from among the wealthy elite. When Matias de Albuquerque was informed of this, he became preoccupied that the denunciations would stir up too much trouble. He ordered the magistrate to stop taking further testimony.

Later that evening Calabar was taken outside and strangled by means of a metal collar affixed to a plank. His head was severed and the rest of his corpse was quartered. The head and other body parts were impaled on the poles of the stockade. Knowing this act would be an affront to the Dutch, Matias de Albuquerque quickly hid, for later use, all of the heavier weapons that he could. He assembled the troops and marched off, together with some of the local landowners.

Seeing the town abandoned, a number of those who lived in the countryside, as well as blacks and mixed race people, came and took all of the weapons and food they could find. None of them felt sufficient pity for the deceased to bury his remains. This failure put them at grave risk of retaliation by the Dutch.

3 PLEAS FOR MERCY

Editor's Note: The Dutch officers are infuriated by the actions of the Portuguese defenders and decree death for the local residents. Calado pleads the residents' case and skillfully argues for the Dutch to show them leniency and thereby gain their cooperation. He points out several factors critical for the long-term success of the Dutch invasion. Only the residents possess the necessary know-how for cultivating and refining sugarcane. Sugar underpins the invasion as a commercial venture. Calado notes with a tone of resentment the relative wealth of the Dutch. We also see the importance of language skills, the near impossibility of overcoming guerilla fighters, and the readiness of slaves to flee captivity when the opportunity arises.

* * *

Three days after Porto de Calvo was abandoned, the Dutch governor Vandscope and his army returned. Vandscope became enraged when he saw his friend Calabar's head and body parts affixed to the poles of the stockade. He ordered his troops to shoot on sight every Portuguese and other resident of the town they encountered. He then had Calabar's remains buried with full honors at the church.

The local people, terrified by the news that the Dutch would kill them all, began to show up at my residence in the countryside. I was getting ready to leave in order to join up with Matias de Albuquerque. With tears they lamented the injustice of the order and begged for God's help.

Even if they could escape the Dutch by hiding in the woods, they couldn't escape death from deprivation and starvation. They shed so many tears that I decided to go back to Porto de Calvo to plead with the Dutch to spare them. In addition to Vandscope, I knew I would also find in town Admiral Lichtart, who spoke good Portuguese, and Field Commander Artixof, who spoke excellent Latin.

When I arrived, the Dutch sentinels seized me and took me to the three commanders, Vandscope, Lichtart, and Artixof. They asked me many questions, and finally: what was my intent in entering the town, considering that the Dutch were there?

I responded that, due to pity and to my zealous service of God, I had come to beg them for mercy, and for their forgiveness of the local residents; and, further, that they suspend the severity of the death sentence for all of the residents.

The officers replied that the death sentence was just, and well deserved, because the inhabitants had helped Matias de Albuquerque to reenter and take over the town, to kill Dutch soldiers, and to execute Calabar in such an offensive way. They said all the inhabitants were traitors who colluded in these evil acts, and all must die, including me.

I was taken aback by this harsh response. For a few moments, I was uncertain of how to respond. I thought to myself: dying in the service of God, for the benefit of my fellow man, and to save so many people, the majority of whom are innocent, is how I should act as a Christian, especially one who has taken the vows of a religious order. I should die for the honor of Him who gives us the most glorious of rewards. I took a deep breath, and replied as follows:

> My Lords, subjects have little fault for the acts of the King or his governing officials. If Matias de Albuquerque committed some offenses against Your Lordships, you have troops and ample resources with which to exact cruel vengeance upon him.
>
> The local residents who went with him, they might have some fault in the opinion of Your Lordships. However, since they were free from any promise of loyalty to either Your Lordships or to the Netherlands, there was no offense committed. They could have acted as they wished. They were free to follow their General, and in fact if they hadn't, it would have been viewed very badly. His Majesty the King of Spain and Portugal could have punished them as wrongdoers.

Those who stayed here as well, had they wished, could have gone with Matias de Albuquerque. They could have done so easily, since they had plenty of time. And even today they could do this, should they find themselves being persecuted, because they can make their way through the forests. They know all of the trails in the backcountry. However, to remain here would be the best for them, because they've chosen to live together with Your Lordships.

If Your Lordships intend to live in this land, and manage it properly, it will be impossible to do so without their assistance. This is because they're the ones who know how to grow crops, maintain sugar cane fields, refine sugar, and tend cattle. None of the Dutch know how to do any of these things. They're in fact incapable of doing so, because in order to do so it's necessary to live in the backcountry.

If the Dutch spread out in small groups scattered across the countryside, separated by long distances, Portuguese soldiers can come at any time and kill them off. There will be no way to stop the Portuguese. They'll burn the cane fields and sugar mills. Even if ten thousand Dutch soldiers patrol in squads, they'll never be able to stop the Portuguese, because the country is huge and the forests are dense. Our soldiers will always be able to move around freely.

Thus, without the support of the local residents, Your Lordships will find it impossible to manage this land. Therefore, taking counsel among yourselves, it would be advisable to suspend the harsh sentence that was issued. You should offer good treatment to the local residents. Show them love and kindness. In this way, they'll offer good will and obedient service.

I said all of this, and more, because I couldn't bear thinking of the poor, dispossessed Portuguese losing everything, while watching the rich Dutch, who had more than enough, take over all of their farms, sugarcane fields, sugar mills, and slaves. The slaves at any rate were disappearing. With all of the disruptions, almost all of them had run off, in order to be free from their work.

I thought it would be better not to have the rich, prosperous Dutch take over everything. Rather, it would be best to have the Portuguese farmers, who didn't seem to be very good soldiers anyway, come back and care for their lands and estates. This would only be until such time as the Kingdom of Portugal could return and offer assistance.

The Dutch officials heard my words with scowls on their faces. They ordered me into a room and put a guard at the door. At this point, I was convinced I'd be killed. I began to repent to God for my sins.

The Dutch held an impromptu meeting, over bottles of wine and rum, to discuss my case. Since it was already afternoon, they ordered that a meal be served. The next thing I knew, Lichtart and Artixof entered my room and extended their hands to me, saying, in Dutch: "Good friend." They brought me out to the table and I joined them for the meal.

After we ate, they ordered me to go out to where the inhabitants were hiding, and to tell them to return to town to get good-conduct passports during the next three days. Those who failed to do so would be hunted down and punished as traitors. I did as they ordered, and the people returned to receive their passports. The Dutch restored everything to the owners and paid a fair price for all the food and supplies they requisitioned. After twelve days, the Dutch forces left in pursuit of Matias de Albuquerque, leaving a garrison of two hundred soldiers stationed in our town.

4 MORTAL ENEMIES

Editor's Note: Calado denounces the Native Brazilian tribe known as the Pitiguares because they hate the Portuguese. Native Brazilians of various tribes were being forced to live in villages under the supervision of Catholic clergy. Some of the tribes collaborate with or submit to the Portuguese, while the Pitiguares, whom Calado calls Caboclos, resist Portuguese domination. Early European accounts attest to the prevalence of intertribal warfare in Brazil. Enemies were at times cannibalized.[4] Calado mentions in several places the fear people have of being eaten by Caboclos. He rages repeatedly against the Caboclos for supporting the Dutch, and for the crimes they jointly commit against the local residents. From the perspective of the Pitiguares, the Dutch are welcome allies in the fight against a common enemy.

* * *

The indigenous Brazilians of the Pitiguares tribe—known to the Portuguese as Caboclos—were our mortal enemies. As soon as they saw that the main forts had surrendered, and that Matias de Albuquerque had withdrawn to a distant location, they offered to assist the Dutch in conquering Pernambuco in its entirety.

The Caboclos forgot how, in the bosom of the Holy Mother Church, the Portuguese had nurtured them. The clerics had worked for many, many years to indoctrinate them in the Holy Catholic Faith. They previously lived as wild animals; they were savages in the wilderness. The Portuguese with deep affection took care of them in their tribal villages, freeing them from captivity, even though they deserved far worse than captivity as punishment for their horrendous misdeeds.

---

[4] See for example Lery, *History of a Voyage to the Land of Brazil.*

Many Caboclos began going out with Dutch squadrons, teaching them all the secret trails. They helped the Dutch ferret out Portuguese hiding places in the forests. They robbed and killed the Portuguese, not sparing even the women or children. Both they and the Dutch committed indescribable barbarities against the women.

The ordinary townspeople began to fear the Caboclos even more than they feared the Dutch because, having lived in the forests, the Caboclos knew every nook and cranny of the land. All they had to say to the Dutch was, "This one accompanied Matias de Albuquerque," or, "That one spoke to his soldiers," and the Dutch would order the person killed. The Caboclos would carry out such orders with cruelty, as inhuman butchers.

From that point forward the Caboclos were always with the Dutch, giving their all to the last drop of blood when fighting against us, to the delight of the Dutch. The attitude shown by the Dutch helped us understand how truly evil their intentions toward us were. The Dutch began to tyrannize the townspeople through their cruelty, which they had previously concealed, not daring to reveal it openly.

Helped by the Caboclos, the Dutch began traversing the backcountry. When they found someone's house, and suspected the householder had money, gold, jewelry, or silver tableware, they'd get false witnesses to allege he was a traitor and then torture him. They'd put his feet in boiling oil, hang him by his arms or upside down by his feet, or release a gun hammer on his fingers, crushing them.

Through these cruel acts, householders were thereby forced to give up everything they had, or to promise to give up what they didn't have. Many were hung, had their throats slit, or were shot for no other motive than robbery. By this means, the wicked, ungrateful Caboclos became the cause of and primary instrument for the Dutch to seize power over the entire Captaincy of Pernambuco, and to maintain control of it for so long.

5 DEFENDING THE FAITH

Editor's Note: It takes Spain and Portugal four years to mount a serious response to the Dutch invasion. Calado directs local guerilla activity against Dutch patrols. He reveals that he himself is a moderately prosperous slaveowner. With the arrival of Spanish and Portuguese soldiers, the Dutch order the local residents to relocate to areas firmly under Dutch control. The conflict becomes increasingly bitter with Calado having Dutch captives summarily executed.

* * *

In 1635, after the passage of some years, His Majesty the King of Spain and Portugal sent a large fleet to recapture the land seized by the Dutch. The fleet carried an army of two thousand Portuguese and Spaniards. Luis de Roxas replaced Matias de Albuquerque, who was called back to Portugal. Luis de Roxas took command of the ground troops. The fleet, which remained anchored in Portuguese-controlled Bahia, was under the command of the new governor, Fernando Mascarenas, Count of Torre.

Word of Luis de Roxas' arrival soon reached Artixof, the Dutch Commander. Artixof was a cautious, experienced military man. He feared his opponent would get support in the backcountry. He therefore ordered—on penalty of death—the relocation of all residents of Porto de Calvo and surrounding districts. They were to take their families, cattle, and supplies to the abandoned houses and farms found in areas firmly controlled by the Dutch. He gave them a deadline of ten days to relocate.

The residents hurried off to my home in the countryside. That's where I conducted mass and preached. From there, I'd go out to administer the sacraments in people's homes. I did so because we no longer had any churches. They asked me to advise them as to what they should do about the edict. I advised them to hide out in the woods with a good supply of provisions. I said they should wait there for the arrival of Luis de Roxas and the troops. I'd received a reliable report that they'd arrive within a matter of days.

I also said that any young men who were free of obligations should join me with their weapons. I issued an appeal to those who treasured their friends, and who were zealous, both in their service to God and in the cause of liberating their homeland. The young men would be placed in ambushes, in order to block the Dutch from proceeding with their campaign. I told them I'd give everyone who joined me plenty of food and drink because my supplies were abundant.

Rather than seeing my supplies seized by the Dutch, it would be better to expend them defending the Catholic faith. Not only did I promise to give the young men food, I also offered to provide slaves to cook it. I had twenty-five of them. Furthermore, I said I wanted to be their comrade in these efforts. I told them to leave if they chose to reject my advice. Personally, I was firmly determined to bury my books and writings. I said I'd head out the next night to meet up with our soldiers, and would return with them. I advised the men to consult their consciences and to do what they thought right.

Seeing my determination, the residents replied in a single voice that my advice was right on the mark. They said it was unjust to leave their farms destitute, to be handed over to the enemy, in order to go live on new lands, in close proximity to Dutch headquarters. Soon seventy-five brave young men offered their services, among them ten of mixed race and six Brazilian-born blacks. All of them had firearms.

The residents left to go erect shacks in the woods in which to hide. The next day, the seventy-five armed men and I went into the forest to set things up. I hid most of my personal belongings. We found a place where my slaves could cook our meals at night. In that way, the enemy wouldn't be able see the smoke from cooking-fires. I divided up the soldiers into five squads.

At night, I placed the squads in ambushes along the principal trails leading to the town. During the day, the soldiers returned to my house to rest, eat, and clean their weapons. Some were assigned to guard duty. During this time, we killed twenty of the enemy, and captured six alive. The latter I sent as prisoners to Luis de Roxas, who sent back his thanks for the good work, along with other correspondence.

Once the ten days were up, a Dutch force of seventy soldiers came to enforce the decree. They found a family and their slaves camped out in the forest. The soldiers burned down their lodging, which resulted in the death of two boys; others were injured. Hearing of this, I ordered that an ambush be set up. However, the main body of soldiers didn't pass that way. Only six did; we killed them all.

The next day being Sunday, I conducted mass. Seven Dutch showed up in the town, having become separated from the larger force. From the time the two boys were burned alive, we made it a point not to offer any clemency, so we killed all seven. We captured three more by the river, and sent them as prisoners to Luis de Roxas.

It took Luis de Roxas twenty days longer to arrive than I had been informed. He was hoping to open a route through the woods so his soldiers could avoid passing close to the Dutch fort. In the meantime, the Dutch went to every house in the district, stealing whatever the residents had left behind. There was no one to stop them, although my men managed to kill a few Dutch soldiers. We left their bodies exposed for the dogs and vultures to eat.

During the delay, one of my spies said that a young man of mixed race informed the Dutch about the hiding place of a landowner's family. A force of one hundred fifty soldiers and sixty Caboclos went out after them. I rewarded the spy, located the family, and set up ambushes. There was a lot of food so my soldiers ate well. We found two Dutch spies who were looking for the encampment and killed them both.

The Dutch managed to capture the owner of the farm, who had remained to guard it, as well as a number of his supporters and relatives. All were hung together. When daylight came and the soldiers marched out, they entered the ambushes we had set and we killed many of them, although we lost some men, too.

I searched for my soldiers to put them back into fighting formation but could only find thirty. The Dutch were afraid of another ambush and therefore didn't chase us. I finally arrived at my house with twenty soldiers, two of whom were wounded. When we could be certain we weren't followed, I took the soldiers, slaves, and supplies to a hiding place in the woods. The spot I chose was close to the route Luis de Roxas would take. We planned to join up with him when he came.

6 FRIENDLY FIRE

Editor's Note: Combatants are at times killed or wounded accidentally by soldiers on their own side during the chaos of battle. It also happens that unpopular or aggressive officers are murdered by their troops, which is known as fragging. The term entered American English during the Vietnam War, in which nearly one thousand such incidents were recorded. The killing that takes place in this chapter could have been either accidental or intentional. Calado has the privileged role of custodian of royal orders. He shows a special affinity for the sensibilities of nobles and justifies himself for having remained behind enemy lines. He once again condemns the conduct of the wealthy. An important figure in the history of Dutch Brazil, Johan Maurits, makes his appearance. He arrives in early 1637.

* * *

The day after we abandoned my house, the Dutch commander led all of his soldiers out to find me. Since there was no one at the house or nearby, he had it burned down, along with everything in it. They burned the slave quarters, and even killed the dogs and cats that remained behind. All of this has been verified in public documents.

At long last, my sentinel spotted a band of two hundred Portuguese under the command of Captain Rebelo, who was called Rebelinho. We joined up with him. The soldiers had been ordered to secure the path and find a place to set up camp for the remainder of Luis de Roxas' forces.

At this time, the Dutch commander Vandscope was in Porto de Calvo together with Artixof, expecting the arrival of Luis de Roxas. Vandscope ordered his personal secretary and some soldiers to bring back a flock of sheep that he'd left at one of the abandoned houses. One of the Portuguese captains with Rebelinho spotted the Dutch and went after them.

Vandscope's secretary asked for quarter, which was given to him, although the others were all killed. There were some murmurings that a few gold coins exchanged hands to facilitate the act of clemency but this was never proven. The Portuguese captain brought the sheep back to the camp, where they made a delightful meal for his comrades.

The Dutch secretary and a Caboclo guide ran back to town, and told Vandscope what had happened. He ordered the sounding of the drums and trumpets. Summoning all four hundred soldiers, he went out after Rebelinho. Recognizing he wasn't well positioned, Rebelinho made a virtue of necessity, put his men in formation, and sounded the drums for attack.

Vandscope feared an ambush. He thought he might be facing Luis de Roxas' entire force. He retreated back to the town. He and his men then raced off to where their boats were anchored, and set sail for Recife.

That night, Rebelinho entered the town without incident. His men ate what they could find. The next day some Dutch soldiers showed up looking for Vandscope. We killed them all. The town was full of gunpowder, lead shot, and tinder, which we confiscated. The Dutch had left it all behind because they were in such a hurry to escape. The next day, the soldiers accompanying Luis de Roxas started to arrive.

I was able to meet up with Luis de Roxas along with my twenty soldiers on the path leading into town. At first he asked who I was. One of his officers told him I was the priest who had sent him the Dutch prisoners. He then greeted me with a joyful look on his face, thanking me for what I'd done. He asked me what motivated me to stay with the enemy. I responded that I did it for the love of God and for the care of those dear to my heart. Had I gone off with Matias de Albuquerque, the residents would have been left with no one to conduct mass, hear their confessions, preach to them the word of God, or exhort them to persevere in the Roman Catholic faith.

If I'd left, then many would have died without confessing their sins. They'd have been led into error because the Dutch preachers were distributing a booklet everywhere, entitled *Catholicism Reformed*, in the Spanish language. This booklet was filled with all of the errors of Calvin and Luther. It was meant to convince the ignorant that the true religion is what books of this type proclaim. I also said that if I hadn't stayed, his Lordship wouldn't have found a single resident still there. There would have been no one left to offer his troops flour, meat, and other foodstuffs. On hearing this, he stood up, embraced me firmly, and said:

> Father, very well done, and very prudent, and for the glory of the King, in that those who left their houses and farms, and withdrew far away, are traitors. Those who stayed in their homes, these are His Majesty's loyal vassals. This is because if they hadn't stayed, there wouldn't be anyone now to help provide sustenance for my soldiers, as well as to lend us slaves and carts to carry our ammunition. In truth, the reason I made such haste to reach this town was not to fight the enemy but to find food to sustain all the people I brought with me.
>
> Those who withdrew, leaving their farms and all of their goods behind, did us great harm. In the first place, they impoverished themselves, without any way to remedy this situation. Secondly, they've consumed food that would have sustained our soldiers. Thirdly, they've made the enemy rich and prosperous. And fourthly, they've made it impossible to render their services to the King at this time.
>
> In the future as well, such people will have no way to aid the King. All of these failings could have been prevented had they simply remained in their houses, with the enemy's good conduct passports. For in the end, they're Portuguese, and when the occasion calls, they must always follow and serve His Majesty, as their natural King and Lord.

I rode into Porto de Calvo together with Luis de Roxas. The nobleman showed me great affection during the four days he remained in the town. I was always in his company. At night, we discussed various subjects. I informed him of many important things. He then set off to do battle with the Dutch.

Their commander Artixof was alarmed that Vandscope had been left exposed with so few men. Artixof led a massive force of fifteen hundred soldiers. He had spies everywhere. Once he determined the place where Luis de Roxas and his troops would arrive, he burned all of the houses and sugar mills in the district. The Dutch managed to ambush some of our rearguard but we turned on them ferociously and killed fifty. The Dutch ran off, leaving many weapons behind.

Luis de Roxas caught up with the Dutch again the next day. He was so determined to destroy them that he ordered his men to attack in hand-to-hand combat. In the middle of the confusion of battle, as he faced the enemy, encouraging on the troops, a bullet that came from our own side hit him in the back. It pierced him all the way through.

He fell to the ground, got up, and shouted, "It's nothing, forward soldiers, so we can defeat the enemy! Give me my horse! Is it possible I could be here among the noble Portuguese?" Shortly thereafter he fell to the ground dead. With help from another man, I pulled his body into the brush and covered it with dry leaves, so that it couldn't be found.

The word began to spread among the troops that the commander was dead. The portly landowners soon turned their horses and rode off. They'd accompanied us from a distance on horseback, not to help in the battle, but to watch from atop a nearby hill what was for them nothing more than a bullfight.

The soldiers, seeing the landowners ride off, imagined we were encircled by the enemy. They turned and fled through the woods. Two of the captains, Camarão and Rebelinho, brought order to the retreat. They faced the enemy, killing two hundred of the Dutch troops and wounding four hundred. The Dutch pulled back and headed down the trail leading to their fort. Most of our soldiers returned to the town.

Many of the Spanish and Italian troops, however, following their officers, retreated without our knowledge. They went south, to an area not under Dutch control. As a result, for several days we didn't know whether or not they'd survived the fighting.

Two days after the battle, a couple of us—as we were ordered—along with my slaves, went to find the body of Luis de Roxas where we'd left it. After viewing the battle debris, we counted the dead, and also recovered the weapons that we'd stashed away earlier. I had my slaves put Luis de Roxas' corpse, which was already giving off a stench, into a hammock. They carried it to a plot in the woods near my house.

Once we were at my house, I had the slaves put the body in a coffin, dig a grave, and erect a cross. I blessed the water, offered prayers, and conducted the burial ceremony according to the rites of the Holy Roman Church, in the best manner that I could under the circumstances. Before the slaves covered the casket with earth, I reached into an opening in my priest's robe, under my left armpit, where I kept a pouch containing relics of the Saints. I removed another pouch in which there were two small golden keys.

The keys opened a small box, which was being carried with our provisions. The box held the King's orders. Once we were back in town, I handed the pouch with the keys to one of the officers, Dias de Andrade. I assured him the grave was well hidden, with no witnesses to the burial.

Andrade opened the box and found in it the orders of the King of Spain, naming the Spanish commander who was to succeed Luis de Roxas in the event of his death. However, this officer was gravely ill and far away. As it turned out, he was already dead, having died the same day as Luis de Roxas. The orders also named the next commander in succession, the Count of Banholo, who was also far away. The King's orders were sent to the Count.

However, even though the entire army was stationed in Porto de Calvo, the Count delayed coming for four months. When he did finally arrive, he brought along additional troops and munitions.

Around the same time an enormous fleet arrived from Holland, bringing Johan Maurits, the Count of Nassau, as the new Dutch governor and military commander. Artixof abandoned the nearby fort and burned it down. He went to Recife to await new orders.

The Count of Banholo took this opportunity to build a massive and impregnable new fort near Porto de Calvo. All of the townspeople and their slaves joined in to build it. We completed construction in the short span of three months. It was outfitted with substantial, high-quality artillery. It was the best fort in all of Pernambuco.

7 COUNTS ATTACK AND FLEE

Editor's Note: Johan Maurits, Count of Nassau, is a seasoned commander sent to Brazil by the Dutch to quell remaining resistance to their rule. Opposing him is the Count of Banholo. At the time, much of southern Italy is under Spanish rule. Portuguese, Spanish, and Italian troops form an uneasy alliance in the battle against the mighty Dutch. Jealousy and infighting paralyze the defenders. Calado praises feudalistic virtues, which seem to matter more to him than competence. In his eyes, it is a testament to the nobility of Count Maurits that his men take pains to handle with respect the disinterred remains of Luis de Roxas. Among the Portuguese defenders are two key figures: Camarão, the leader of indigenous troops, and Henrique Dias, the leader of African, African-Brazilian, and mixed race troops.

* * *

Once the Count of Nassau recovered from his sea voyage and had been fully debriefed, he set about to crush the Portuguese resistance, as he'd been sent to do. He assembled an army of five thousand men, plus a massive number of Caboclos. By land and sea he set out to dislodge the Count of Banholo and seize Porto de Calvo. He issued a proclamation to the residents of the surrounding district that it would be impudent to withdraw into the backcountry with their wives and children, and likewise to send away their cattle. Such acts would be punished as treason, with their belongings subject to confiscation.

However, even before the Dutch forces arrived, the Count of Banholo had already sent away all of his goods and cattle, broken up into small lots to escape notice, to an area far away that was under Portuguese control. He assigned Italian soldiers to guard his belongings, which were moved at night to avoid any commotion. He especially wanted to ensure that I didn't see what he was up to. He also set up a secret hiding place, together with an escape route, that he and a few high officials could use when needed.

The Count of Banholo called a war council. In attendance were the nominal Portuguese Governor of Pernambuco, and the officers Andrade, Rebelinho, Camarão, Henrique Dias, and others. Camarão was captain of the allied indigenous Brazilians. Henrique Dias led the black soldiers. Andrade proposed setting up numerous ambushes between where the Dutch would make landfall and the town. Those who were more courageous among the officers supported this strategy. The Count of Banholo, however, decided to station all of the troops in the town, where they were to await the enemy. This plan caused the Governor much grief because, as a man of prudence and wisdom, he had a presentiment that it would lead to ruin.

The landowners, local officials, and officers saw that the Count of Banholo was doing almost nothing to prepare to resist the enemy. They also observed that he had three watches of Italian soldiers guarding his house every night. Through his conduct, they recognized the signs that he was planning to flee. They decided to seize the Count of Banholo, and to nominate Andrade as the new field commander.

The plotters went to Andrade's house and offered him the command. They pleaded with him to accept. He replied that he couldn't possibly do so because he prided himself on being the King's loyal subject. He wouldn't disobey orders since this would ruin his reputation. He said further that he had no aspirations for recognition or high office, unless they were awarded for loyal service to his King. He persuaded everyone to halt the plan.

In light of everyone's disappointment with his response, he said to me and the three officers who remained with him that no matter what danger there might be, it would have been worse to stir up a revolt among us, especially with the enemy so close. However, if everyone had acted first and imprisoned the Count of Banholo, before offering Andrade the position, then he would have accepted it. In such a case, there could be no accusation or assumption that he'd been involved in the plot. But, since they tried to get his support first, there was no way he could accept what they offered.

We soon heard the nearby pounding of the enemy's drums. The Count of Banholo said it wasn't the enemy. This statement was contradicted when a couple of sentinels arrived, reporting that they'd seen the massive army just a short distance away. The townspeople raised an uproar, gasping and crying. Women ran with their children, slaves carried their master's furnishings, officers yelled for their sergeants to order the troops into formation, and some confessed their sins, out of fear that their lives would soon end.

The Count of Banholo rode back and forth on his horse, without giving any orders. A number of soldiers pulled back to the fort, which was well supplied. They secured the gate just as the Count of Nassau appeared on the hilltop above the town.

Seeing the enemy, a number of courageous officers led their men to fight them. Notable among them were Rebelinho, Camarão—who with a lance in one hand led a horse carrying his wife Dona Clara— and Henrique Dias, whose skin was black but who was white in deeds and force of will. Others guarded the rear.

The Count of Banholo, once these actions were taken, ordered the town to be burned down. This was a sure sign he had no intention of ever living there again. The flames quickly consumed it. Nothing remained except ashes and dust. The fort, which was on high ground, escaped burning.

The Count retreated to his hiding place on a hilltop, together with the Governor and a few soldiers. He ordered Andrade to come with him. He refused to release Andrade to go fight. He did this to prevent the officer from achieving any glory in battle. The Count was also afraid the other officers and men would revolt and proclaim Andrade their field commander.

As the enemy descended into the town, a fierce battle arose. Our men fought courageously but were outnumbered. Many were killed and wounded on both sides. Seeing the enemy gaining ground, Andrade finally arose with furor, and, disobeying the Count, rode his horse into the battle, entering the fray with his sword drawn. Those in the fort began discharging the artillery, firing sacks of nails and musket-balls that caused great damage to the enemy, to the point that they were forced to sound the retreat and pull back.

By nightfall, our troops were in the town, and the enemy forces were on the other side of the river. The Count of Banholo snuck off with the Governor and some soldiers by his secret escape route. When the troops found out what he had done, they went after him. The Count, gripped with fear, kept on the march by candlelight, ordering that no one speak. A group of women along the pathway, waiting for daybreak, saw him go by. They shouted insults at him, calling him infamous, cowardly, traitorous, treacherous, perfidious, and other such slanders. All he could do was order his men to keep marching.

Andrade continued to fight a rearguard action against the advancing Dutch. Others defended the townspeople, including women, children, and slaves, as they made their way to Portuguese-held territory. Their sufferings along the way, through the forests and along the beaches, were immense. Many were killed or died. Things were indescribably bad. Those who were eyewitnesses, like me, were left so heartbroken that they couldn't thereafter recall the images without shedding innumerable tears.

When the enemy found the town burned down and abandoned, they encircled the fort and began blasting it with artillery. After twenty days and nights of bombardment, our men, badly outnumbered, seeing the town abandoned, with no signs of assistance or hope of receiving any, at last surrendered the fort. They were allowed to do so with honor.

The Dutch took control. Their soldiers combed the charred remains of the town for anything of value. In the church, they found a painting of the coat of arms of Luis de Roxas. The Dutch knew he'd been killed. They asked where he was buried. A nephew of his questioned me about this. I showed him the site of the makeshift grave.

Luis de Roxas was disinterred. His coffin was brought to town. The nobleman was given a dignified burial inside the chapel, under his coat of arms. The soldiers later presented the coat of arms to the Count of Nassau, who valued it highly and hung it on his own wall. He did this out of respect for the courage and nobility of Luis de Roxas.

8 BAHIA BESIEGED

Editor's Note: Brazil's capital at the time is Salvador da Bahia. As the Dutch drive imperial troops south from Pernambuco, Count Maurits becomes confident that he can land a knock-out blow on his opponent by seizing Bahia. Portuguese civilians are advised by the retreating officers to return to their homes and wait for the return of Portugal's forces. The Vicar of the Church in northeastern Brazil orders the remaining priests to go to Bahia. Calado laments the destruction of churches and the absence of clergy to perform the sacraments. He fears the demonic influence of Protestant propaganda on the Christian faithful. Count Maurits takes on the New Christian Gaspar Dias Ferreira as a close advisor. Bahia's defenders repel the massive Dutch assault at a great cost in lives. Fighters under Camarão and Henrique Dias are decisive in the defense.

* * *

The Count of Nassau, after resting for a few days and securing the fort, pressed on with his campaign. He sailed with most of his forces south to the San Francisco River, in an attempt to attack the Count of Banholo and our retreating forces. The poor townspeople expected to be caught up in the fighting. In their despair, they asked Andrade what they should do.

Andrade said that those who wished to, and who had the means, could continue on with the soldiers to Bahia, and he would defend them. However, for the others, it would be better to hide out for a bit, and then request good-conduct passports from the Dutch. In this way they could return home, and continue to live peacefully, although in subjugation.

Their subjugated status would continue until God chose to help them in their misery, with the return of the Portuguese to reclaim the lost territory. They could take care of their farms, produce food, and supply the King's soldiers when they arrived. Many decided to take this advice and requested passports, which the Count of Nassau graciously conceded to them. Thereafter, they returned to their homes.

Assisted by the Caboclos, who with great cruelty killed every Portuguese they found, including children, the Dutch captured the entire region bordering the San Francisco River. The Portuguese soldiers made their way further south, to Bahia. It appeared to the Count of Nassau that he was close to seizing all of Brazil. The key was to take Bahia, Brazil's capital.

The Count of Nassau ordered up a powerful force of thirty-five warships, plus auxiliary vessels, carrying six thousand combatants, fully stocked with ammunition and supplies. A New Christian named Gaspar Dias Ferreira, who lived among the Dutch, in support of this effort provided cunning assistance to the Count. Hoping to gain more land, Ferreira offered to accompany and advise him. The Count accepted this offer and made Ferreira quartermaster.

When the fleet embarked, Ferreira sailed on board the Count's ship and was given the honor of dining with him. Both men assumed the Dutch would be victorious and thereby accrue great riches from pillaging Bahia.

With all our fighting men in retreat to Bahia, the residents of Pernambuco and the other Captaincies of northern Brazil were subjected to the harsh measures imposed by the Dutch. Among our sorrows was the destruction of the churches, which were converted into horse stables, with the holy images being smashed to pieces.

What was even more pathetic than this destruction was the lack of priests. No one could administer the sacraments of the Holy Mother Church, indoctrinate the residents, or encourage them to persevere in the Catholic faith. This was because some of the priests, out of fear of the enemy who had killed a few of them, fled with the Count of Banholo. Others, who would have stayed behind in their zeal to save souls and out of Christian love, were ordered by the Vicar to leave. The Vicar said this was the command of the Bishop of

Brazil. He threatened to punish any priests who remained in enemy territory.

I honestly didn't know the reason for this order, or its justification. I could ask: What would have been better and of greater service to God? Would it have been best for the priests to stay with their faithful Christian flocks, comforting them in their struggles by administering the sacraments? By consulting Scripture, we would have found written in every relevant passage that when God punished His people with captivity, as merited by their sins, He permitted the Holy Prophets to accompany the wicked captives. God did this so that they could be consoled in their sorrows. By their prayers of supplication, God's wrath was appeased, and His rod of justice was placated. Bestowing mercy on the captives, God gave them liberty.

Was it truly best for our priests to run and hide, whether forced to do so or by choice? They abandoned the miserable Christians and their eternal souls in total distress. Weren't the Christians left without Mass or Confession, in the midst of the countless heresies and perverse rituals that filled Pernambuco? The priests deserted the simple residents, who were at obvious risk of falling into the hands of the Devil. The One who has perfect knowledge must answer these questions. Those who lack such knowledge should judge the matter honestly and without prejudice, in the spirit of justice.

Be that as it may, a favorable wind carried the Count of Nassau and his massive fleet south to Bahia faster than expected. They entered the harbor unimpeded. After disembarking soldiers and artillery pieces on the beach, the Count ordered an attack of such ferocity that his men quickly reached the city gate. However, they were stopped by the rigorous defense hurriedly implemented by the Governor, Pedro da Silva. He launched counterattacks, sending officers and men who had experience fighting the Dutch in Pernambuco. Despite many deaths on both sides, the Count of Nassau wouldn't desist in his attack. He managed to set up eight cannons in two batteries on land, which were used, together with artillery on his ships, to bombard the city savagely. The Portuguese fired back in reply, but were clearly outgunned.

The Count, having demonstrated his power, sounded drums calling for a parley. His representative sailed to shore in a small launch, carrying a letter demanding surrender. Many who were with the Governor and read the letter commented that the writing appeared to be that of the New Christian Ferreira, who they knew well.

The letter stated that another fleet of equal size would soon arrive from Pernambuco. The Portuguese would be allowed to surrender on favorable terms if they didn't delay, but should they fail to capitulate within three days, they would be attacked and given no quarter. The Governor Pedro da Silva replied in more or less the following terms:

> The cities of the King, our Lord, don't surrender without bullets and without sword in hand, and only after much blood has been spilled. The strong-spirited Portuguese aren't made cowards by words not backed by deeds. They aren't humiliated by bravado and empty threats. Here we are, and whoever survives will claim success.
>
> If I were to advise Your Lordship—even though I know it would be rash to advise someone who hasn't requested it, or doesn't seem to think they need advice—it would be for Your Lordship to save your life. Go home to enjoy the richness of your years. You shouldn't be putting on comedies, which are going to turn into tragedies. I have plenty of gunpowder and bullets, which I will give to you as a gift. My many soldiers will wait on the tables at this party.
>
> However you might find me, no matter how easygoing I am, it would be better that you think about my soldiers, who are fierce by nature. They are, after all, the Portuguese, accustomed to never being defeated, ready and able to bring down the overbearing pride of the most arrogant men of the entire world.

Deal with your weapons, which are the only things that matter now to Your Lordship. Stop believing in dreams, which will soon be turned into ashes. Forgive the brevity of my response, because what I lack in words will soon be made up for by my hands, not only mine, but those of my soldiers. They don't want any more parleys, and in fact didn't want me even to read the letter sent by Your Lordship. May God protect you from your insane imagination.

As soon as the Count's representatives returned and delivered this message, he unleashed a blistering attack, supported by horrendous bombardment from both sea and land, with many killed on both sides. Two captains went out from the city, Camarão with his indigenous Brazilian fighters, and Henrique Diaz with his regiment of blacks and men of mixed race. They engaged the enemy with such courage, killing so many of the Dutch, that both captains deserve the honor of ceaseless praise. Governor Pedro da Silva seemed to be everywhere, encouraging the troops, distributing ammunition, and displaying the boundless courage he had within.

After three days of relentless combat the Count saw that he was on the verge of utter defeat, having lost so many men. As night fell, he withdrew all of his remaining men to his ships, including the wounded. He blasted away at the city throughout the night, setting sail before dawn. The beaches were littered with the dead and abandoned war materiel. The Count returned to Recife not quite as content as he had expected to be when he set out.

9 FREEDOM OF CONSCIENCE

Editor's Note: Following the failed attack on Bahia, the Count turns his focus to the governance of Pernambuco. He realizes that to secure the cooperation of the residents, the Dutch must allow Catholic clergy to perform the sacraments. This is difficult because the clergy are suspected of engaging in treasonous communications. In fact, two friars are arrested for transmitting letters, some of which contain embarrassing details about infighting among clerics.

The Portuguese view the Count as sympathetic to them, and they begin to call him Prince, as do the Dutch. The Prince invites Calado to dine with him and then to move into his house. Calado declines but relocates to a nearby house in Recife. He begins to conduct mass in a small chapel. With the changing atmosphere, the leading members of the Portuguese community pledge obedience to the Dutch Republic, and the Dutch grant the Portuguese freedom of conscience.

The Prince proposes a governing body for the Church. Since communication with Bahia and Brazil's Bishop is prohibited—due to the state of war—the Prince believes Calado will be elected to lead the local Church. Calado explains that this arrangement would be impossible among Catholics. Only by the authority of the Pope or Bishop of Brazil could such an appointment be made. Religious governance by council reflects the distinctive environment of the Netherlands.

However, the Dutch decide to banish Catholic clergy due to their inciting disobedience among Catholic soldiers in Dutch service. Although freedom of conscience prevails in the Netherlands, public worship by Roman Catholics is restricted due to suspicions about their loyalty. The same concern seems to have arisen in Dutch Brazil.

The Prince founds a new city, Mauritsstad, which Calado praises for its beauty, like a city in Holland. Calado seems to admire some aspects of Dutch culture. The Portuguese see the Prince as almost a father figure.

* * *

Around the time of the Count of Nassau's ignoble defeat, he began to let up on the oppression of the Church. A few priests had remained in the occupied lands, despite the Vicar's orders. At first, they went about secretly. The Count allowed them to appear in public, and to conduct rites in churches located in the countryside. He did this in response to numerous petitions from the residents, who asserted that either the Count would need to permit priests in the occupied territories, or else authorize the residents to leave Pernambuco, because they'd refuse to remain without priests to administer the sacraments.

The residents directed their petitions to the Count because he was a good-natured person, and had royal blood, which caused him to be inclined toward the good. However, his authority was limited. He couldn't go against the decrees of the governing body set up by the Dutch, known as the Supreme Council. Calvinist preachers, who hated Catholic priests and couldn't bear to see them, had strongly influenced the Councilmembers. The Council refused to allow public Mass to be conducted within their fortified cities, even though it permitted the Jews to have synagogues in them.

Some prominent residents of Pernambuco sent requests to the Bishop of Brazil in Bahia for priests to administer the sacraments. I also wrote to the Bishop on their behalf, making powerful arguments and citing the Saints as authorities, with the intent of bringing forth the piety one would expect from someone as educated, virtuous, and full of Christian zeal as the Bishop to whom I wrote.

The ordinary townspeople also sent petitions to the King by way of Holland, because for several months no priests arrived from Bahia, nor did we receive any response to our letters. Finally, news arrived in Pernambuco, by way of Holland, that the King had sent orders to warn the Bishop against his negligence in this regard. After six months, a few priests began to appear, and the residents at last felt relief in their hearts.

During such a difficult time, when the remaining clerics should have focused only on serving God, a priest named Friar Cruz sent Friar Junipero, a monk under his command, to Bahia with a number of letters. He had been warned by some cautious people not to do this because the Dutch had published a proclamation promising death to anyone in Pernambuco who wrote to someone in Bahia. The death penalty also applied to those who received letters from Bahia or who sheltered or assisted a soldier or anyone else arriving from Bahia.

Furthermore, anyone who knew of someone who did any of these things was required to denounce them or else suffer the same penalty. Despite having witnessed the severity by which the Dutch enforced these measures, including executions, Friar Cruz proceeded to send Junipero to Bahia. Junipero delivered the letters and brought back others on his return.

Within a few days of Friar Junipero's return to Pernambuco, the Dutch learned of his trip, and ordered his arrest, as well as that of Friar Cruz. Both were brought to Recife. They decided to rough up Junipero, who was afraid of being tortured on the rack, which was set up right in front of him. He admitted to everything, including the contents of the letters he'd carried. Under threat of torture, he said he acted on the orders of his clerical superior, Friar Cruz.

The Dutch confiscated the letters and had them read in translation by a Portuguese Jew. From them, the Dutch learned about clerical matters that the priests had wanted kept secret. Among the clerics, to their discredit, there was much hatred and resentment. Knowing all about the two clerics' secrets, as they were being sentenced to death by hanging, the Dutch mocked them and looked on them with scorn. However, many prominent landowners pleaded with the Count to pardon the two. He relented, out of his good nature, but in addition, a lot of money exchanged hands, which is how the Dutch get things done. Although the death sentence was lifted, the two clerics remained imprisoned.

I had been hiding out in the backcountry, far beyond the reach of the Dutch, waiting for the King's forces to return. Somehow the residents of Pernambuco found out where I was, and pleaded with the Count to bring me back. They offered him gifts and made various arguments to him on my behalf. I should note that the Dutch called him Prince, which was deserved, and the Portuguese residents likewise began using this title and other respectful forms of address when dealing with him. I likewise have adopted the convention of referring to him as Prince, and will do so for the duration of my account.

With all of the praise heaped on me by the Portuguese elite, the Prince became desirous to see me and to speak with me. He not only gave permission for the landowners to request my return but also wrote to me personally. He promised to protect me. However, in reading these letters, I recalled how I had sent soldiers to fight the Dutch, and had caused them so much harm. Their hatred for me was likely to be such that on the slightest excuse, no matter how minimal, they would take vengeance on me. I became scared and, overwhelmed by fear, decided to move somewhere I couldn't be found.

As a subterfuge, I sent the messenger back with word that I'd arrive in a few days. I then prepared to flee. Before I could go, I received a second letter from the Prince, in which he asked me to come promptly, at the request of the residents. He assured me, by his word of honor, that I'd live under his protection, free from oppression.

Feeling reassured, I set off without delay and arrived at the Prince's home. Since the Prince didn't know me, one of his guards, with whom I'd previously spoken, made the introduction. I was received with great courtesy, not because of my position, but because the landowners had spoken so highly of my virtue and learning.

That same day he invited me to eat at his table, in the position of honor at his right hand side. We spoke on a range of matters in Latin, at which he excelled. He offered to let me live in his house and pressured me to accept his offer. I gave many solid reasons why this wouldn't be a good arrangement. The Prince accepted my arguments but only on the condition that I'd live nearby and visit him frequently.

During the three days I stayed with the Prince, I kept puzzling over why he was treating me so well. In the end, I concluded it was due to his kind nature, and to his desire to gain the good will of the Portuguese, who had requested my presence. One of the Portuguese nobles provided a small house for me next to his. He sent for my books and belongings. There was a chapel nearby, where I began to conduct Mass for all those in the vicinity, and to administer the Sacraments.

Within ten days the Prince called for me, to let me know that the leading Portuguese had by petition promised obedience to the United Provinces of the Netherlands, and had been granted freedom of conscience. They could live in the purity of the Holy Roman Catholic Faith, and would be allowed the services of priests. However, among the priests none were well educated or capable of providing leadership. Since there could be no communication with Bahia, it would be necessary to set up a governing body. The Prince had no doubt that I'd be elected by the faithful to take charge.

I explained to him that it would be impossible to appoint someone to a clerical role in this manner. Although the Prince and Supreme Council could govern the secular realm in this way, in the spiritual realm such actions must be taken by the proper authority, which in this case belonged to the Bishop of Brazil, who was in Bahia. The only other such authority was the Pope as universal Priest of the entire Church, the successor of Saint Peter and Vicar of Christ. The Prince asked me whether I would accept the role, if it could be obtained via Holland, with proper authorization by Portugal or Rome. He told me that not even he was permitted to communicate with anyone in Bahia, due to the orders from Holland and the decree of his own Supreme Council.

I agreed but on the condition that I'd be permitted to return to Portugal via Holland, in order to deal with the matter. When the Portuguese landowners got wind of this, they petitioned the Prince to prevent me from leaving. They promised to manage the request to the Pope, via Holland. Jumping ahead a bit in my narrative, in the year 1641 I received a Papal letter from the Pontiff, Urban VIII, authorizing me to exercise religious authority in Pernambuco. For those who might doubt this, I've recorded a copy in the Open Records of Notary Public Manuel João de Neiva, and retained the original.

Returning to the events of 1637, once the Prince recovered his composure following his ignominious defeat in Bahia, he had to address the fact that small bands of guerilla fighters were entering Pernambuco from Bahia to carry on the conflict. They'd roam about the countryside, attacking the homes and farms of the Dutch and Jews who lived in the backcountry, robbing and killing them. The guerillas would then escape back into the woods. The Prince called the full Supreme Council to decide on a course of action. The Council members were fearful of the damage caused by Friar Junipero's trip to Bahia and the information he'd passed along.

The Supreme Council also noted that some Friars were refusing to grant absolution to Dutch and French Catholics who were serving the Netherlands because they'd taken up arms in an unjust war against Catholic Christians. The Friars were advising these soldiers to stop fighting for the Dutch, or else to flee to Bahia, from which they'd be given passage back to their home countries. Given this state of affairs, the Council commanded that every Catholic cleric, of every religious order, vestment, and status, who was to be found in lands under Dutch control, must gather on an island adjacent to Recife. They were given one month to do so, a timespan of fixed and certain duration. There were to be no exceptions, under penalty of death.

The clerics who assembled were badly mistreated and deprived of food. Hearing of this, the Prince sent them sustenance. At the end of one month, all were put on ships in a Dutch fleet. The sailors took the clerics' robes, abandoned them on deserted beaches, and otherwise abused them so badly that nearly all perished on the journey. After this, the Dutch ordered the confiscation of all weapons from the residents. In addition to being disarmed, the residents were now bereft of spiritual support from their clergy.

I was also sentenced to exile, and would have been forced to depart, had it not been for the intervention of the Prince. He told the Supreme Council that it wasn't acceptable to exile me. In his view, he'd given me his word that I'd be protected. If it were to be perceived that his word couldn't be trusted, then the landowners and other residents, who had petitioned on my behalf, would become aggrieved. He said it was necessary to get along with the local people because they produced the crops and provisions on which the Dutch relied.

The Prince went on to state that he'd carefully observed how I lived. He was convinced I didn't involve myself in matters of war or government, and sought only to carry out my duties as a priest, preaching to the Catholics. The Dutch, after all, had granted liberty of conscience to the Portuguese, as well as to the Jews. In fact, they showed greater generosity to the Jews, who were allowed to have synagogues within the fortified towns, including Recife. The Portuguese, in contrast, were prohibited from openly conducting Mass within the fortified area of Recife. In this way, I was allowed to remain in Pernambuco.

The Prince again invited me to come live in his house but I objected on many grounds, which he accepted as reasonable. He then offered to build a house for me, within the fortified area, on another island adjacent to Recife, where he was erecting a new city called Mauritsstad. I accepted his generous offer. The house was soon completed. From there, I'd go out to preach in various locations, and at religious festivals where my presence was requested. By living there, I was able to perform greater service to God—and sustain many more souls—than I possibly could have had I lived in hiding somewhere in the countryside.

The Prince became preoccupied with constructing his new city. He encouraged the Portuguese landowners to build houses there. The Prince personally helped lay out the street grid. He had a dike built to provide ample water for canoes and boats, and docks at which they could berth. He had a house for his own leisure built there, with a garden, filled with every type of fruit tree that existed in Brazil, and many from elsewhere. At his direction, two thousand coconut palms were dug up, hauled in, and planted. The city had a beautiful layout, landscaped with plants and flowers, and places for celebrations, entertainment, and games. It resembled a city in Holland. The Prince loved it so much that he moved most of his household staff and dependents there.

In addition, he brought in all types of birds and animals. The residents of the backcountry, who knew how to care for these creatures, would send him parrots, macaws, cuckoos, ducks, turkeys, chickens, panthers, anteaters, monkeys, goats, rabbits, and eventually every strange animal that could be found in Brazil. The people did this out of good will because they saw how the Prince was favorably inclined toward them. They helped him construct his two houses and garden. He showed the Portuguese such appreciation, and such favor, that he seemed to them like a father. This greatly alleviated their sorrow and discomfort in living under foreign occupation.

10 INTERMEDIARIES GET RICH

Editor's Note: Calado admires the wealth pouring into Pernambuco, although he disparages merchants and Jews. Nowadays we recognize the value of those with cross-cultural skills. The Sephardic Jewish community in Amsterdam retained its knowledge of Portuguese. Subsequent generations were fluent in Dutch. The know-how of Portuguese New Christians in Brazil, who had experience running sugar plantations and refineries, combined with the bilingualism of Jewish merchants from Holland, creates excellent opportunities for brokers and other intermediaries. Calado indicates that some of the Dutch resented Jewish commercial success. However, Calado admits that without translators the Portuguese and Dutch can't trade with one another, and the Portuguese can't go to court.

* * *

Pernambuco prospered greatly at this time. So much wealth flowed in from Holland that even blacks had money. When the Dutch conquered Pernambuco, some Jews came along with them. They were so poor they had nothing but the rags on their backs. However, in a short time they became rich with their shrewd dealings and frauds. When their relatives learned of their success, they began to pour in from Holland and other parts of Northern Europe. Each was smiled on by fortune in some little way, so that in a matter of days they all became rich.

The Jews succeeded because they were once Portuguese, having fled out of fear of the Holy Inquisition. They knew how to speak both Portuguese and Dutch. Serving as translators, they could make lots of money because the Portuguese and Dutch couldn't understand each other without their assistance. No business deals could be made without Jews being involved.

As a result, Jews could spot opportunities to buy land cheaply. They could then resell it at a high price, without any risk, ensuring a good profit without performing any work at all. They also got all of the jobs to serve as brokerage agents for the Dutch. In this way there wasn't a single piece of merchandise that didn't pass through their hands. They managed anything that rendered an easy profit. Only the more risky items were handed off to third parties.

When the Portuguese had to petition Dutch authorities about something, Jews would both draft the petitions and act as legal representatives. By this means, they came to know everything that was happening in Pernambuco. They made money from inside information. The Jews, in order to ingratiate themselves with the Dutch, passed on to them every secret that existed in the occupied lands.

The Jews would propose business ventures to the Dutch, to enrich themselves and impoverish the Portuguese. Eventually, with the Jews padding their pockets, the Dutch merchants began to realize that, due to their lack of fluency in Portuguese, they couldn't buy or sell anything without the involvement of Jews. This made the Jews rich. The merchants began to take collective action against the Jews, with the intent of banishing them. The merchants failed, however, because the Jews were numerous and influential. With all of their money they could grease the palms of the Supreme Council.

The Dutch residents claimed that Pernambuco had been conquered at the cost of Dutch lives and blood. A high price had been paid in terms of their personal welfare and Holland's resources. The Jews were latecomers, showing up after most of the fighting had taken place. It was only due to the Jews' knowledge of the Portuguese language that they were so successful in their business dealings, enriching themselves. The Dutch, for lack of language skills, had to run their shops from out-of-the way places that no one frequented, except for the Jews. The Jews would buy Dutch merchandise at liquidation prices before everything rotted. The Dutch then had nothing but junk left to sell. In this way, the Jews, without either work or expense, became ever richer. The Dutch were losing out.

The situation was a mess because the Jews who came from Holland had many relatives in Pernambuco who had lived according to the Law of Christ up to the time of the Dutch invasion. Once the Dutch conquered the land, these people took off their masks, so to speak, underwent circumcision, and publicly declared themselves to be Jews. They had deep roots in the land with many farms. They made common cause with their relatives, the newly arrived Jews from Holland. Aided by their relatives, who helped them acquire and operate sugar mills and plantations, the newly arrived Jews prevailed. They assumed control of the best assets, with the Portuguese thereafter reduced to a lowly status.

The good Christians were scandalized when the New Christians were circumcised and declared openly they were Jews. These people had been tenderly nurtured within the loving embrace of the Holy Mother Roman Church. Many said that all New Christians were in fact Jews. The only reason some didn't come out openly at this time was because they were afraid the Portuguese would eventually return and retake Pernambuco. However, I had knowledge that some New Christians didn't follow the Jewish Law, and in fact remained faithful to the Law of Christ. The doors of the Church have always remained open for such true Christians, who deserve our respect.

11 TURNING AGAINST YOUR OWN

Editor's Note: The name of João Fernandes Vieira appears for the first time in Calado's account. He's a major figure in the story of Dutch Brazil. Ana Pais, a Portuguese woman of good family, draws Calado's ire for having married three times, twice to heretics. Otherwise, we see growing evidence of the double-dealing and corruption that beset both sides in the conflict.

* * *

The Prince received a batch of letters from Holland, sent by the Dutch government, the West India Company, and his brother. The letters were critical of how he was governing Pernambuco. Count Johan Arneste of Nassau, the Prince's brother, wrote that he was astonished by what people were saying and writing about the Prince. Word had it that the Prince was out-of-bounds in some of what he was doing, carried away by his personal interests.

He was acting this way, it was said, on the advice of a Portuguese with whom he'd become too close. The Prince was known in Holland for being very gentle but in Brazil he'd become a rampaging lion. He was accused of harassing the local residents or consenting to their harassment, in order to amass personal wealth through illicit practices that would never pay off in the long run.

The Prince's brother informed him that the officials in Holland were aware of everything he was up to in Brazil. This was evidenced by their detailed knowledge about three great friendships the Prince had among the Portuguese. I was named as the first such friend, João Fernandes Vieira as the second, and Gaspar Dias Ferreira as the third. In my case, I was said to provide him with relief and diversion because he enjoyed my good and honest conversation, all the more so because I didn't intervene in matters of war or government. However, since I was well educated and prudent, I was thought to offer him sound advice on many topics related to his good name and reputation, and also on matters of benefit to the local residents, among whom I was highly esteemed and loved.

Regarding Vieira, the second of the three, he had won the Prince's favor by giving him many gifts and remembrances, some of great value, but all paid for by Vieira himself. The third, Ferreira, was causing the Prince to commit unjust acts, some of which were outrageous and deeply prejudicial to the local residents. These acts in fact bore the mark of tyranny, rather than being the works of a person of royal and imperial blood. The path down which Ferreira was leading the Prince was solely that of amassing wealth, at the cost of the blood of the poor and innocent.

Ferreira was, in short, making the Prince rich, and enriching himself at the same time. Ferreira had previously been so poor that he didn't have a plate of manioc flour to eat. However, under the shadow of the Prince's authority, and enjoying his favor, this man had been raised to higher status and received more respect than the Prince himself. Acting in the Prince's name, without his knowledge, Ferreira committed many foul deeds.

Finally, the Prince's brother said that the main source of all this intimate knowledge came by way of a certain woman. However, rather than blame her, he said the Prince should take a look at how he as a noble should conduct himself. He needed to acknowledge his own failings, which were giving rise to such accusations. It was his duty to renounce the riches and baubles that were tarnishing his good name and noble reputation.

Showing me the part of his brother's letter touching on these matters, the Prince was very offended and irritated. He knew, or suspected, that those among the Dutch who said these things were jealous, seeing him so rich, and that his own private Secretary must have sent all of this malicious gossip to Holland. He was certain the source was someone within his own household. He soon settled on a likely culprit, the Captain of his guards Carlos de Torlon, who was quickly removed from his position.

Captain Torlon had previously led an assault on Bahia, sailing a small fleet into the large bay known as All Saints Bay. He caused great damage to the sugar mills located on the coast at points where navigable rivers entered the bay. He looted and burned them. It took many days for our infantry to arrive from the city of Salvador da Bahia to assist the residents, who had fled into the forests. Using the driveshafts, fittings, caldrons, and other mill components he had seized, Torlon set up his own mill back in Pernambuco, next to the house of Ana Pais, who he had recently married.

Ana Pais was the most brazen woman there was among many such women in Pernambuco during this time of subjugation. I say this because although she was from a wealthy and noble Portuguese family, and had previously been married to an honorable nobleman, after her husband's death, being still young and newly widowed, she chose to marry a Calvinist. Rather than say she married him it would be more accurate to call her his concubine, since a preacher of a false sect conducted the ceremony. Her purported remarriage to a heretic caused a terrible scandal among the Catholic population.

As a consequence of Torlon's attack, the Viceroy Mascarenas decided to retaliate by sending small bands of soldiers back into Pernambuco, where they were to burn down sugar mills and plantations, and kill cattle. He sent additional fighters under the leadership of Henrique Dias, who commanded the blacks and men of mixed race.

Mascarenas then wrote to the Prince that a number of deserters were making their way to Pernambuco, with the objective of finding passage on ships to Holland, and from there back to their homelands. He said the men were likely to cause some damage along the way, since they had no officers to govern them. Mascarenas asked the Prince not to grant them passage but instead to hang them upon capture. He wrote this, however, because he knew that it would be impossible for the Dutch to capture any of these soldiers. Unfortunately, some of our soldiers, because they had no commanders to supervise them, accepted bribes in return for sparing the property of Dutch and Jewish landowners in Pernambuco.

Following the receipt of his brother's letter, the Prince went after Torlon, charging him with the crime of plotting to hand over Pernambuco to the Portuguese. Rebuking him and having him violently seized, he had Torlon shipped off to Holland in chains, where he soon died in captivity. His wife, Ana Pais, was pregnant and gave birth to a child. Finding herself widowed again, she married for a third time, to a member of the Legislative Council set up by the Dutch.

This third wedding was held in the French Calvinist and Lutheran Church in Mauritsstad. Another preacher of the same heretical sect conducted the ceremony. The wedding exhibited such impudence and so little modesty that even the Dutch who participated were astonished by Ana Pais' audacity. Once she was married for the third time, or rather once again became a concubine, she turned into such an enemy of her own people that she would bring charges against them to the Supreme Council. She advised the Councilmembers to rob the Portuguese and to kill them all.

12 CHRISTIAN IMPOSTERS

Editor's Note: Calado disparages the Protestant funeral held for the Prince's brother. He notes the lack of belief in purgatory and compares the poverty of its rituals with the sumptuousness of Catholic ceremonies. It's noteworthy how greatly the outer practices and inner beliefs of these two forms of Christianity came to differ after barely a century of schism. The turn away from pageantry by the Dutch owes much to the influence of Christian Humanism.

The order of the funeral procession is strange in Calado's eyes. Members of the Supreme Council, who are merchants, precede the landowners. Jews take precedence over military officers and the mass of ordinary Christians.

Calado's sharp tongue turns to the Catholic clergy. He directly criticizes the Chief Vicar and implicitly denigrates his superior, the Bishop of Brazil. His description of clerical incompetence, sexual improprieties, and misuse of donations differs little from criticisms of the Church leveled by the Dutch. We see evidence of differing Dutch and Portuguese attitudes toward clerical authority. Portuguese landowners pay to avoid Church exactions for keeping mistresses, while the Prince says the Dutch will in effect rebel if anyone attempts to impose something similar on them.

* * *

The Prince's brother, Count Johan Arneste, became ill and died while sailing with a squadron of freebooters. A ship brought his corpse to Recife for burial. The Prince gave orders for the body to be embalmed. He sent out a request for all of the leading citizens of Pernambuco to attend the funeral.

When the time came, they began a formal procession, with most dressed in black as a sign of mourning. The corpse was placed in a casket, followed by the Prince, then his guards, followed by his household, the Supreme Council with their Secretaries, the members of the Legislative Council, the Judges and Court officials, the military officials, the leading members of the Portuguese community, then the Dutch, French, and German merchants, then the Jews, followed by the military officers with their companies in order, the indigenous Brazilians carrying both guns and traditional bows and arrows, and finally the mass of the ordinary people. In this order they proceeded without speaking, in profound silence.

At last they entered the Church of the Holy Host, in which the Dutch preached their false religion and conducted their diabolical ceremonies. There they buried the body, without music, or tears, or any other demonstration of petitioning or intercessory prayer. The soldiers then discharged their guns in salute three times, as did artillery gunners on land and at sea. The mourners thereafter returned to the Prince's house, where a buffet was laid out, including many trays of cooked meat, fish, cheese, butter, sliced bread, both Spanish and French wine, beer, and rum. Each could eat as he pleased, and they offered many toasts in memory of the deceased. They also offered prayers for his sake, even though this was done after the burial rather than before.

These bizarre practices are based on the teachings of their false sect, in which they preach and believe that there's no Purgatory. Therefore, they assert there's no need for petitioning or intercessory prayer on behalf of the dead. They claim that all who believe in Christ will go to heaven, even if they don't perform good works. In support of this, they cite from the Gospels Mark 16:16: "He that believeth and is baptized shall be saved." However, they ignore such passages as James 2:17: "Even so faith, if it hath not works, is dead." It does a man little good to believe in Christ unless good works accompany his faith. Faith without works is dead.

The solemnity of Roman Catholic burial, on the other hand, deeply impressed the Dutch. The Viceroy Mascarenas, before the death of the Prince's brother, had sent a delegation to discuss various matters with the Prince and Supreme Council. One of the delegates passed away while in Pernambuco. The Chief Vicar happened to be in Olinda at this time. He, together with other priests, conducted the funeral service in Olinda with the permission of the Prince, with a full church choir, the crosses of the various orders, and a great display of pageantry and ceremony. The Dutch had nothing to compare with this in their country.

It's worth pausing to consider the background of the Chief Vicar. His name was Father Gaspar Ferreira, and he normally resided in the Captaincy of Paraiba, which was under Dutch control. The Bishop of Brazil in Bahia had appointed him to this senior role. He was an idiot, who didn't know how to recite the breviary or how to offer Mass. His impudence in his personal life and manners was so great that I hardly dare to write about it, so as not to tarnish the good reputation of the Priesthood or to diminish the respect owed to it.

Nevertheless, someone might ask the question: How could this incompetent cleric be appointed as the Chief Vicar? I'd have to answer that the Bishop issued secret orders, due to the Dutch occupation and suppression of priests, for the appointment of a different priest as Chief Vicar, Father Simão Ferreira. He was the Vicar of Olinda, a man of deep learning and exemplary character. However, since the Bishop didn't know his full name, he wrote only Ferreira on the instating order. The order was smuggled into Pernambuco by way of Gaspar Dias Ferreira, who I'll refer to simply as Ferreira, in order to avoid any confusion with the two priests of the same surname.

In place of the name Simão, Ferreira inserted the name Gaspar, since Father Gaspar Ferreira was his friend. Although Father Simão Ferreira complained to many about this trickery, he decided not to make an issue of it, since he was an honest priest devoted only to his calling.

At the time when the delegation sent by Viceroy Mascarenas arrived in Pernambuco, the Chief Vicar Gaspar Ferreira traveled to Olinda, which is why he was there to preside over the funeral ceremony. The Chief Vicar sent a letter to the Bishop of Bahia, by way of the head of the delegation, offering warm greetings and thanks for his appointment. In addition, he included various gifts, such as several costly rosaries, with the ends made of finely worked gold, and a hefty supply of silver coins. Ferreira also sent a letter to the Bishop, in which he spoke favorably of the new Chief Vicar. In this way, the Bishop found that all was well with Father Gaspar Ferreira serving in the role of Chief Vicar.

The shameless conduct of the Chief Vicar, this Father on whom fortune had smiled, became so extreme that leading residents of Paraiba journeyed twice to Olinda to lodge charges against him with the Prince and Supreme Council. Even two Calvinist preachers came with them in support. They extensively documented fifty-two serious offenses he had committed, testified to by witnesses, and asked for his banishment.

The accusers said no married man could feel safe, in regard to his wife or daughters, so long as the Chief Vicar remained in Dutch-controlled lands. They asserted that, should the Prince and Supreme Council fail to banish him, they would kill him. Despite the numerous charges, nothing was done because the Chief Vicar, through his friend Ferreira, bribed the Dutch. He gave an expensive gift to the Prince and made a sizeable offering to the members of the Supreme Council. The men of Paraiba appealed to the Bishop and Governor of Bahia to remove the Chief Vicar from his position but neither responded, due to their affection toward him.

The Dutch found out that the Chief Vicar had been sending quite a bit of money to the Bishop of Bahia, which came from such sources as offerings from mourners on the deaths of clerics, fees received in connection with his official duties and office, fees and asset seizures received as a consequence of punishments meted out by the Church, and bribes paid by those who wished to become Vicars. Seeing how much money was being generated from these sources, and wanting to skim it off for themselves, the Dutch called the Chief Vicar and demanded he turn the booty over to them. He denied that he had sent any money to the Bishop. The Dutch threatened to banish him, based on the many well-documented accusations against him. They rubbed his nose in the low opinion people had of him.

The Dutch then asked the Chief Vicar who was it that he recognized as his lord and superior: Was it the Dutch or his Bishop? He acknowledged that he served the Dutch. At this, the Dutch made an entry into the records of the Supreme Council that the Chief Vicar no longer recognized the Bishop of Brazil as his superior. From this point on, he would no longer have any communication with the Bishop or obey his commands. Going forward, he would take no action as Chief Vicar without being ordered to do so by Dutch authorities. By submitting to these conditions, he was allowed to remain. The Dutch ordered him to carry out no further excommunications. They also told him to deliver the funds and assets he received from fees and seizures to the Supreme Council.

The Supreme Council also came up with an innovative way to generate more funds. They ordered their bailiffs to seek out Portuguese landowners who had or were suspected of having mistresses. The bailiffs were to inform the landowners that the Chief Vicar would carry out his duties diligently. They'd be forced to pay significant penalties although thereafter they'd be promptly absolved of any guilt and exempted from further punishment.

One afternoon I was passing time with the Prince, engaged in conversation. Jokingly, I said to him that since the Supreme Council gave power to the bailiffs to mete out punishment on the wallets of the Portuguese who had mistresses or were suspected of such, and since the punishment was only money and not beatings, why not have the so-called Father Bailiffs also go after the Dutch? After all, the Dutch all had mistresses. They weren't punished for it and it didn't cause any scandal. The Councilmembers and the Prince could divvy up the penalties that would be collected from this source.

The Prince laughed at my suggestion. He said that among the Dutch, womanizing and drunkenness were the normal state of affairs. He wouldn't take the chance of implementing any new laws along such lines, since my own life would be put at risk for having proposed the idea. The women would rise up against me and throw stones at me, or I'd be forced to fight with some drunk, which would cause people to lose respect for me. Respect is something that can't be purchased at any price.

I had two serious doubts about the Chief Vicar, which I expressed to certain prominent individuals. The first doubt was, how could this Priest carry out his office in good conscience, after having negated his obedience to the Bishop who gave him the position? Further, how could he have assented to the conditions noted in the records of the Supreme Council, by which he no longer recognized the Bishop as his superior? How could a Priest refuse to obey his Bishop or to follow his orders, but instead only recognize the Dutch as his true superiors, following their orders and working on their behalf, in accord with their statutes and commands?

Ferreira addressed this first doubt of mine by noting that the Chief Vicar agreed to these conditions and signed off on them because he feared the Dutch would remove him from his position and his holy office, and banish him. The Chief Vicar didn't agree to these conditions in his heart, but only as a matter of form. Ferreira, in order to salve the Chief Vicar's conscience, petitioned the Bishop for a pardon and written exoneration, which the Bishop sent.

I challenged the value of the pardon, pointing out that to be a Christian, that is, one who believes in and professes the Law of Christ, is to proclaim faith to the point of dying for it. When a tyrant holds a sword to the chest of a Christian, threatening to kill him unless he recants faith in Christ, such a man who continues to profess faith in Christ, even though he is killed because of it, will be a martyr. According to Saint Augustine, suffering a painful death isn't what makes one a martyr but, rather, one becomes a martyr by virtue of the cause for which one dies in pain. A man who denies Christ to escape death is an apostate to the faith. The Bishop, while standing as Prelate and Prince of the Church, represents Christ, and whoever denies the Bishop, especially while facing a tribunal instituted by the enemies of the True Faith, is as a consequence denying Christ.

My refutation of the Chief Vicar's position was augmented by the fact that the Dutch hadn't threatened him with death, or even torture, but only with banishment to a non-Catholic land, or removal from his clerical office. Neither of these threats had any urgency, nor were they of the type that would instill fear in a resolute man. Furthermore, given the fact that the Bishop might have issued a pardon and absolved him of fault, it would still have been necessary to show the document to the residents.

Without showing the residents the pardon, they couldn't be expected to believe one had been issued. They would have rejected the Chief Vicar as a true Prelate, and would have refused to obey his commands and orders of excommunication. In the eyes of the residents, his wrongdoing was obvious, in that he publicly denied the authority of his Bishop. The secrecy of the Bishop's absolution of his fault was useless as a consequence. In the end, the document remained hidden and was never produced. The Chief Vicar continued to serve in that role.

The second serious doubt I had about the Chief Vicar was, why did he have to prance about in white slippers, with scarlet stockings, colorful velvet shorts, a raised collar of fine fabric, and a cassock and cloak made of silk? Priests and other clerics should always dress modestly to show their integrity, which sets a good example for their subordinates. This would especially be the case at a time when we found ourselves among the enemies of the Priesthood and the Holy Faith.

In response to this concern, I was told that the Chief Vicar dressed this way either because he suffered from depression, and was simply trying to cheer himself up by wearing elegant clothes, or else because he was a young man who lacked experience, who therefore wished to project a polished and dapper appearance. He might have thought his lavish dress would cause him to be taken more seriously and to be viewed as being dignified or wealthy. Those who might wish to know the truth of the matter should ask him. As a first-hand witness, only he could explain why he dresses as he does.

13 PORTENTS OF RESTORATION

Editor's Note: Calado recounts Portugal's history in mythic and religious terms, from the time of its first king. Following the death of an infant heir, Castilians claim Portugal's crown and install Philip II of Spain simultaneously as the king of Portugal. They later intend to seize the crown and scepter in a plot to reduce Portugal to a Spanish province. As Calado tells it, the Dutch foil the plan when they destroy the Spanish Armada in 1588.

Portuguese women, who were formerly secluded much like Muslim and Sephardic Jewish females, under Spanish rule begin to take on the brazen behavior of Castilian women. Calado's views about women were once prevalent. Those who appear in public without a male guardian are disreputable and subject to molestation. The relative freedom enjoyed by Dutch women and those from elsewhere in Europe is notable by comparison.

The lands of Portugal's vast empire, acquired at great cost in lives and resources, are surrendered by the Spanish without resistance. They show no compunction in squandering Portugal's wealth. God severely punishes the Portuguese for their sins.

However, because the Portuguese are God's chosen people, their king will be restored. There are portents that this will occur in 1640. In describing one such omen, Calado shares his own background and relationship to Portugal's nobility. The Duke of Bragança is so impressed with the young Calado that he awards the youth scholarships for both his Bachelor's and Master's degrees. Unlike his disdain for spending by merchants or Spanish nobles, for Calado the lavish outlays by Portugal's aristocrats denote nothing but virtuous conduct.

* * *

Our Lord and Savior Jesus Christ, having overcome the sufferings of hell and death, triumphantly liberated us. Concerned for the progress of our salvation, which was entrusted to the power of His cross, He revealed Himself to the afflicted and anguished caretaker and defender of His Holy Catholic Faith, Don Afonso Henriques. Our Lord promised to him glorious victory over a vast number of Muslims.

Our Savior gave him the title of King of Portugal, secured by the force of arms, as evidenced by His holy cross and by the emblems of our redemption, which are the five piercings of His body and the thirty coins for which He was sold. Our Savior certified to holy King Afonso that he was chosen as the first of a succession of Kings to the throne of the Portuguese monarchy. Our Savior likewise certified that the Portuguese people were chosen for the purpose of carrying His name and His faith to the ultimate corners of the world. Nevertheless, Our Lord had foreknowledge of their eventual ingratitude and lack of piety, and threatened them with punishment.

The time arrived for the crown of Portugal to be eclipsed, on account of our sins and ingratitude. This occurred as a result of the disgraceful military campaign of King Sebastião in Africa, and the succession to the throne of the infant Cardinal Henrique. Upon the latter's death, the Kingdom was assailed by—so to speak—the horrible battering rams and powerful cannons of divine castigation.

The first punishment was seventy years of subjugation by the Castilian Spanish. The Dutch captured our ports in the East Indies; in Brazil they took the city of Bahia for a short period, and thereafter Pernambuco and the entire northeast; and, they seized the Portuguese colonies in West Africa. At sea, each day the Dutch, English, French, Ottoman Turks, and North African Muslims took our ships. No one lacked for enthusiasm when it came to attacking the Portuguese, so long as we lacked our own king.

As Saint Augustine said, Christ wished to save us by His stigmata, not only for the glory of His own triumph over sin but also for our sake. His love for us is attested to in the wounds He received on His feet, side, and hands. Our Lord God didn't abandon the Portuguese in all respects but only wished to punish us for our ingratitude. He had shown us many favors, choosing us as His beloved children. Lashing us with the rod of His justice, He sought to guide us by His mercy away from the path of suffering we were on.

Our burdens became many when the crown and scepter of Portugal passed to the hands of the Castilians. The Castilians, following the death our saintly Cardinal and King Henrique, pretending to be virtuous and luring us with promised benefits backed by intimated threats, moved unjustly against the legitimate heir to the throne, the Duchess Catarina de Bragança. The Castilians seized the crown for themselves. Thereafter, Portugal was so disgraced that the injuries deserve the shedding of tears of blood more than to be written down on paper. Those who supported the cause of Catarina de Bragança were arrested and killed. Official offices, positions, and honors were no longer awarded on the basis of merit but were, rather, given to those who were the greatest traitors to Portugal. Theft of Portuguese property by Castilians became the norm.

First among these affronts was the loss of all modesty by our women. Portuguese women had been an example of good morals to the women of other countries because they wouldn't tolerate women who'd gone astray. Portuguese women previously would never leave their houses, except to attend Church. They'd never show themselves in their windows, unless they were married—even then only rarely—and only with their husbands beside them. Until they were married, young women would never speak to or even look at unfamiliar men.

Castilian women, on the other hand, were accustomed to going out in public and walking the streets. They did so in greater numbers than did the men. Hiding their faces and averting their eyes, they hoped to avoid being recognized. (This behavior shows how brazen women truly are in their hearts.) The Portuguese women, once they came into contact with Castilians, in order not to feel left out, boldly began to follow in their footsteps. They entered into secret liaisons with and accepted money from men, not because of love, but to have a good time and enjoy themselves.

The Spanish lost many of the colonies in Africa that the Portuguese kings had conquered at a great cost in lives and treasure. The same thing happened in India, which the Spanish put at risk of being lost in its entirety to the English and Dutch, due to their failure to come to the aid of the Portuguese in a timely manner. That is, they failed to have the ships set sail from Lisbon at the time of the monsoon winds. Pirates of many stripes, including Turks, Muslims, and Dutch, constantly plundered the Portuguese coast and port cities, with great success. Morocco, the land of the Berbers, became filled with Portuguese captives. The ransoms paid each year cost so much that they would have been sufficient to outfit numerous warships that could have been used to rid the coast of pirates.

All revenue, from every source, including conquests, navigation, and commerce, was spent on Castile; none went to Portugal. In the end, an investigation of Castile's swindles, which were obvious to anyone, showed that the wealth of the land was wasted on costume balls, favors given to personal friends and mistresses, and luxuries of all sorts. After the great sacrifices that were necessary to build the Portuguese Empire, everything was being taken by the Spanish Court. The Council in Madrid concluded it would be best to give up on defending India, since the conflict was hard to sustain and the situation was dire.

The Kings of Castile and their Council only discussed how they could wipe Portugal off the map. They wished to put it in such a lowly state that it could never rise again. They hoped in this way to block God's promise to the Portuguese that they would have their own kings.

King Phillip of Spain summoned the Portuguese nobility, including the Duke of Bragança, who was the legitimate heir to the Portuguese throne, to fight against the Catalans on his behalf. The Catalans had risen up against the tyranny of Castile. The King's hope was that the Portuguese nobles would all be killed in the war or at least kept under Castilian control. This would deprive Portugal of any capacity for self-defense.

The King ordered the seizure of silver ornaments from Portuguese churches. He had Lisbon blockaded to enforce compliance.

The final step in the King's diabolical plot to eliminate Portugal was to seize by brute force the Portuguese crown, conveying it from Lisbon to Spain. Portugal was to be reduced to a Spanish province, like Catalonia. To carry out this scheme, he ordered Don Antonio Orquendo to enter Lisbon on his return voyage from England. Orquendo was headed to Flanders in the Spanish Netherlands with an enormous fleet. He was carrying the funds necessary for provisioning the fleet and transporting the King's army from Flanders to England. The King's troops were to subdue the heretics.

He would have been successful but God intervened. God allowed the Dutch to destroy the Spanish Armada in the English Channel, at very little cost. The Dutch succeeded because against Heaven's will there's nothing that human effort or ingenuity can achieve.

Due to the fact that Christ our Savior promised our first King, Dom Henriques, that when the Kingdom of Portugal suffered its worst setbacks, at the very last moment, when it was about to disappear, He would look on the country with loving eyes and rescue it. Our Lord Jesus Christ would give Portugal a new king and great happiness.

It's likely many Portuguese almost stopped believing this blessing would occur. Some gave up because they'd already passed seventy years of subjugation, with no relief in sight. Others didn't expect a new King because they were awaiting the return of the former King Sebastião. They continued to doubt he'd been killed in Africa. Still others had become Castilian in heart and deed, remaining Portuguese in name only. The rest saw Portugal reduced to such a pathetic state by the King of Spain that it could no longer hope to recover its sovereignty.

However, because the word of God is fixed, firm, pure, and never fails, so that the Portuguese wouldn't lose heart, individuals continued to receive divine revelations. These revelations made many men holy, so that they could encourage their friends and relatives. All were waiting for the year 1640, during which they hoped to receive this wonderful blessing from God.

God sent many signs that something great would occur in 1640. I'll share two examples, one from Portugal and the other from Bahia in Brazil. The one from Portugal was connected to the town in which I was born. I'll discuss what led up to it in some detail. First, though, I'll describe the example from Bahia.

The omen from Bahia, in its main city of Salvador, happened between the months of August and September 1640. An old priest named Antonio Viegas lived there. He was virtuous but happened to believe strongly that King Sebastião would return. He was highly outspoken that there would be a Portuguese king. Hearing him discussing these beliefs and various prophecies, the commander of the Castilian troops in Bahia responded that only when horses began to walk on tile rooftops, without breaking the tiles, would the Portuguese have their own king.

The priest excused himself, perturbed by the conversation. He dismissed the commander's words with a laugh, joking about the preposterous circumstances. Within a few days, however, a horse was actually seen walking on the roofs of some beach houses, without breaking any tiles. The people who came running from the city to witness the event were deeply impressed. Within a matter of months, we received news that João IV had been proclaimed King of Portugal.

Regarding the other omen, by way of background, my hometown is Vila Viçosa in Portugal. I grew up in the shadow of the House of Bragança. My primary school studies commenced in this town. The curriculum developed by the Royal Court spread to all of Portugal and to other provinces and kingdoms throughout Europe. At school, I learned the basics of Latin, which the Dukes of Bragança had directed to be taught in two parallel courses, grammar and rhetoric, by clerics from the order of Saint Augustine.

During religious festivals the nobles would sponsor various types of entertainment, including some riddles with prizes for those who solved them. I tackled one of the riddles and answered it correctly, explaining my solution in a forceful and entertaining way. His Excellency the Duke presided over the event. Joining him were other members of the House of Bragança, as well as other nobles who served the Royal House. Seeing me explain the riddle, His Excellency viewed me so favorably that soon he ordered me to attend the University in Evora, where I studied logic and philosophy at his expense. I earned a Bachelor's degree and Master of Arts degree, both of which were paid for by His Excellency.

In the year I received my Master's degree, his Excellency the Duke Teodosio married Lady Ana de Velasco, the daughter of the High Count of Castile. Their wedding festivities included the most luxurious and majestic parties that were ever to take place in our times in Europe, with special guest houses for relaxation and open banquet tables overflowing with delicacies beyond imagination. Honored guests and many others in attendance received gifts at these parties, according to their degree of nobility. The House of Bragança covered all of the expenses out of its own funds. The Castilians were amazed by the display of generosity.

The numerous Castilian nobles who attended took note of the varied and elegant parties, the quality and quantity of gold and silver tableware, the excellent manners of the servants, the accouterments and bearing of the Portuguese nobility and military officers, the number of guests, and the caliber of the royal ceremonies. The nobles agreed among themselves that in terms of sheer magnificence, majesty, and grandeur, the House of Bragança far surpassed the Spanish Royal Court.

The festivities included steeplechase competitions, bullfights, and other outdoor contests, with the town illuminated by lanterns hung from windows. The castle, which is impregnable and the best fort in Iberia, discharged all of its artillery, which was so loud it shook the earth. The soldiers held tournaments. Some went about on stilts, dressed as giants. Others, in lion, griffin, or horse costumes, pulled flaming carts, wearing costly harnesses.

Everything was enchanting and enjoyable. The Castilian nobles returned home filled with admiration for the greatness of the House of Bragança. What impressed them most was that the Duke returned the sizeable dowry sent to him by his bride's father. In doing so, the Duke stated that he spent that much money and more in one day, and that if he chose to marry her, it was because of her virtue, honesty, reputation, honor, and noble blood. He said these traits were her true dowry and not the money that had been offered.

Duke Teodosio eventually had four children, three of them sons. The eldest and heir was named João. After the Dutchess Ana de Velasco passed away, the Duke didn't remarry, because he was truly chaste. He never had a relationship with a woman other than his wife. He raised his three sons in the purity of the holy Catholic Faith, as well as in good and laudable customs. The Duke prayed intensely every day, and in many ways lived more as a cleric than as a noble. He was also very generous, always giving money to the poor. He prayed to God that His promise to the Portuguese would be fulfilled and that the monarchy would be restored. He didn't want this for himself, even though he was the legitimate claimant to the throne. Instead, he asked God to choose one of his sons or another worthy Portuguese noble to become king.

The omen appeared one night, while the Duke was at prayer. Three horsemen, riding three white horses, passed by his window. They were resplendent in their elegant dress. The first said: "I've chosen one of the three." The second said: "One of the three is under my care." And the third said: "In one of the three I'll fulfill and keep my word." God, through his angels, gave the Duke certainty that one of his sons would be crowned King of Portugal.

The next morning, all of the poor people who that night had been in the hallways below or on the palace steps, began clamoring about what they had seen and heard. The news spread throughout the town. While the Duke was eating lunch, a court jester said to him: "Duke, do you know what they're saying out there?" The Duke asked, "What?" The jester said, "They say that last night three horsemen spoke to you, saying these words …". At this, the Duke shouted, "Shut up, you lunatic, you always say idiotic things. You're a witless dunce. You don't understand that these horsemen are here for the festival of Saint Anthony. They're in training for the steeplechase and other equestrian events I've prepared for this day." At the end of his outburst, he punched the jester in the mouth. He then moved on to discuss other subjects with his guests.

With the occurrence of these and many other portents, finally, in the month of December 1640, before the celebration of Christ's birth, the nobles of Portugal proclaimed the Duke's eldest son, João, as King of Portugal. They offered to him the crown and scepter, and shouted triumphant cheers. His ascension to the throne was greeted joyously in Lisbon and throughout all of Portugal. Everyone gave God thanks for this magnificent blessing. Thereafter, notices of the wondrous news were sent to Portugal's colonies in India and elsewhere. The notices admonished the local governors to protect the King's subjects and to fight his enemies, as might be necessary.

The King sent ambassadors to the northern countries, seeking alliances and treaties of peace and friendship. Pope Urban VIII recognized King João IV as the legitimate and Catholic ruler of Portugal. The ambassadors met with great success, especially with the Most Christian King of France, and Her Excellency Queen Cristina of Sweden. The various rulers of the northern countries pledged support. They provided weapons and troops, to help Portugal defend itself against the wrath and fury of the Castilians, who wished to strip the King of his throne.

14 KING AND ARMISTICE PROCLAIMED

Editor's Note: There is a dramatic turn in events. With its unilateral proclamation of a new king, Portugal is at war with Spain. The Portuguese concede much of northeastern Brazil to the Dutch in return for tacit support and a cessation of hostilities. Not everyone on the Portuguese side is fully prepared to commit treason against the Spanish king. The Dutch occupiers, at the direction of the Prince, celebrate the news together with their former opponents. Calado marvels that northern European women, both married and single, join in the banquets and drink toasts with the men, as is their custom. We see another extreme example of clerical treachery and profiteering. The Supreme Council in Recife and colonial government of Bahia reach ceasefire and communications agreements but trade arrangements remain a sticking point.

* * *

The joyful news of the ascension of King João IV reached Brazil at the end of January 1641. It arrived by a letter from the King, delivered to the Viceroy, Marquis Jorge Mascarenas. As soon as Mascarenas read the letter, he ordered his Council to assemble. He invited as well the Prelates of the various religious orders and the military commanders. He read the letter to them all. Then, he asked that each of them take a position regarding the proclamation, which would be recorded and made public.

Some wanted an extra day to consider their response, given that it was such a serious decision. They said it was necessary to weigh the pros and cons as to whom they should follow, since the King of Spain was also the King of Portugal. He was extremely powerful and could be expected to punish them severely as traitors.

Hearing such vacillation, the Viceroy said they would have to decide quickly. No one would be permitted to leave the assembly until the matter was resolved. One of the field commanders stood up and raised his sword. Putting on his helmet, he shouted: "We have a king of the Portuguese nation, and he is the noble João the Duke of Bragança, to whom belongs the legitimate right of kingship, as the whole world knows. We don't need to wait for any other opinions. Long live King João IV who by this name is King of Portugal!" The Viceroy seized this opportunity to declare: "Long live King João IV of Portugal, with no one opposed!"

Without further delay, before anyone could leave, the Viceroy ordered all of the soldiers, who numbered about five thousand, to march out in order, as though they were headed into battle against some hidden enemy. He ordered the Castilian and Italian troops to march in the vanguard, and as they passed by the officials, they were compelled to stack their weapons. As soon as they were disarmed, he ordered the Portuguese soldiers to assemble in Bahia's main plaza. The officials all gathered, with the Viceroy in dress uniform. The townspeople were called to assemble, without knowing why.

Drums were sounded, and then a town crier proclaimed firmly: "Listen, listen, listen, and be attentive!" At this, the Viceroy spoke: "Royal, Royal, Royal, the noble João IV who by this name is King of Portugal!" And the crowd shouted back, "Royal, Royal, Royal, long live João IV who by this name is King of Portugal!" The Portuguese troops gave three volleys with their guns, the flag was raised again and again, and the people cheered without stopping. The Viceroy had the artillery at the fort and on the ships discharged. The people hung lanterns in their windows that night and celebrated by dancing, playing music, engaging in equestrian competitions, and otherwise showing their happiness by all means possible.

Soon thereafter, the Viceroy sent his sons to Portugal, to kiss the King's hand in his name and offer his congratulations. He also dispatched ships to the other Captaincies along Brazil's coast, sharing the wondrous news, so that they might celebrate as well. He likewise sent notice to Prince Johan Maurits in Pernambuco, whom he treated as a close friend. He also notified the members of the Supreme

Council, as representatives of the Dutch West India Company, due to the secret agreement that was now in place.

When the Viceroy's representative arrived aboard a ship festooned with Portuguese flags, it caused quite a commotion among the Dutch. The men on board discharged numerous volleys into the air. Without requesting permission, they sailed right up to the Prince's house and dropped anchor. Upon landing the men were soon surrounded by many Dutch and Jews, who had rushed to the beach to see what was going on. On entering the Prince's house, the Viceroy's representative delivered his letter. Upon reading it, the Prince was so joyful that he gave the messenger a valuable jewel, and invited the Viceroy's men to stay and rest. During the next eight days they celebrated continuously.

In order to better commemorate the joyous news, the Prince ordered bleachers to be set up around a field near his house. He sent invitations throughout Pernambuco for all of the best horsemen and other vigorous young men to come join in a series of competitions to be held in the field. The Prince asked that they use their finest livery and decorative harnesses in honor of the new king.

Many of the men arrived with costly adornments that appeared to be far beyond their means. Some had been borrowed. When all were at last assembled, they were presented to the Prince, who was beaming with happiness. He offered them a feast featuring the most marvelous delicacies, which was accompanied by diverse forms of musical entertainment.

The Prince divided up the horsemen into two squads. He personally led the squad made up of Dutch, English, French, and German riders, while the other consisted entirely of Portuguese horsemen. Everything was put in order for the competition. The foreign ladies from all parts of northern Europe were allowed to watch from behind the windows of the houses bordering the field. Men of importance sat in the bleachers and review stands. The ordinary people found places wherever they could. The adjacent river was filled with various types of boats from which men and women could enjoy the spectacle.

As the horsemen entered Mauritsstadt, the trumpets bid them welcome. The Prince led the way through the streets of the town, followed by the horsemen, in pairs. The Dutch and Portuguese were mixed together. They at last reached the field, lining up at the judges' stand, which was brightly decorated.

As the competition began, even though the Dutch had the better horses, their level of skill was much below that of the accomplished Portuguese riders. The Portuguese rode with such grace and dignity that all eyes followed them, especially those of the women. None of these Northern European women, however, could boast that any Portuguese man of Pernambuco had developed any attachment to her.

I'm not speaking of one of these men going so far as to marry such a woman. Rather, none of these men would even have had an affair or other such illicit relationship with one of them. Conversely, around twenty Portuguese women had married Dutchmen, or more correctly, became their concubines, since they married heretics, in ceremonies conducted by heretical preachers. The Dutch in these cases lied, stating they were Roman Catholics. When the fathers of these young women complained, they were threatened with unjust punishment, based on false charges of misconduct.

Many valuable rings with jewels were displayed as prizes for the victors. Pairs of competitors, one from each squad, jousted with wooden lances. The Portuguese won most of the prizes, showing thorough mastery of equestrian skills. With their triumphant air and gallantry, in the end, the Portuguese made such an impression that some of the English and French women pulled off their rings and offered them as prizes, just to see the men ride again. After this, the men broke up into squads and engaged in mock battles. So ended the first day of celebrations.

The next day, the Prince ordered the repeated discharge of all of the artillery, both on land and at sea, and invited the horsemen to join in celebratory drinks. This is a Dutch custom, and there's a certain ceremony to it. Anyone who made an error in the routine had to down three drinks as punishment. With each round they toasted the good health of King João IV. Everyone would stand, hat in hand, and none were allowed to sit or cover their heads, until everyone at the table had offered a toast. As long as the toasting continued, there were drumrolls and trumpets blaring.

Similar events took place throughout the town. If the banquet involved a mid-day meal, the drinking went on until nightfall, and if supper was served, the drinking continued until the wee hours. Among those invited to the banquets were the most beautiful young ladies and most important women to be found in Pernambuco. They hailed from Holland, France, and England. They happily drank even more than the men, which they justified as being the custom of their home countries.

On the third day of the festivities, the Prince arranged for various equestrian events and more mock battles. At nightfall, the Prince had a French comedy put on, with much fanfare. The following morning he dismissed the Portuguese horsemen, thanking them for participating in the celebration. Eying them as they left, many Dutch were filled with envy, due to their elegant outfits and the prizes they'd won. The Dutch began to plot ways to rob the Portuguese. This, after all, had always been their intent, from the time they first arrived in Pernambuco. By their deeds, it was obvious they never wished to husband the land or care for its people but, rather, to rob and kill the residents by every means possible.

These festivities took place in April 1641, between Passover and Easter. They were scarcely over when a Dutch ship arrived with news that King João IV had agreed to a peace treaty of ten years duration between Portugal and Holland. On this news, the Prince set sail for Bahia, to meet with the Viceroy, and also to welcome three new Governors who had been selected.

The Prince, when he arrived in Bahia, learned that the Viceroy had already been stripped of his position. There was some trickery behind his removal. When the priest Father Vilhena brought to Brazil the happy news of King João IV's ascension, the King also sent on the same ship the three new Governors. They were prepared, in case the Viceroy didn't show sufficient enthusiasm in support of the King, to have him arrested and brought back to Portugal as a traitor.

As it turned out, the Viceroy did in fact display strong support for the new King. He even sent his sons to Lisbon as his representatives to pay obeisance to the King. However, Father Vilhena acted disreputably in furtherance of his own interests. He held back the King's letter that would have affirmed, based on his display of loyalty, the Viceroy's continued service. Father Vilhena instead delivered to the three new Governors only the second letter, by which the Viceroy was dismissed and the new Governors were instated. The Viceroy accepted his dismissal gracefully and withdrew to a monastery, where he awaited orders to return to Portugal.

More Dutch officials arrived in Bahia, to bid farewell to the Viceroy, to welcome the new Governors, and to begin discussions about implementing the peace treaty. The Dutch asked that all Portuguese troops fighting in the backcountry of Pernambuco be withdrawn. Other steps to restore trade and communications were also taken.

The Governors agreed to send a senior military officer, Pedro da Gama, to Pernambuco to work out the details for the withdrawal of the soldiers. Father Vilhena requested permission from the three Governors to accompany Pedro da Gama, for the purpose of digging up silver that the Jesuits and military commanders had buried in Pernambuco when they fled during the early stages of the Dutch invasion. He promised to bring it back to Bahia, for transport to Portugal.

When Father Vilhena arrived in Recife, the Dutch assumed he had some important matters to share related to the King, since it was he who had brought news of the King's ascension to Brazil. For various reasons, it was Dutch policy to prohibit Jesuit priests from entering Pernambuco. Therefore, he was restricted to dealing only with matters related to the King. As soon as Father Vilhena saw the Prince, he embraced the Prince on behalf of the King and said various things in the King's name.

The Prince, however, was somewhat taken aback by these actions. Later, he confided to a few intimates that what Father Vilhena said was pure flattery and lies because, should the King have wished to send greetings, he would have done so via a personal letter, to show his high regard and esteem. The Prince said that he would await such a letter as a token of the King's propriety and personal regard for him. Nevertheless, the Prince offered effusive thanks to the Priest, and provided him and his companion with a house where they could rest and be well cared for. The Prince actually enjoyed spending time with Father Vilhena because he was knowledgeable, and spoke both Dutch and French, which he had learned during many years of service in the Spanish Netherlands.

Father Vilhena had been given many letters of commendation bearing the King's name, issued in blank, which he had been entrusted to fill in and award to those identified as persons of importance who merited recognition as good and loyal subjects. The Priest decided to turn these letters into merchandise. He took bribes in return for issuing letters to those who didn't deserve them. He brought many of these letters to Pernambuco, where he sold some to people who merited not recognition but instead to be hung as traitors.

Proclaiming that he was an intimate of the King, Father Vilhena went about Pernambuco promising false grants of privilege and other nonexistent awards. As a consequence, many clerics and laymen gave him large sums of money, for the purpose of having him obtain various offices and grants on their behalf from the King, upon his return to Portugal.

However, his evil acts were justly rewarded. En route to Lisbon, he decided to change ships on arriving at the island of Madeira, thinking a larger ship would help him better guard the vast sum of money he was carrying. As it turned out, God permitted Turkish pirates to capture the ship he was on. He died as a miserable captive in Algeria. The smaller ship that carried him from Brazil, which he abandoned, sailed with a favorable wind and arrived safely in Lisbon.

Returning to our account, the officer Pedro da Gama, after he had rested for eight days, went with the Prince to the Supreme Council. There, he pleaded as follows:

As the world well knows, when Portugal had its own kings, it always had peace, friendship, and alliances with the rulers of northern Europe, who variously assisted Portugal in times of crisis. It came to be that Portugal, due to the sins of its people or for other reasons known only to God, had its legitimate queen, Duchess Catarina de Bragança, stripped of her crown, which was claimed by the kings of Castile.

Out of hatred for the kings of Spain, who made themselves likewise the kings of Portugal, the same rulers of northern Europe went about seizing many ports in the East Indies. They robbed Portugal of its trade, which belonged to it, because the Portuguese are the ones who first discovered and conquered the lands of the East. For a short period the Dutch seized Bahia but were driven out by force of arms. They now are the rulers of Pernambuco and other Captaincies in the region.

They've committed many unjustified injuries, with no wrong having been done to them by the Portuguese. Today, this damage is no longer of consequence, because of the ascension of His Excellency King João IV. He promptly ordered the establishment of peace and friendship with all of the rulers of northern Europe. The States General of the Netherlands ratified a cessation of hostilities for ten years. Because of this, there's no reason to continue the wars started previously.

The Governors of Bahia ordered me here to explain to Your Excellences that they cannot enter into formal agreements absent orders from the King. However, until such orders arrive, they agree with Your Excellences to a ceasefire, and the establishment of open communications. As assurance of their agreement, I've come here to order the withdrawal from Pernambuco to Bahia of all our soldiers who've been carrying on the military campaign.

As Your Excellences ordered to be described to our Governors, these soldiers have been moving about in small squads throughout the land, harming many and causing much damage. The Governors have also ordered that Portuguese shipping be allowed into Pernambuco, paying the appropriate duties on merchandise. This shall be carried out on the same terms as agreed to between the Portuguese and Dutch. From Pernambuco, we'll ship locally produced goods, under a free trade regime, as is the custom among all nations.

The Supreme Council accepted the ceasefire and communications agreements. However, regarding the shipping provisions, they said these could not be agreed to without orders from Holland. The Councilmembers committed to seek authorization promptly and said they expected resolution of the matter very soon. However, this was a pretext, because until authorization was received, they'd require all merchandise traded by the Portuguese to pass through their own hands.

The Portuguese were prohibited from negotiating with any other parties. The port fees, tariffs, and so on, would also be those declared by the Supreme Council. With the assertion of these commercial and shipping requirements, the meeting ended. Pedro da Gama said he would advise the Governors in Bahia about the Supreme Council's position. This sort of double-dealing was typical of the Dutch. They were always looking for ways to extort excessive profits from the local people and Portuguese traders. It was a no-win situation for the Portuguese merchants.

15 TREACHERY ABOUNDS

Editor's Note: Efforts are made to demobilize Portuguese guerillas in Dutch Brazil. The West India Company violates the truce to seize Angola, Portugal's west African ports, and additional land in Brazil. This gives the company control of the trade in slaves and gold. Dutch piracy continues unabated. The Prince has been lured into moneymaking schemes by Gaspar Dias Ferreira, who employs sorceresses—possibly performing *macumba* rituals from Africa that are still common in Brazil—to control the Prince. Calado schools the Prince in the proper use of noble titles and forms of address. This is evidence that the distinctions of social caste are much more pronounced at the time in Portugal than they are in the Netherlands. The Prince informs Calado of accusations that he's a spy. However, the Prince has found no evidence of the charge and remains Calado's loyal friend. Calado feels great relief.

* * *

Former Viceroy Mascarenas, following his removal as Governor of Bahia, at long last received orders to depart for Lisbon. He had many complaints against the new Governors as regards their treatment of him. They, in turn, accused Mascarenas of treason because after his sons arrived in Lisbon to kiss King João IV's hand and offer fealty on behalf of their father, they ran off to Castile and pledged loyalty to the King of Spain. Like father like son, as they say. However, King João IV, in his prudence, good faith, and wisdom, as well as due to his vast experience in governing and awarding positions of influence, welcomed Mascarenas and treated him honorably.

The new Governors also had to deal with the seven hundred Spanish and Italian soldiers who were still present in Bahia. They were given a suitable transport ship. However, the Governors were afraid that these seasoned fighters, on arriving in Spain, would promptly be sent into battle against King João IV. Therefore, they were given only enough food and water to make it to the Spanish West Indies. They weren't allowed to buy any additional supplies on their own.

Shortly after departing Bahia, the soldiers set sail for Spain despite their lack of supplies. Due to contrary winds and currents, they ended up in the Captaincy of Paraiba. Hoping to take advantage of this unintended diversion, they thought they could take on additional water and other provisions. However, because this area was under Dutch control, they were forced to disembark.

The Dutch, as mortal enemies of the Spanish, considered hanging all of the soldiers. Instead, the Dutch put them on limited rations and forced them to work on their fortifications. The Dutch allowed a senior officer to sail to Recife to plead with the Prince and Supreme Council. His protests against the Portuguese of Bahia were effective.

The Supreme Council decided to let the ordinary soldiers sail on to the Spanish West Indies. There, without leaders, they could be expected to desert and disperse themselves into the backlands. Several months later the Dutch sent the Spanish officers back to Holland. They eventually made it to Spain, where they lodged numerous complaints against the Portuguese. They proposed a strategy to the King of Spain for conquering Brazil.

While all of this was going on, the Portuguese officer Pedro da Gama continued his work in Recife. He ordered on behalf of the Governors the withdrawal of all Portuguese combatants from Dutch-held territory. Bulletins were posted in every shop for them to withdraw to Bahia. Noncompliance would be punished as treason. They could take the overland route or go to Recife, where they would be carried back by ship. The Dutch promised them safe passage. Since the Portuguese didn't trust the Dutch, who had repeatedly broken their word, most went back by land. However, one captain did go to Recife with his fighters. They were treated well by the Dutch. The Prince even invited the captain to his home for dinner, together with Pedro da Gama.

When they arrived the table was already set, so after perfunctory greetings all were seated and began eating and toasting each other. With great charm, and a bemused attitude, the Prince said, "Is it possible, Captain, that you were so bold as to offer a significant cash reward to whomever brought you my head or killed me?" To this, the captain responded:

> Your Excellency is astonished that I would offer this amount to whomever might kill you. Yet I see you aren't astonished by your own promise of a sizeable cash reward to whomever might have killed me. If I did make such an offer, I'd have the money ready and would have paid it the instant I saw you dead, or upon proof of your death.
>
> What surprises me is that, with so many soldiers, Your Excellency didn't order them to come after me in the forests and remote pathways, where I marched with my men. You could have ordered them to kill me like a soldier.
>
> What surprises me even more is that, since I'm a Captain in service to the King of Portugal, and of noble blood for many generations, Your Excellency holds me in such low esteem that you would put such a paltry price on my head. For if I were you, and knowing the mortal enemy I faced in someone like me, I'd offer the entire income of my estate to have you killed, and thereby be free of you forever.
>
> And if I did offer the amount you stated for your head, it would be to resign myself to my own poverty. It would negate my courage, status, and pride, in failing to acknowledge what I owe to you as a nobleman and person of honor. In the end, it surprises me that Your Excellency places so little value on the Captains of João IV, King of Portugal, my Lord.

The Prince smiled amicably and took these words in jest. He offered the captain a toast to the good health of His Majesty, King João IV. In truth, no matter what crimes the Dutch committed, or what rewards they offered, they couldn't defeat or even manage to find our soldiers in the backlands. However, once all of our soldiers had withdrawn from Pernambuco, the Prince and Supreme Council were freed to resume their treacherous and traitorous acts.

The first major action they took was to send four large warships filled with soldiers and laborers to the Captaincy of Sergipe, which had been depopulated during the fighting, in order to build a fort. This was in violation of the ceasefire agreement. Sergipe still had some crops and was full of stray cattle, which the Dutch wanted for their food supply.

What was worse, the famous Dutch pirate Peg-Leg, who usually raided Spanish shipping and the silver fleet in the West Indies, arrived in Recife. He was made commander of a large fleet, which sailed to Africa and seized Angola and São Tomé from the Portuguese. They managed to take over all the ports along Africa's west coast, which gave them control of the trade in gold and slaves. The Dutch also sent forces by sea from Recife to Maranhão, which lies to the northwest of Brazil proper. Pretending friendship, through betrayal the Dutch captured the fort and surrounding areas, killing many, although eventually the local residents regrouped and drove out the invaders.

Pedro da Gama knew that the Dutch had built a fort in Sergipe, in violation of the ceasefire agreement. When the time arrived for him and his aides to depart for Bahia, he drew up a letter addressed to the Prince and Supreme Council. In the letter, he demanded that they abandon the fort because what the Dutch had done reeked of fraud, deceit, and treachery.

While da Gama and his aides were in Recife, the Prince's Portuguese friend Ferreira made it a point to visit them repeatedly. Under the cloak of friendship, Ferreira pretended to be a loyal vassal of the King of Portugal. All the while, he carried out various schemes, in order to discover what was in their hearts. He intended to reveal their secrets to the Dutch. During one of these visits, da Gama showed Ferreira the letter he planned to present to the Prince. Ferreira replied that the Dutch couldn't abide by the conditions contained in the letter without first advising Holland. As he knew with certainty, the Dutch in Brazil were under orders to seize everything possible and to surrender nothing.

The next day, Pedro da Gama presented his letter to the Supreme Council. Although he demanded a written response, the Council refused, and replied orally that they couldn't respond without writing to Holland for directions. They said they'd need to provide an explanation to the States General and to the Board of Nineteen Directors of the illustrious Dutch West India Company. With this response, da Gama came to understand the truth of what many had informed him. That is, Ferreira was the one who could make things happen or block them before the Supreme Council. Beneath his feigned friendship and pretense of virtue, he was the greatest enemy the Portuguese had in Pernambuco. His facility with treason is why the Dutch took him in as an advisor.

I had been aware of Ferreira and his treachery for some time. As I described previously, Ferreira intended to help Holland conquer Bahia, accompanying the Prince in the command ship during his failed attack. He was the first Portuguese who, together with his wife and children, had mingled with the Dutch inside their fortifications. He led the Dutch to extract much wealth from Pernambuco. He was so notable in this regard, as I personally witnessed, that the pirate Peg-Leg bragged about what good terms they were on and how much land he'd thereby amassed. There wasn't a scheme Ferreira wouldn't come up with to help the Dutch make money or to usurp farms from the Portuguese owners. All the while, he'd take a cut for himself.

An early subterfuge Ferreira employed to enrich himself and the Prince was to persuade the owners of sugar mills and plantations to offer crates of sugar as gifts to the Prince, in order to win his favor. He or his agents collected the sugar personally. Ferreira took credit for the gifts and absconded with most of the sugar. Within a few years the owners caught on to what was happening. Thereafter, they made the gifts directly to the Prince. Ferreira was irritated because his methods had been exposed.

The night before Pedro da Gama's departure, the Prince invited him to a private dinner. He asked da Gama to leave his sword to the side. Upon leaving, when he requested the return of his sword, the Prince's chamberlain instead presented to da Gama a costly, highly ornate sword, with a luxurious sheath, embroidered with gold thread. It was the sword the Prince wore to festivals.

When da Gama said the sword wasn't his, the Prince replied: "My dear sir, this sword is my treasured possession, which I customarily wear as decoration on occasions of honor. I now place it at your service, so that it can be held in your courageous and honorable hand. I hereby give orders that it be taken to your home." Offering deep thanks, da Gama departed, accompanied by the Prince's chamberlain, who handed him the sword upon arriving at his place of lodging. The next day, da Gama and his aides departed by sea for Bahia.

A few days later, a Dutch officer named Andre Son arrived from Angola. He brought back three black ambassadors from an African count who had rebelled against the Portuguese. He was seeking Dutch assistance and an alliance. The Dutch sent the ambassadors to Holland to make their case to the Board of Nineteen Directors of the Company. Son also brought a large amount of gold and silver, plus jewels, ornaments, and household goods, all looted from the Portuguese residents in Angola.

Following the conquest of Angola by forces under Peg-Leg's command, during which many were killed in cold blood, the Dutch shipped captured officials, clerics, and leading citizens back to Pernambuco as prisoners. They were badly mistreated. However, Peg-Leg and the Dutch got what was coming to them. Departing Angola, Peg-Leg sailed to the island of São Tomé and captured it. There, both the Dutch and the indigenous Brazilian Coboclos who fought with them contracted a local disease that killed many. Peg-Leg issued orders that the dead not be buried in such a pestilential place. He had the bodies committed to the sea. Although the Dutch managed to hang on and also to seize the port cities of West Africa, the disease killed Peg-Leg.

In the meantime, Antonio Teles da Silva returned to Bahia as Governor of Brazil. On being informed of the plight of Angola, he sent a ship with supplies and munitions to where the Governor of Angola had retreated. After unloading, the ship picked up some slaves for the return trip. Teles da Silva also sent notice to King João IV of the treacherous acts committed by the Dutch following the ceasefire and peace treaty.

The King ordered the Governor of Angola to stop fighting the Dutch and to treat them as friends. On these orders, the Governor of Angola entered back into contact with the Dutch, who were occupying the city of Luanda. The Portuguese began trading slaves with them in return for food, clothing, and beverages. However, the King then lodged complaints in Holland and demanded the return of Angola, São Tomé, and the West African ports, because they had been seized unjustly, in violation of the ceasefire.

The Dutch not only seized land, they also engaged in piracy. Taking advantage of the ceasefire, they seized sixteen ships sailing between Portugal and Brazil, bringing them and their crews into port in Recife. Protests were lodged, but nothing was done. In one significant case, a massive Dutch warship en route to Angola from Recife intercepted a cargo ship laden with sugar that was sailing to Lisbon from Bahia.

The Dutch seized the ship's captain, merchants, pilot, and some passengers as prisoners, and continued on to Angola. They put fifteen soldiers onboard the cargo ship and ordered the Portuguese sailors to head back to Recife. The Dutch captain sent on the ship some letters to the Supreme Council describing how he'd captured the ship and prisoners, and that he was entitled to his cut of the booty. The cargo ship happened to be loaded with supplies, including wine. The Dutch soldiers on board the ship got drunk one night while en route to Recife. The Portuguese sailors attacked the intoxicated soldiers and bound them up. They then rerouted the ship back to Bahia.

When they arrived, they gave Governor da Silva the letters from the Dutch captain. The Governor locked up the Dutch soldiers. He planned to hang them but then realized they might be more useful alive. He had the soldiers interrogated. Their statements and the letters were translated and read publicly. He retained copies of everything. Thereafter, the Governor sent an educated man to Pernambuco with the originals, in order to shame the Prince and Supreme Council with the enormity of Dutch treachery and betrayal. The Governor's representative did more than deliver the documents. He snubbed the Dutch by refusing their offer of hospitality. He instead lodged with a friend while in Recife.

The Governor also sent a personal letter to the Prince, advising him that Dutch treachery must stop. He demanded that losses to Portuguese shipping be indemnified and that the perpetrators be punished. The Prince and Council denied any knowledge of these matters and promised to write to Holland about them, which of course they never did.

Displeased by the lack of a Dutch response to his demands, as well as their failure to abandon the fort in Sergipe as Pedro da Gama had previously required, the Governor gave orders to the indigenous commander Camarão to set up camp in Sergipe. His native Brazilian forces were to disarm any Dutch they found outside of the fort. They were to warn the Dutch that on the third time they went out, they'd be killed. Camarão's men acted so effectively that the Dutch never again left the fort. They had to be supplied with food by ship from Recife.

Included in the letter the Prince sent in response to the Governor's complaint was an invitation to the Governor to visit Recife, with an offer of hospitality in the spirit of friendship. On reading the Prince's letter, the Governor could tell it had been written by Gaspar Dias Ferreira, due to the recognizable wordplay and flourishes. The Prince obviously couldn't have come up with these touches, since he didn't speak Portuguese very well. The letter also somewhat inappropriately referred to the Governor as Lordship, whereas in the Governor's letter he had referred to the Prince as Excellency.

Together with the Prince's letter arrived one from Ferreira, in which he bragged about being on intimate terms with the Prince and of being a trusted advisor to the Supreme Council. He claimed he could accomplish whatever the Governor might need and would be delighted to be of service to him. When the Governor read Ferreira's letter, he said to those with him, "This letter is from Gaspar Dias Ferreira. How am I to respond to it?" He picked up his quill and jotted down the following: "I received your letter, in which you told me you have good health, which God gave you according to your needs. I have good health, thanks be to our Lord God. Etc."

To the Prince, the Governor responded courteously, thanking him for his kind offer of hospitality. If the letter had thirty lines in total, it included the term Lordship twenty-nine times. One of the sentences read: "Regarding some of the things Your Lordship said to me in your letter, I won't respond to them for now because I know Your Lordship wasn't at fault but, rather, it was your Secretary. Your Secretary, after all, is the one who transcribed your letter and in fact wrote it, although I could see he tried hard to alter his handwriting so that I wouldn't recognize it."

Ferreira was badly upset by the Governor's brief and dry response to his letter. He began trying to make the Prince hate the Governor. He made a big deal about the Governor's use of the term Lordship in his reply to the Prince, rather than referring to him as Excellency, as all others did. The Prince became a bit agitated by what Ferreira had said.

The Prince's agitation wasn't surprising because everyone said Ferreira had cast spells on him. Ferreira could make the Prince do anything he wanted. In order to administer the spells, it was said Ferreira maintained two powerful sorceresses in his house. He paid them well, so they would make certain potions at his request. I would say that the spells he had cast were very effective for filling his own pockets, as were his self-interested recommendations. Equally effective were his schemes to disguise his cunning intent, which was to suck the blood from the poor.

I saw the Governor's letter once when visiting the Prince, who was deeply disturbed and saddened, and remained alone. He kept opening the letter and reading it over and over. When he saw me, he called me over, and had me take a walk with him in the garden. When we were alone, he asked me if I knew the Governor and what sort of man he was. I responded that I knew his parents very well, and knew him even better. He was an illustrious nobleman, related to the royal family. The Governor was a man of great accomplishments, prudent, kindly, and powerful, and above all dignified and courageous. He wouldn't put up with deceit or schemes, or fail to assuage with gifts those who were treated unjustly. To this, the Prince replied, "I'm angry at him, because he disrespected my personal honor and has highly offended me."

I questioned the Prince, what offense had been committed? What form did it take? At this, he asked me, "With what degree of courtesy, acknowledgment of eminence, and title do the Portuguese greet and speak to the Governor of Bahia?" To which I replied, "As Lordship, because he's Governor, as well as being Military Commander of all of Brazil." The Prince then stated: "He wrote me a letter, calling me Excellency, and in order to respond, a knowledgeable Portuguese friend of mine, whose opinion I sought, told me that the proper salutation to use in this case would be the title Lordship. I did this, and now I see in his response to my letter that he now addresses me as Lordship, not just once but many times. He also said that I'm not at fault for various improprieties in my letter because it had been written for me by my Secretary, who had also advised me on its contents."

The Prince then showed me the letter from the Governor and asked for my unbiased opinion on the specific matter of the form of address. I read the letter and paused. I gave it back to the Prince, without uttering a word. After a few moments, the Prince queried of me, "My dear Father, why don't you respond to my question?" In reply, I said to him: "My dear Prince, there are two options here, either Your Excellency would like to be spoken to in a fawning manner, which I will never do because I detest flatterers, or else you'd like to be spoken to in a disinterested manner, with neither love nor hatred, as to what I understand about this matter." At this, the Prince said, "My dear Father, tell me what is just and reasonable in your understanding." With all due courtesy and respect, I explained to him the following:

> Your Excellency in Holland signifies nothing more than Lordship. If here in Brazil the local residents refer to you as Excellency, it's because they see the Dutch referring to you that way. The Portuguese will also use as forms of address Eminence, Highness, and Majesty, if they see that this brings you pleasure, because a person who finds himself subjugated, overcome, and captured, will do anything, even that which shouldn't be done, to bring pleasure to the one who dominates him.
>
> However, Your Excellency by law signifies nothing more than Lordship. They refer to you here as Excellency as a form of flattery or out of the ignorance of common people.
>
> Since Governor Antonio Teles da Silva is a prudent man, he's obligated to render what is due to those who merit it. He knows the rules of precedence maintained in royal courts, and the titles held by each caste of the higher and lower orders. He knows that to give elevated titles to those who don't deserve them is not only flattery but is also pretentious on the part of the one who gives the title, as well as being shameful and an insult to the one to whom it was given. It reflects nothing but ignorance on the part of the one who receives it.
>
> Because of this, the Governor ceased to employ flattering terms and switched to referring to you as Lordship rather than Your Excellency. For in truth it is Lordship that is fitting for you and not Excellency.
>
> Your Excellency could say as a retort that since the Governor employed a certain manner of address in his first letter, he shouldn't change to another manner in the second. To this I would respond that in the first letter his use of Your

Excellency was in the way one would address an intimate friend. Among close friends one would say Sir, or Your Grace, as well as Lordship, Excellency, and Highness.

Seeing that Your Excellency didn't treat him as a close friend, he gave to you the title of Lordship, which is also his title as Governor and Military Commander. He also chose to give Your Excellency the title Lordship, which was your due, and not Excellency, to which you had no right, no matter how the Dutch might care to address you.

And I will say more, trusting in the permission Your Excellency granted me to speak freely, regarding the meaning of titles. Your Excellences is the title by which the Board of Nineteen Directors of the West India Company expects to be addressed. They are no more than a bunch of merchants and some of them are Jews.

You, the Prince of Orange, address the Directors as Sir, and ordinary people refer to them as Your Grace. And since none can give what they don't have, how is it possible that those who deserve no more than Grace or Sir can be referred to as Excellences?

The Governor of Bahia represents His Majesty the King of Portugal João IV, one who can give titles of Lordship, Excellency, and Highness to whomsoever he chooses, as well as Principalities and other grants merited by such titles. Assuming that he gave a title no greater than Lordship to his Governors in Brazil, nevertheless, there's a huge difference between a Governor as the representative of the King's sovereign authority and a band of merchants.

Because Governor Antonio Teles da Silva chose to continue using the title by which the Dutch and residents of Pernambuco refer to Your Excellency, he addressed you as Excellency. Nothing would have been lost by Your Excellency had you replied to him equally, respecting not only his nobility and noble lineage, which are illustrious, but also the fact that he's a Governor General of His Majesty and of a state as immense as Brazil.

At the very least, you have very little cause to be offended by him referring to Your Excellency as Lordship, which is after all the appropriate title, noting that it would be offensive had he referred to you as Grace, as likewise it would have been an insult for him to call you Excellency, given that the two of you weren't conversing with the liberties taken by close personal friends.

Turning to another matter raised by the Governor, he wrote that Your Excellency has no fault in regard to some of the things that were in your letter to him but, rather, the fault lies with the Secretary who wrote it and to the Counselor who gave you poor advice. I tell you that the Governor knew by the handwriting and the letter's contents that Gaspar Dias Ferreira was both the Secretary and the Counselor. Since he has a bad reputation in Bahia for his numerous misdeeds here in Pernambuco, the Governor's response was actually a cannonball directed at him.

Having spoken at length, I finished my discourse by recounting to the Prince some of the history of noble titles as employed by the King of Spain and the superior rights retained by the Dukes of Portugal. In the end, I reaffirmed to him the complete propriety of how he had been addressed by the Governor. The Prince warmly took my hand and said to me in Dutch: "Good friend." Reverting then to Latin, he said to me:

> My dear Father, I've come to believe that Your Grace is the only one who speaks the honest truth to me, with all sincerity and without self-interest, hatred, or undue affection. But now I want to share with you a secret, which is that a certain person affirmed to me that Your Grace is a spy. He said that everywhere you go, you're taking notes as to what

we're up to, and you order that Bahia be advised of everything we do.

I've conducted a thorough investigation, taking great care in determining Your Grace's conduct, manner of dealing with others, and lifestyle. I've found that you do nothing more than pour over your books. You're devoted to clerical duties and preach the sacred scriptures to the Portuguese according to the Roman Catholic religion.

I've never been able to find anything about your conduct that would cause you to be blamed for any misdeed, for which I would have seized and punished you. I've now concluded that those who are making these complaints are filled with jealousy over the favor I show Your Grace. I invite you to sit at my table and converse with Your Grace, for I find your discourse enjoyable. What they're trying to accomplish with this malicious gossip is to break up our friendship. You can be certain that in whatever way I can be of service to you, I will do so in good faith.

I kissed the Prince's hand and excused myself from his presence. I felt tremendous relief and great satisfaction, for I was, from the perspective of the Dutch, which they realized only later, the greatest traitor among them in Pernambuco.

16 REPRESENTATIVE GOVERNMENT BETRAYED

Editor's Note: The Prince and Supreme Council in Recife receive instructions from the Netherlands to establish a local legislative council. Appointed Portuguese landowners gather to represent the interests of their parishes. Calado admires the proceedings and customs that replicate the practices found in Holland. The members discuss various proposals over a span of three days. The proceedings are documented and become official records. The council's work is meant to help pacify the residents of Dutch Brazil. However, the new arrangements last for only a few weeks. Local Dutch officials are determined to extract as much wealth as they can from Pernambuco. They violate the newly agreed regulations. Even the Dutch preachers collaborate in the oppression of the residents.

* * *

There's another subject to which I'd like to return. The Prince, following the receipt from Holland of his brother's letter and other accusatory correspondence, began taking steps to implement certain direct orders from his superiors. The Prince and Supreme Council were commanded to establish a Legislative Council composed of Portuguese residents. The Legislative Council was empowered to propose statutes and regulations for peaceful self-governance.

The Prince and Supreme Council duly issued orders for the highest and most prominent nobles of Pernambuco to assemble on a specific date, three or four of them from each parish. Once all had arrived in Mauritsstad, the Prince held a banquet in their honor. It was fabulous. The members of the Supreme Council attended, as well as officials and war ministers. While they feasted, trumpets played, drums were sounded, and artillery was discharged, both on land and

127

at sea. In order to maintain their customs, the Dutch comported themselves as they would have in Holland.

For the next three days all representatives gathered together in one room. Each Portuguese proposed what was needed in his local district, together with steps that were necessary for good governance and the pacification of the populace. Above all, they requested permission to have priests come to administer the sacraments. The Dutch conceded to this request, so long as the priests didn't come from Bahia but, rather, from France or Portugal by way of Holland.

The representatives listened intently to the proceedings, during which the Portuguese read the petitions aloud and debated them. The attendees slaked their thirst with ample supplies of wine and beer. They yielded on certain points in order to preserve others and acted decisively, never surrendering to exhaustion. In order to solemnize the proceedings, everything was drawn up under official seal and signed by all, so that in the future no one could question what was agreed upon.

The legislative concessions granted by the Dutch, which took up a stack of paper, were copied and then distributed throughout Pernambuco. These documents can be found in the records of local councils. My own copy is still there, since I had to leave so quickly.

I would like it to be widely known the Dutch put everything possible in place to serve their own interests. The concessions they granted were full of booby-traps, designed to rob the local residents. The Dutch violated all of the provisions repeatedly, without punishment or correction, whereas when a Portuguese man failed in the smallest degree to fulfill any of the requirements, he would promptly be imprisoned, harassed, and punished. His punishment consisted of both torture and seizure of assets, the latter being the main target toward which all of these abuses were directed.

When the Portuguese notables who participated in the Legislative Council returned home, they imagined that they'd be protected. With all of the Dutch concessions firmly in place, the constant stream of new laws and other impositions by which the Dutch had been robbing and killing them should have stopped. However, it took no more than fifteen days for the Dutch judges and military officers who lived in barracks throughout Pernambuco to return to their old ways. They engaged in thievery and harassed the local residents, accusing them of crimes and arresting them. They'd haul their prisoners off to Recife, where the accused hoped the Prince would intervene on their behalf. However, for the most part, they were left in cruel hands that sought only to exploit them.

In one case, Jeronima de Almeida, the wife of a landowner who'd withdrawn to Bahia, had to pay a bribe to Gaspar Dias Ferreira of ninety crates of sugar in order to escape a death sentence. She was hauled from Porto de Calvo to Recife on charges of having given food and lodging to a squad of Portuguese soldiers. They'd come from Bahia to carry on the fight against the Dutch. The soldiers also carried letters from her husband. The Dutch had no proof, other than the word of a black man who was her slave. She'd previously ordered him whipped because of a robbery he'd committed. The slave decided to come forward with false testimony in order to get revenge against his owner. For the Dutch, just one word from a black was all they needed to bring charges against a resident.

In any case, they took this poor woman, the mother of nine gorgeous daughters and three sons, and threw her into a ramshackle prison cell, where she was prevented from speaking to any Portuguese person. She was condemned to death by decapitation. To prevent this sentence from being carried out, it was necessary for all the wives of the noblemen and other leading residents, who lived in the vicinity of Recife, to go en masse to the Prince and bow down at his feet. At the same time, they delivered crates of sugar, which were stacked against the battlement wall, in order to secure her pardon.

The Prince greeted the women with a joyful countenance, which he always showed to everyone. Displaying great courtesy, he signaled for them to rise from the ground. He said that had he known he was going to have such beautiful and honored guests, he would have prepared a banquet, as they deserved. However, since they'd taken him by surprise, he would have to invite them to dine with him at his ordinary table. The women kissed his hand for his show of kindness.

They told him that the only banquet they hoped to be served in his home, should they have found favor in his eyes, was to obtain His Excellency's assistance in regard to an immensely cruel act. What they sought to receive was his forgiveness of Jeronima de Almeida.

The women said further that although they appreciated the gesture of the Prince's offer for them to dine with him, it was against Portuguese customs for women to eat with men other than their husbands. Even at home, they could only sit at the table with their husbands or fathers if no guests were present. However, the Prince's kind offer put him in a cherished place in their hearts.

The Prince was touched by their courtesy and honorable response. He dismissed them, saying that in regard to their petition he would do everything that he could. He soon issued a decree, stating that he pardoned Jeronima de Almeida, by the authority vested in him as Governor and Military Commander of Pernambuco.

I write this to assemble examples for the pious reader of the tyrannical abuses and cruelties employed by the Dutch. For the slightest excuse, they would mistreat and hang the Portuguese. In another case, there was a man who was already on the block, with the executioner ready to decapitate him, on the charge of simply having spoken to soldiers from Bahia. His wife was prostrate on the ground, tears pouring from her eyes, surrounded by their five children, the oldest of whom was no more than twelve. The Prince took pity on them all and issued a pardon.

Another evil committed by the Dutch was to refuse to permit final confession for the Portuguese who were condemned to death. They wouldn't even allow priests to be present or to walk to the gallows with the condemned. The Dutch instead exposed the poor souls to Lutheran and Calvinist preachers, who tried to pervert them, leading them toward their false sects. I, however, was able to obtain permission from the Prince to hear the confession of and accompany some of my parishioners. Of necessity, I kept this authorization concealed, due to the difficult circumstances.

In truth, the heretic preachers had such malice toward and hatred for our sacred Roman Catholic religion that as soon as the Dutch seized a Portuguese suspected of a crime, the preachers would descend on him like ravenous wolves. They'd put it into the prisoner's head that they were true priests and confessors. Since the suspects were imprisoned, they'd confess their sins to these preachers, thinking this might help them to be freed. With their cynical arguments, the preachers would get the poor ignorant prisoners to vomit up their offenses, which couldn't be verified, other than by their confessions. The preachers would then turn this information over to the authorities, who would proceed to condemn the accused to death.

17 VILE TRAFFICKING

Editor's Note: Pernambuco is facing a shortage of slaves. A constant supply of new slaves is necessary to keep the sugar-based economy going. It repels us that anyone, let alone someone ordained in a religious tradition, can speak so casually about human beings as a commodity. Calado is more concerned about usurious lending than the cruelty inflicted on abducted Africans. Slaves were worked to death in Brazil, which is why new slaves, even at exorbitant prices, were always in demand. Both the Dutch and Portuguese were complicit in this vile institution.

Whatever nobility the Prince might have had—even in the eyes of someone like Calado, who reveres nobles—is compromised by his schemes and blatant self-dealing. As a side note, Calado mentions a "spy glass," which was something relatively novel at the time. It's a small telescope, a device invented in Holland in 1608. The commercial and intellectual freedoms of the Dutch Republic stimulated many such innovations during the seventeenth century.

* * *

In the midst of these many difficulties, two ships arrived from Angola. They were loaded with blacks, to be sold as slaves. The ships carried news that the Portuguese Governor of Angola and those with him had, under the terms of the peace treaty, taken good-conduct passports from the Dutch. The Portuguese had settled by a port. The Dutch acquired slaves from them in exchange for trade goods and provisions. Everything in Angola seemed to be in a state of peace and tranquility.

The landowners in Pernambuco, however, were suffering from a great shortage of slaves. Slaves were needed to work the sugar mills and plantations, as well as to cultivate crops. The Dutch took advantage of the situation and sold the Angolan blacks, even the young and sick, for very high prices. Those who had to buy on credit were charged ridiculous amounts and had to pay interest at the rate of four percent per month. Those who couldn't pay by the end of the month were charged compounding interest, causing the debt to multiply exponentially.

The same thing happened with the farms and provisions, as well as basic necessities, such as supplies for the sugar mills. By these methods the Dutch were sucking the lifeblood from Pernambuco. The slaves died off quickly in the hands of the landowners because the Dutch made them sick from drinking salt water while at sea. The Dutch did this intentionally in order to cause the landowners to suffer the loss after the slaves were acquired. Burdened by the need for more slaves, the landowners would then have to buy others.

The landowners became increasingly impoverished and unable to keep up with their payments. There were many who obligated themselves to the Dutch for loans, say for example in the amount of ten thousand silver coins, who after four years of notching up compounding interest, would find in their ledgers that they'd paid forty thousand back yet still owed the same ten thousand of principal. Most landowners ended up in this situation, some owing more and some less, depending on how much they'd borrowed. They had no alternative because the only ones they could trade with were the Dutch or Jews.

Gaspar Dias Ferreira, taking note of the high prices being fetched for blacks in Pernambuco and also of the shortage of wine, recognized that a killing could be made dealing in these two commodities. He persuaded the Prince that they should go into business together. His idea was to send a ship to either the Cape Verde Islands or else the island of Madeira, with plenty of money and trade goods such as sugar, brazilwood, and tobacco. There, the ship would load up on either slaves or wine. Portuguese sailors would man the ship. They'd claim to be sailing out of Bahia, not Pernambuco. That way, the Portuguese ports would allow the ship to take on cargo.

On the return voyage, the ship would anchor somewhere in Pernambuco, other than Recife. They'd discharge the cargo, store it in a remote location, and sell it without being detected. The goods would be under the protection of the Prince, who would thereby accrue immense profits.

The Prince's self-interest made him bet on this outlandish scheme. He directed Ferreira to buy a large damaged ship from the Supreme Council. They managed to have it refurbished quickly and rigged the sails. Recife was filled with Portuguese pilots and sailors at that time, due to the number of ships the Dutch had seized in violation of the peace treaty. The ship was to set sail under the pretense that it was going to Setuval in Portugal to load salt, which would be carried to Holland. In this way, Ferreira hoped to keep the scheme hidden from the Supreme Council.

Before the ship left, the Prince showed great favor to the Portuguese pilot, even dining with him and promising him rewards. The pilot, however, told some of his friends that he had no wish to go on this voyage but was being forced to do so. He wanted to remain on good terms with Ferreira and the Prince. However, it was his intent to sail straight to Lisbon or another Portuguese port, denounce the plot, and deliver the ship to the King's representatives.

Somehow word of the pilot's intent leaked out and reached Ferreira, who quickly had the pilot imprisoned in solitary confinement. Ferreira wanted to hang him but was afraid the pilot's friends would disclose the plot to the Supreme Council. Later that night, Ferreira had the pilot taken from prison, and along with his friends, put them in a boat that sailed out past the reef. They were never heard from again.

Not taking any further chances, Ferreira placed his nephew on the ship as the chief merchant and his brother-in-law as the captain. He asked the Prince to put some soldiers and a Dutch pilot on board the ship as well, in case of any treachery by the Portuguese pilot and crew. The ship arrived in Cape Verde. The Portuguese pilot exposed the fraudulent scheme to the Governor, who had the ship confiscated. However, the captain and merchant, who were Ferreira's relatives, swore that they were returning to Bahia and paid a surety of six thousand silver coins. The ship was released and loaded with cargo. The Portuguese pilot refused to sail back.

When the ship, laden with slaves, was within sight of Recife, it gave a signal. It was flying a Portuguese flag and feigned that it was sailing toward Bahia. It then cut back. Guided by a fishing boat sent by Ferreira, it entered a river next to Porto de Calvo. However, using a spy glass, from Recife it could be confirmed that it was the same ship Ferreira had purchased. Ferreira's people scrambled to unload the ship and hide everything. They stripped the ship of its rigging, sails, and other fittings, and then sank it.

Despite Ferreira's diligent efforts, the Supreme Council found out about the scheme. They only smoothed things over with Ferreira out of respect for the Prince, whom they understood to be behind the venture. They decided to let the matter rest for the time being.

The slaves were divided up into lots, to be sold for excessive prices. At first, though, using letters bearing the Prince's signature, Ferreira distributed the slaves to owners of sugar mills and wealthy landowners. The letters stated that the slaves were gifts from the Prince. They could be paid for whenever and at whatever price the recipients might choose. Some accepted the slaves out of their respect for the Prince and need for slave labor. Others knew Ferreira well and declined the gift, although with an expression of thanks and gratitude to the Prince. However, after eight months had passed, Ferreira went after those who had accepted the slaves with a vengeance, demanding astronomical prices.

The slaves that Ferreira couldn't sell off secretly in this manner were sent to the sugar mill of his mother-in-law. He then, with the Prince's assistance, joined with a Jewish merchant to buy another shipment of slaves from different parts of the West African coast. He mixed these new slaves with his original shipment from Cape Verde. The whole lot was then sold off in Mauritsstad. The gimmick was obvious to everyone. There's actually an incident I'd like to recount that illustrates how ridiculous it all was.

Some Dutch and French merchants passed in front of Ferreira's shop in Mauritsstad. There they encountered the heretical French preacher Vincent Soler, a native of the Spanish province of Valencia, who had been an Augustinian friar. He deserted the faith and made his way to France, where he became a Calvinist preacher and then married. He was serving as a preacher in Pernambuco.

At the time, Soler had a grievance against the Prince, who had spurned the love of the preacher's daughter, Margaret Soler. The Prince had instead taken up with the daughter of a low-level officer. Margaret's feelings for the Prince caused her to die from heartbreak and sadness. One of the merchants commented to the preacher about the mixture of blacks from different regions of Africa that Ferreira had for sale. The merchant also said that the well-known fraud would catch up with the Prince and Ferreira at some point. The preacher then shared the following story:

> Gentlemen, in my homeland there was a married woman, who became the mistress of a young man, who was attentive to her and treated her well. She wasn't satisfied with him and fell in love with another. She therefore spurned the love of the first man and broke off her relationship with him. The first man was aggrieved by this insult. When he met up with her on the street one day, he cut her face with a razor.
>
> The scandalous woman fainted and fell to the ground. A neighbor picked her up and took her into his home. He summoned the local surgeon, who gave her some stitches. He stopped the bleeding with a salve made of egg whites. She then regained consciousness.
>
> Seeing many people at the doorway who were admiring the success of the procedure, the woman got down on her knees, and with raised hands said: "Gentlemen, by the stigmata of Christ, I beg your Graces, that my husband be told nothing of this." The surgeon replied: "Whore, deceiver, if you'd been cut on the arm or leg, you could very well have hidden it with your dress but, since it's in the middle of your

face, there's no possible way to cover it and hide it from your husband."

What I say to you now, gentlemen, is that if Gaspar Dias Ferreira has here in his shop, displayed openly in the doorway, these blacks from Cape Verde to sell, some of whom are saying where they came from because they've picked up a smattering of the Portuguese language, how is it possible for him to hide what he did? It doesn't matter what strategies he might employ or how many other kinds of Africans he mixes them up with.

At the time of this business with the Cape Verde slaves, a ship arrived from Holland carrying orders for the Prince to cut his expenditures in half. He was informed that he would no longer be given a blank check to run Pernambuco, since the Dutch West India Company was running out of funds and could no longer support the Count and all of his dependents.

In addition, the members of the Supreme Council had come to hate the Prince. They wanted him sent back to Holland. They felt this way because the Prince gave all the orders. He had a chokehold on all of the commercial advantages and revenue streams. The Councilmembers had been pushed into a corner and deprived of opportunities to turn a profit. However, they didn't dare try to block the Prince or interfere in matters under his jurisdiction because he was the cousin of the Dutch Stadholder, the Prince of Orange.

The Prince was very upset by the order to cut costs. In secret, he soon began to prepare to depart, sometime during the next six months. He started selling off his horses. He had thirty of high quality, for which he'd paid nothing, since the landowners had given them to him as gifts. As soon as the Dutch figured out the Prince was getting ready to leave, they began harassing the Portuguese again. Even the hangers-on started to threaten them. They said they would exact vengeance on the Portuguese as soon as their protector, the Prince, had departed from Pernambuco.

Another ship from Angola arrived. It was filled with Portuguese from Angola, including priests, friars, and Jesuits. In violation of the good-conduct passports granted to the Portuguese, the Dutch ambushed and robbed them, killing many. Others were shipped to Pernambuco as prisoners. Among the clerics that came from Angola was a cousin of Ferreira's wife. She was half New Christian. Her cousin had been ordained using false documents sent to Angola by Ferreira.

Ferreira wrote to the Bishop of Brazil in Bahia, requesting that the cousin be formally ordained. Some men from Pernambuco who were in Bahia told the Bishop that this young man was more than half New Christian. The Bishop decided not to ordain him and said: "God doesn't want me to sell the blood and honor of Christ for mere human considerations." Ferreira wouldn't give up and wrote to the Bishop again. Ferreira stated that without his personal intervention, all of the clerics would have been expelled from Pernambuco. Those who knew Ferreira and his schemes could only shake their heads at his insulting attitude toward the Bishop.

18 FERREIRA'S TANGLED WEB

Editor's Note: The Prince leaves Brazil. Ferreira departs with him, knowing that he will probably be murdered if he remains. Calado hears of the plans of Protestant preachers, who were drawn into a plot hatched by Ferreira, to expel all Catholic clergy. He coordinates with a Dutchman of noble character, one who cares for the Portuguese, to derail the expulsion.

* * *

The time finally came for the Prince to depart. He hosted a series of going-away parties. Ferreira realized that if he remained in Pernambuco, with the Prince gone, either the Dutch would imprison him in order to seize his assets or else the Portuguese would murder him. He put his affairs in order quickly so that he could depart with the Prince. He took with him two sons and two daughters, claiming that he was going to take them to receive the blessing of King João IV. Before leaving, he met with the Supreme Council and recommended that they banish all Portuguese priests, supplying various reasons for them to do so.

As the Prince sailed out of Recife, in May of 1643, many Dutch and Portuguese accompanied him. They saluted him with guns and artillery. He had tears in his eyes, showing his grief at being pulled away from Pernambuco, where he had "honestly" acquired such a vast amount of gold. Ferreira snuck away separately, accompanied by a dozen soldiers, due to his fear of being murdered along the way. No one came to bid him farewell. He said with great sadness as he departed his house: "I never imagined that I had so many enemies, as I can now see by this experience." He eventually caught up with the Prince, and refused to leave his side until the ship was at full sail, on its way to Holland.

After the Prince had left, all of the Calvinist and Lutheran preachers came to Recife to hold a religious convocation. They needed to resolve various matters about their false sects and also to carry out the expulsion of the Roman Catholic clergy that Ferreira had proposed. One member of the Supreme Council, Manuel Code, was elected as chairman of the convocation. He was a young man of good intentions and nobility, who cared deeply for the Portuguese. Code always defended the suffering Portuguese before the Council.

I went to visit Code one day because he was sick. He displayed his friendship by telling me what the preachers were up to. I made it very clear to him the trouble that could be expected if this clique were to succeed in their plot to expel the priests. I said that should it be appropriate, I'd like to present my thoughts on the matter to the assembled preachers, so that they might understand the situation better and desist from their plan. Code agreed with my suggestion. He said he'd arrange for me to speak to the convocation. I kissed his hand in thanks for his kindness.

The next day, I appeared before the convocation, with all of the preachers in attendance. Code asked me to say whatever I considered to be necessary. I spoke with the level of courtesy and deference that I thought would be appropriate for the occasion, even though such respect wasn't owed to heretics:

> Illustrious Lord, and Highest Preaching Authorities, it has come to my attention that Your Lordships have decided at this convocation to banish all Portuguese priests serving here, who conduct the sacraments for residents in the lands under Dutch control. First of all, this act would break the word and violate the assurances given to the residents that they would continue to live with the liberty to embrace the pure Holy Roman Catholic faith. By banishing the priests and breaking your word, you'll have no cause for complaint should the Portuguese decide they no longer owe you obedience and choose instead to rebel.

After all, the Portuguese wish to remain your subjects and friends, provided that you don't interfere with the faith they profess, nor mistreat their women. Anyone who is bold enough to offend the Portuguese in these two areas will need to prepare to have them as mortal enemies forever.

Secondly, it's well known throughout the land—or at the least appears to be the case based on ample evidence—that Gaspar Dias Ferreira is the author of this plot, which makes it necessary for me to clarify for Your Lordships the following: Ferreira by race is a Jew; his wife is a New Christian and by race is Moorish. Here they worked the land with a double-tipped plow. In Recife, they engaged in both licit and illicit business dealings. In Bahia, they constantly wrote to the Bishop and Governors that only the two of them were protecting the Roman Catholic faith and clergy.

At this point Code interrupted me, and said:

It was Ferreira who threw all this dirt at the Roman Catholic priests. He caused the uncertainty that led us to plan to banish them. We've been well informed that the priests ran to him seeking his favor and they gave him substantial gifts to be used as bribes, most of which he kept for himself. A small part he gave to us so that we'd be less severe with the priests.

With these schemes, he made himself rich, and ingratiated himself with the Prince. He tricked the Portuguese priests into thinking he was the one shielding them. However, in Holland where he's headed, he'll be held to account for all that he's done. Here, he's going to pay with all of his property because we've already opened an official inquiry against him. We have sworn testimony about his serious crimes.

After Code had spoken, I continued my discourse:

Your Lordships need to know that the ship filled with Portuguese prisoners from Angola included a young man who is Ferreira's or his wife's nephew, who had taken Holy Orders. The Bishop of Angola had ordained him on the basis of forged papers that came from Pernambuco.

Ferreira wrote to the Bishop of Bahia requesting the perfection of the nephew's ordination to Holy Orders and renunciation of secular life. The Bishop refused to do so, on the basis that the nephew is Hebrew. I must note that this is an impediment to the taking of Holy Orders, according the Supreme Roman Pontiff.

Ferreira wrote again to the Bishop, challenging his decision. Ferreira stated that he was the defender and protector of the priests operating in Pernambuco. Since the Bishop had failed to reward him justly for his extraordinary service, the Bishop would come to see what would happen upon his departure for Holland in the Prince's company. Without his favor, Ferreira predicted the priests would soon be expelled from Pernambuco.

I then pulled out a copy of Ferreira's letter to the Bishop of Bahia and showed it to the preachers. I said, "Here's the reason Ferreira left in place this tangled web of a scheme, so that the Governor of Bahia and His Majesty the King of Portugal would believe in his influence." I went on to recount in detail another of Ferreira's schemes, by which he siphoned off for himself ecclesiastical funds that were to be distributed to all the parishes. In the end, I told them:

Returning to the expulsion of the priests, I implore Your Lordships, in the name of God, don't issue this order. If you abuse them, then you can rightly assume that you'll no longer possess Pernambuco. In an instant the entire populace will rise up against you in rebellion, taking up arms or abandoning the land. These people, if you treat them well, can be governed with the tip of your toe. Once they've rebelled, however, you'll have to expend enormous resources to bring them under control. This is my message to the convocation.

The preachers were so impressed by my arguments that they halted their nefarious plan to expel the priests. Not only that, they also from that day forward ceased insulting or harassing the priests. In fact, they treated them perfectly, with complete courtesy.

19 GROUNDWORK FOR INSURGENCY

Editor's Note: Dutch defenses are in disrepair. The best officers and soldiers departed with the Prince. Key players make their opening moves in the pending revolt. Its instigator, the wealthy but indebted João Fernades Vieira, begins recruiting an army and appointing officers. Andre Vidal de Negreiros is the military commander in Bahia who privately supports the rebellion. Teodor de Estrate, who appears but isn't yet named, is a Catholic officer in service to the Dutch. He wishes to serve the Portuguese king and surrender a fort he commands.

Although the king's orders command obedience to the Dutch, the abuses under their occupation are so great that Vieira and others are willing to face royal punishment for rebelling. They hope to create "facts on the ground" by quickly defeating the Dutch before the king receives word of their uprising. In reality, the king maintains the pretense of cooperation with the Dutch while secretly condoning the rebels' efforts.

The arguments for rebellion rely heavily on religious justifications. Stamping out the heretical teachings of Calvin and Luther is important, but above all else eliminating Judaism is a sacred obligation incumbent on all Portuguese. Calado equates Dutch rule with permissiveness and freedom of conscience, which the Dutch value and the Portuguese detest.

* * *

With the Prince gone, all restraints on Dutch abuses were removed. It would take many reams of paper to recount in detail how they oppressed the pathetic residents of occupied Pernambuco. The Dutch committed countless acts of cruelty and extreme outrages. The sight of this situation moved the heart of the wealthy João Fernades Vieira. He was a man of noble character who had often helped the unfortunate. Vieira was at one time a friend to the Prince and highly respected by the Dutch. He realized that there was no other recourse but to take up arms against the occupiers, even at the cost of his life and the lives of his fellow Portuguese.

Vieira began laying the groundwork for an insurgency. He secretly acquired weapons and ammunition, which he stored in hidden sheds in the forests. He also bought foodstuffs: manioc flour, rice, beans, dried corn, salt-cured fish, smoked meat, wine, olive oil, vinegar, salt, and other necessities. He ordered his sugar mills to convert all their production to rum. He disguised his stockpiling activity by sending the supplies into the woods in carts used for harvesting brazilwood, along with slave laborers. He posted cattle, sheep, and goats in his corrals in the backlands. He blamed their disappearance on death from eating poisonous herbs.

While Vieira was setting things in motion, in September of 1644, the Portuguese Commander Andre Vidal de Negreiros came to Pernambuco from Bahia for the purpose of visiting his father and mother. While in Recife he asked for permission to visit his friends, which was granted. Vieira met with him and disclosed his secret plot and determination. He told Negreiros that the Dutch had let down their guard. Their defensive infrastructure was in disrepair. They had few good soldiers. All the best officers, soldiers, and officials had left with the Prince. They did so either at his request or else because their time of service was up. There was nothing left for them to rob in Pernambuco.

According to Vieira, the only Dutch who remained in Pernambuco were merchants and tavern-keepers, plus those who had usurped Portuguese landowners and had taken up sugar cultivation and processing. The Dutch and Jews in the countryside were spread out. They no longer lived within fortified areas. The majority of those living within the walls of fortified towns were Jews and their families.

Most of the Jews were people who'd fled Portugal for Holland. In an act of supreme impudence against the Christian religion, they'd erected synagogues. The Portuguese were duty bound at all costs to put a stop to this blasphemy, sacrificing even their lives if necessary.

They were obliged to exert themselves wholeheartedly in devoted service to our Lord and Savior Jesus Christ, in order to preserve the honor of Christ's holy faith.

Commander Negreiros heard everything Vieira had to say. He could see for himself the state of the enemy's fortifications. He noted the current conditions of the land. In all cases, he exercised prudence and masked what he was doing. On his return to Recife, as he was preparing to sail back to Bahia, he got word that four of our soldiers were captured in Porto de Calvo, where they'd been denounced by spies.

The soldiers had been secretly attacking the Dutch wherever they could, disguising their identities by associating with some deserters from Bahia. The news got out that they were to be hung. Negreiros and I went before the Supreme Council, where I made an excellent presentation, during which I reminded the Councilmembers that they were currently at peace with Portugal, with an armistice in effect.

I said it would be better not to hang the four because it would cause a commotion among the people. Rather, it would be best to send the four to Holland, or else to Bahia with Negreiros, so that they could be punished as deserters. Three of the four were ultimately hung anyway, with one first having his hands chopped off on a butcher's block. The fourth, a Castilian, paid a bribe and was released.

On his return trip to Bahia, Negreiros carried with him a letter to the Governor of Brazil. It had been written by Vieira and signed by the leading men of Pernambuco, both the clergy and laity. In it, they attested to the pathetic condition of the Captaincy and the atrocities committed by the Dutch against the residents. They asserted their loyalty as vassals of the Portuguese king. However, they also claimed their right as honorable Portuguese to take up arms to fight against the Dutch enemy.

The petitioners asked the Governor, as Chief Military Commander of all Brazil, to assist them in their efforts. They requested help both in their defense as the King's loyal vassals and for the protection of the Holy Catholic Faith. It was his duty, they claimed, to put a stop to the false sects of Luther and Calvin. Worst of all was Judaism, which had been taking control of the hearts and souls of so many Christians in Pernambuco. The letter ended with a plea for ammunition, weapons, and experienced soldiers in support of the planned rebellion.

At the same time, Vieira wrote to Camarão, who was still camped out in Sergipe with his indigenous Brazilian fighters. Entreating Camarão with kind words, Vieira appealed to his past loyal support of the King, the Portuguese, and the Catholic faith, that he might come to the aid of the rebellion. Should he fail to do so, Vieira warned, Pernambuco was at risk of being lost forever, with the True Faith of Christ dying out as parents were killed off. Their innocent children would be abandoned to the diabolical sects and false doctrines followed by the Dutch.

One might ask, who was this Camarão? I would respond that he was the King's most loyal vassal in all of Brazil, a courageous commander who, as soon as he was called, summoned all the indigenous Brazilians loyal to him. Camarão's men descended from the backcountry to attack the Dutch. Before long, the Dutch were filled with terror even hearing his name. Their Field Commander Artixof said that in more than forty years of fighting, whether in Poland, Germany, or Flanders, where he always held positions of high command, none had deflated his pride or caused him such dishonor as this man.

Camarão led the fight to defend Bahia in 1637, during the Prince's attempted invasion. Through stealth and bravery, he drove off the Prince in defeat. Beyond all of that, he was a man of good character, courteous of speech, accomplished in reading and writing, with some knowledge of Latin, devout in the Catholic Faith, and highly respected. The King in fact gave him honors, including noble status. He was named Governor of the indigenous Brazilians. As soon as Camarão received the letter from Vieira, he replied that he was ready to fight. He would send his men by secret pathways through the forests as soon as the winter floods subsided.

Vieira also wrote to Henrique Dias, the Governor of the Brazilian-born blacks and people of mixed race. He also led Africans of various regions who'd been imported from different slave entrepôts. He'd fought with great courage, losing a hand in an early battle against the Prince. He was an emancipated Brazilian-born black and greatly feared by the Dutch.

Dias also led the resistance to the Prince during his attempted invasion of Bahia. He fought with such bravery that the King likewise gave him honors. He too received the title of Governor. Government funds were used for the emancipation of those of Dias' black soldiers who were still technically slaves of Portuguese landowners. This occurred at the time Matias de Albuquerque was leading the initial resistance to the Dutch invasion. In later years, Dias was sent as Captain of the troops for the reconquest of Angola.

However, Dias wasn't in Bahia at the time Vieira wrote to him. He was instead out in the backcountry with his soldiers, since technically the Dutch and Portuguese were still at peace. Dias and his men were hunting down runaway slaves who'd settled in a large encampment, known in Brazil as a mocambo or quilombo, where they'd built a fort. Vieira's messenger finally caught up with Dias. On reading the letter, Dias responded that he assumed Vieira had an insufficient number of men. Dias, therefore, planned to set out immediately for Pernambuco.

In Bahia, the Governor read Vieira's letter and heard Negreiros' report. He ordered several officers and a small force of experienced soldiers to Pernambuco by way of the backcountry, where they could pass through in secrecy. He told them to find Vieira and to follow whatever orders he might give them. In writing, though, he replied to Vieira that he couldn't provide any assistance because the King had given express orders, in light of the truce, to maintain peace and friendship with the Dutch in Pernambuco. The King's order couldn't be disobeyed.

The Governor knew, of course, of the truce violations committed by the Dutch. However, he ordered the officers not to make war on the Dutch but, rather, only to engage in self-defense until directed otherwise. The officers met up with Vieira in December 1644. Vieira asked the chief officer to return to Bahia with a secret letter. In it, Vieira pleaded for more ammunition and guns due to the dire situation. The officer departed in January 1645.

Before this, back when Commander Negreiros left Pernambuco to return to Bahia, many Jews started sounding the alarm that his visit hadn't been for the purpose of seeing his parents. They claimed, rather, that he'd been sent to spy on the condition of Dutch defenses. The Jews said he'd stockpiled munitions and weapons in Pernambuco.

The Jews petitioned the Supreme Council to send a ship to Bahia, carrying a protest to be lodged with the Governor. The protest asserted that the Governor's plan to wage war against the Dutch was well known in Pernambuco. The Governor had been part of a faction that opposed the ceasefire between Holland and Portugal. His plotting was known to the Jews by way of New Christian spies they had in Bahia.

The Council agreed to lodge the protest. They sent representatives to Bahia. The Dutch ship arrived at the same time Vieira's letter reached the Governor.

With full knowledge of Dutch oppression and cruelty as reported by Vieira, the Governor listened impassively to the complaints lodged by the Dutch representatives. He responded that he had express orders from the King to preserve a state of friendship and peace with the Dutch who were occupying Pernambuco. The Governor said he'd be beheaded should he disobey such orders.

However, the Governor noted that since the Dutch were committing on a daily basis the same vicious acts they feared would be committed by the Portuguese, it would only be natural for the Portuguese to refuse further obedience. It could be expected that they'd attempt to liberate themselves. So long as the Dutch wanted the Portuguese to live quietly and in peace, it would be necessary to put a stop to the constant theft, oppression, and abuse the Dutch committed. Then everything would be calm.

The Governor showed the Dutch representatives the King's order by which the Portuguese were prohibited from fighting the Dutch. Nevertheless, the Governor said he'd need to inform the King of the harm the Dutch had caused along the coast of Brazil following the ceasefire. He would report how the Dutch constantly abused the residents of Pernambuco, in violation of the solemn commitments entered into between His Majesty and both the United Provinces of the Netherlands and the Prince of Orange. The Governor then dismissed the representatives.

Before they departed, one of the representatives asked for a private conversation with the Governor. It weighed on his conscience how the Dutch abused the residents of Pernambuco. He knew that in their desperation the Portuguese would have no choice but to fight for liberation. The representative said that he was of noble birth and good family. In addition, he was a captain in command of one of the Dutch forts.

As a direct witness to the destruction happening in Pernambuco, he concluded he could no longer serve the Dutch. He wished to depart for Portugal to serve the King. He would henceforth pledge his loyalty to João IV as his sovereign lord. However, before departing Pernambuco, there was a great service he could perform for the King, which he'd disclose only if the Governor would tell him whether or not he intended to attack Pernambuco.

The Governor, who was a clever and cautious man, suspected the representative's offer was a ruse to get him to reveal his plans. He replied that he greatly respected the courage shown by the representative in wishing to serve His Majesty. He would let the King know, so that the King might show the representative favor at some future time. At present, there was no plan to attack the Dutch in Pernambuco because His Majesty had commanded the maintenance of peace and friendship. However, if things were to change in the future, he would certainly let him know in time to be of service. With this, he presented the representative with a valuable gift, bidding him farewell.

Once the Dutch representatives made the return voyage to Recife, they reported to the Supreme Council that everything in Bahia was quiet. Their spies hadn't come up with any new information. They'd seen with their own eyes the orders from the King of Portugal to maintain peace and friendship. Although the Governor objected to Dutch conduct toward the residents of Pernambuco and planned to report it to the King, there was no intent on his part to begin a war. The rumor was a falsehood and crooked plot cooked up by the Jews.

The Governor of Brazil, conversely, upon the Dutch representatives' departure, commanded the chief officer whom Vieira had sent to return back to Pernambuco. He was ordered to tell Vieira that the Portuguese were ready to fight, should the Dutch continue in their abuses. The Governor also sent word that he'd provide the necessary assistance for Vieira and his men to defend themselves. Further, the Governor said that if they wanted to do so, the men with Vieira could send their wives and children to Bahia for safety, under the escort of Camarão and Dias, who would soon be arriving.

In addition, the Governor directed Vieira, in the event that he and his men ended up on the verge of total defeat, to burn down every sugar mill and all the plantations, kill all the cattle they couldn't take with them, destroy all the crops, and proceed to Bahia, leaving Pernambuco in total ruin. By doing so, the Dutch would have no sugar to ship and would starve. They'd be forced to return to Holland because the cost of ships and soldiers would become unsustainable. If despite all of this the Dutch were to persist in their occupation, and managed to cultivate the land, then the Governor said he would send Camarão and Dias back with their troops, to rob and kill everyone they could find outside of the forts. As regards ammunition and weapons, Camarão would bring them shortly.

On receiving the Governor's letter, Vieira was delighted, for it authorized him throughout the districts of Pernambuco to appoint as captains those who in his estimation merited the positions. He was also authorized to appoint other military officials.

In great secrecy, Vieira dispatched the newly appointed captains to the various districts so that they could appoint qualified men to local command positions. Everything was put in order as quietly as possible, to lull the Dutch into remaining inattentive, with their defenses down.

In preparation for launching the rebellion, Vieira and his closest advisors decided to present to the King a written justification for the absolute necessity of their actions, given the horrendous abuses they suffered at the hands of the Dutch. It was their hope that by the time the document reached the King, they would have already succeeded in the glorious undertaking. Many copies of the letter were circulated, so that signatures could be obtained from all of the leading men, both clerics and laity.

Among the abuses detailed in the letter, the worst were how the Dutch forced the daughters of the Portuguese into marriage, engaged in dishonorable acts with the wives of Portuguese men, and were attempting to exterminate the Roman Catholic Faith in Pernambuco. The Dutch sought to replace the Holy Faith with the false sects of Calvin and Luther, as well as treacherous Judaism, which was being practiced openly.

Recife was filled with Jews. Many lived in rural outposts, where they'd become owners of sugar mills, having usurped them from the Portuguese by means of their diabolical plots. The Portuguese proclaimed loudly that all men of Hebrew ethnicity in Pernambuco were Jewish in faith. The only ones who hadn't declared themselves Jews and been circumcised were those who wanted to but were afraid that the Portuguese might somehow return, and punish them severely. This latter claim, however, might have been malicious, and offensive to honest men of Hebrew ethnicity, who had chosen not to follow the path of error.

I say this because I know of many who, even during this time of permissiveness and freedom of conscience, enjoyed true satisfaction in maintaining their loyalty to the Holy Faith of Jesus Christ. I would boldly swear this on their behalf, to the extent I'm capable of judging them by their acts.

In any event, those who were zealous for the common good all signed copies of Vieira's letter. Two men, however, refused to sign. Both had collaborated with the Dutch and remained on good terms with them. One was so cowardly, he once asked the Prince to send him to Holland as a prisoner, so that it would appear to the other Portuguese that he wasn't in fact a traitor. They both ran off to tell the Supreme Council about all that was happening. The two traitors gave them the names of all who had signed the letter.

The Dutch kept this information under wraps in the hope of keeping things quiet because they realized they were short on manpower and resources. They knew that their fortifications were in disrepair. Regardless, they hurriedly began making repairs and stocking up. Together with the Jews, they began to collect rigorously all outstanding debts from the Portuguese, storing the sugar and other in-kind payments within their fortified areas. Under the cover of debt collection, the Dutch also began seizing people who had signed the letter and holding them in Recife. They hoped in this way gradually to detain all of those who had signed the letter. Once all were rounded up, they were to be killed in one fell swoop.

The Jews soon began proclaiming that the Portuguese were all traitors. They said the Portuguese planned to rise up and murder the Dutch. Aware of the risks to his safety, Vieira began to sleep in a different place each night. He was guarded by a handful of men he could trust. He put hidden doorways in all of his lodging places so that he could quickly escape.

Whenever he traveled, he sent scouts out ahead. He kept at hand about one hundred of his slaves, armed with spears, bows, and arrows, so that they could free him if the Dutch somehow managed to capture him. He continued to prepare diligently for the uprising, putting everything in order. Vieira sent his wife away to stay with a relative. All of those who had signed the letter to the King were advised to use extra caution. The men awaited the arrival of Camarão and Dias, together with their accompanying troops.

20 REBELLION IS A DUTY

Editor's Note: The rebellion is delayed due to torrential rains. Camarão and Dias take months to reach Pernambuco. In the meantime, the Dutch—well informed by spies—make efforts to round up the plotters and kill or capture Vieira. Calado finally openly preaches in favor of revolt. Catholic Portuguese must rise up to free themselves from Dutch tyranny, even at the cost of their lives. The congregation is moved to tears and is resolved to fight.

The uprising begins with the murder of a Jewish merchant in the town in which Calado resides. The locals, some armed only with sharp sticks, kill another Jew and a few of the Dutch soldiers who respond to the incident. The Dutch launch a retaliatory attack. They also lodge a protest in Bahia. Brazil's governor is unsympathetic. Teodor de Estrate, who is part of the Dutch delegation, communicates in confidence his proposed collaboration with the Portuguese.

* * *

Passover of 1645 came and went. The troops still hadn't arrived. The rainy season had been terrible, worse than anyone could remember. All of the rivers were flooded. It took Camarão and Dias four months to descend from the backcountry.

Between Passover and Easter, I was approached by a man who had forty men-at-arms. He wanted to set up an ambush to kill Dutch soldiers. I advised him to desist with this plan because it wouldn't help the broader cause. Instead, it would bring great harm upon all of us. Besides, the Dutch were closely monitoring him. I asked him to be ready for the proper time. Then, he could show his bravery and determination to serve His Majesty. I promised to advise him as soon as we were ready.

At last, I preached openly in favor of rebellion. In the past I'd hesitated because I knew the Dutch typically had informers planted at the services I conducted. I spoke of the abuses, cruel acts, thefts, and treachery of the Dutch. I exhorted everyone to prepare to defend the Catholic Faith and to free themselves from their current state of tyrannical subjugation. I advised them to take up arms, in the full knowledge of their heritage as Portuguese. They were the descendants of heroes who'd conquered the remotest parts of the earth. In the end, when I'd finished conducting Mass, everyone left the church shedding tears of joy, firmly resolved to stand up against the enemy, ready to die in battle if needed.

In the countryside, Vieira met up at a sugar mill with a number of the leaders of the rebellion in order to work on their strategy. All of these men had armed slaves and other dependents with them. Vieira told his most trustworthy slaves that he'd emancipate them if they were to fight courageously in the rebellion.

With a small force of one hundred thirty men, Vieira marched to where there were several mocambos. He sent out word that all of the runaway slaves who joined them and fought bravely would be emancipated. He asserted he'd pay their former owners a just price for their liberty out of his own funds. Although this helped Vieira build up his forces, they were still insufficient to take on the Dutch directly.

Vieira learned that spies had informed the Supreme Council of his whereabouts. Therefore, he moved on to another set of mocambos in a different district. There, he recruited some more blacks to join him.

The Dutch kept rounding up prominent Portuguese, some whom were sworn to rebellion and others who weren't. The Dutch would release them on payment of a penalty. The Dutch required the Portuguese to take a loyalty oath and would then issue passports to them. Even some of the Portuguese who'd been denounced by informers were released, due to the large amounts they paid.

On 18 June 1645 the Dutch issued a proclamation, which they ordered posted on the doors of all churches in Pernambuco. It read more or less as follows:

> The illustrious and noble Lords of the Supreme Council of Pernambuco hereby declare: It has come to our attention, much to our distress, that some of the residents of this jurisdiction have fled to the uninhabited forest areas.
>
> They've done so as the result of a false rumor, which has been spreading, to the effect that our soldiers have been ordered to go out and kill and rob all residents who live outside of our fortifications. They're understandably overcome with fear and dread. We wish to put a stop to the suffering and misfortune the residents, especially the innocent, are likely to experience by fleeing in this way.
>
> By this proclamation, be it known to all that it is our intent to defend, sustain, and conserve in peace and tranquility all of our subjects. We hereby solicit on behalf of God, and in our own right, that all residents under our jurisdiction, who have taken to the forests in fear, return promptly to their homes.
>
> We pledge to give full pardon for all wrongs committed against us in our official capacities by traitors and rebels, provided that they comply within nine days. This term is fixed and irrevocable. As soon as those eligible for pardon receive notice of this proclamation, they must appear before the Supreme Council to take a new loyalty oath and to receive passports.
>
> The pardon hereby granted doesn't extend to the leaders of the rebellion and uprising. Those who fail to return to their homes or appear before the Council by the deadline will be subject to violent reprisal. They'll face death as traitors, without forgiveness or any show of mercy.

When this proclamation was posted, nearly all of the residents presented themselves to the Supreme Council. These were people who couldn't withdraw to the forests due to the severe rainy season. They hadn't hidden provisions for their families because they had no knowledge of the planned rebellion. When the time came, they would of course stand up for liberty. They paid for and received the Dutch passports.

Once the nine days were up, Dutch soldiers went about confirming that people were in their homes. The soldiers warned the residents that anything they'd left hidden in the countryside would be seized. The Dutch set loose their indigenous Brazilian allies, the Caboclos, to roam the forests. They stole anything they could find and killed anyone they came across.

As the Dutch intended, the threat of raids by Caboclos caused the residents to bring all of their belongings from the countryside into their homes for protection. Unfortunately, this made it much easier for the Dutch to rob everyone. Despite the threats, a number of residents and their families went out to join up with Vieira.

The Dutch posted another notice, offering a large sum in gold coin for Vieira, dead or alive. They promised emancipation to any slave who might kill or capture him. Vieira responded by offering an even larger bounty for the heads of the three members of the Supreme Council. He also wrote to them. In his letter, he called them tyrants and deceitful thieves.

Vieira threatened to hunt down the Councilmembers without a moment's rest. He promised to soon have his hands on them because he had under his command 14,000 white soldiers and 24,000 blacks and men of mixed race. The Supreme Council and Jews treated Vieira's letter as a big joke. Due to intelligence passed on by informants, they knew exactly how many armed men he actually had.

On 5 July 1645, Vieira finally received word that Camarão, Dias, and their soldiers had crossed a major river and would soon arrive. He shared the joyful news with the trustworthy leaders of the rebellion. Unfortunately, the same pair who had informed the Dutch previously did so again. They asked the Supreme Council to arrest all of the ringleaders but, first, to arrest the two of them. The two wanted to allay suspicion among their fellow Portuguese that they were traitors.

The Dutch sent all of their soldiers, in squads of twenty to forty men, to carry out the arrests. The rain was terrible and the roads were mired in thick mud. They encircled the houses of the suspects at night. Their plan was to arrest them at daybreak, bring them to Recife, and hang them all. However, aware of the risks and despite the rain, all of the men went out to hide in the forests. Not a single suspect was arrested.

The men of the town where I was staying openly began the uprising. Several Dutch boats had arrived to pick up shipments of sugar, manioc flour, and other produce of the Dutch and Jewish planters. I also had some crates of sugar to ship to Recife. The town had a number of merchants' shops. One of the Portuguese exchanged harsh words with a Jewish merchant. They came to blows and the Jew was killed. Another Jew entered the fight and was killed by some of the residents.

The Dutch soldiers stationed in town went after the Portuguese involved in the killings. They too came under attack by the residents, who managed to kill some of the soldiers and wound others. The soldiers scrambled back to their barracks, grabbed the rest of their weapons, headed to the boats, and set sail. They sank the cargo boats and killed some of the seamen. They continued on to the nearest Dutch fort. The local Portuguese commander ordered everyone, for self-defense, to gather what weapons they could. These were often no more than sticks with fire-hardened points.

When news reached Recife about the uprising, the Jews wailed in lamentation for the two who were murdered. The Jews began petitioning the Supreme Council to launch a retaliatory attack. They offered to pay for the costs of the expedition. Before long, a force of six hundred soldiers and three hundred Caboclos set out from Recife, under cover of night. They encountered some light resistance. Fearing an ambush, they hesitated to advance.

In the meantime, Dutch spies continued to inform the Supreme Council about Vieira and the weakness of his position. The Dutch kept up their threats against those who supported Vieira. They offered clemency to those who turned against him.

In early July the Dutch sent another ship to Bahia with two representatives to meet with the Governor. Their true mission was to determine whether or not any warships had arrived from Portugal. The representatives, who were military men fluent in Portuguese, complained to the Governor about Vieira's rebellion.

The Dutch officers said that if Bahia were found to be supporting Vieira, they would make a firm request to Holland for an invasion force. It would be employed not only to kill all of the Portuguese in Pernambuco for treason but, also, to take Bahia. They asserted that it was open knowledge in Recife that various commanders and numerous soldiers from Bahia had already crossed into Dutch-held territory.

After hearing their complaints, the Governor sent for the commanders named by the Dutch representatives, in order to show how badly informed the two were. He then said:

> The Lords of the Supreme Council, who lack any knowledge other than how to engage in trade, care only for serving their own interests. They think nothing of committing treason and treachery or of breaking the word they give to Kings and Christian Princes, especially to one so distinguished as my Lord, King João IV. He has clearly seen the treason and treachery you've committed in Brazil and the surrounding seas following the ceasefire.
>
> I would have exacted harsh vengeance for your crimes but have been impeded from doing so by the express orders of His Majesty. He commanded that we are to preserve peace and friendship with the Dutch in Pernambuco.
>
> However, I'm also under orders to remain vigilant and well informed. It's impossible to have much confidence in the trustworthiness of merchants. Looking at what you've done,

we see that in violation of the peace treaty, in bad faith, you've seized Angola, São Tomé, and Maranhão. You've come here to deliver a pack of lies and fraudulent claims that these commanders have passed into Pernambuco. You can see here before your eyes that all are here in Bahia.

Those who can lie so shamelessly will have even fewer qualms when it comes to breaking their word to His Majesty. What you must understand is that if you continue to tyrannize the residents of Pernambuco, robbing them, curtailing their liberty, and impeding the practice of the divine Roman Catholic Religion, as you have been doing, I will wage all-out war against you. This I swear by the cross I wear here on my chest, even knowing that in doing so His Majesty will have my head cut off for disobeying his commands.

Hearing this, the two Dutch representatives responded:

Illustrious Lord, our superiors on the Supreme Council never believed that Your Lordship would order war to be waged against us. However, since everyone among the local people says so vehemently that war is your intent, it's natural they're afraid. It's for this reason we were ordered to petition Your Lordship on behalf of the Lords of the Illustrious West India Company.

The Lords in this respect have a common purpose with His Majesty King João IV, being that Your Lordship should order the residents of Pernambuco to be tranquil. Your Lordship must also carry out the arrest of João Fernandes Vieira because with him imprisoned everyone else will quiet down. To achieve this, the Lords of the Supreme Council promise to give free passage through their lands in Pernambuco to all the soldiers Your Lordship might choose to send in the cause of peace, for the pacification of the land.

The Governor replied to them:

These Lords of the Supreme Council, who have repeatedly betrayed His Majesty and have looted and harmed the people of Pernambuco, have committed great evil. Because of this, they now suffer from guilty consciences. They're filled with fear and dread. Although I could assume they're trying to deceive me, I wish to set all deception aside at this point.

So go back to Pernambuco. Tell those of the Supreme Council that, within fifteen days, more or less, I'll order the residents of Pernambuco to calm down. I'll also order them to seize João Fernandes Vieira. They'll send him as a prisoner to Recife. The Supreme Council can then send him to His Majesty with a list of the crimes he's committed. They should leave it to His Majesty to order his punishment.

The Governor dismissed the Dutch representatives. As they were leaving, an officer in their service approached the Governor. His name was Teodor de Estrate. He was the same officer who'd previously met in secret with the Governor. Estrate was in charge of a Dutch fort in Pernambuco. He requested a private audience. Once alone together, Estrate said to the Governor:

Illustrious Lord, as Your Lordship knows, as soon as I learned that His Majesty King João IV gained the Crown and scepter of the Kingdom of Portugal, there arose in my heart a great desire to go serve him in the war against the King of Spain. However, although this was my intent, the Lords of the Supreme Council in Recife refused to grant me leave to do so, due to their great need for my services in Pernambuco.

I have much experience in positions of command and military affairs. At present, I'm a Captain and also Commander of the fort at the port of Point Nazareth, on the Cape of Saint Augustine. This is one of Pernambuco's principal ports. João Fernandes Vieira, knowing of my desire to serve King João IV, asked me three times in the past year to surrender the fort to him, offering me large sums of money and promises of other favors to do so.

I hesitated due to my uncertainty and wariness. I felt there was little hope of his ambitions achieving lasting success. However, during this time, I've seen the extreme level of harm, insult, theft, damage, and oppression that the Dutch authorities have inflicted on the local people. They're obligated to rebel on account of pure necessity and duress.

The residents have no other remedy but to rise up in armed revolt against the Dutch. I've now seen the people in a state of rebellion, with Vieira assembling a substantial army in the forests. His soldiers all vow either to win freedom from captivity or else to die in the attempt. I see that Vieira and all who follow him are willing to lose their estates, wives, and children. They'll fight as one in their attacks on the Dutch.

Because of what I now see, what I offer to Your Lordship is to surrender the fort at the Cape of Saint Augustine. In doing so, I'm committing no fault against the law of Christ because I'm Catholic, the son of Catholic parents. For this service I request no reward, except that His Majesty might be informed of the courage with which I serve him. As regards my promise, I hope that God will bless our fight for liberty, which Vieira is leading.

The Governor thanked Estrate for his dedication to serving His Majesty. He promised that Estrate would be rewarded when the right time might come. He and the other Dutch representatives set sail for Recife the next day.

21 PILLAGE, RAPE, AND MURDER

Editor's Note: The Dutch believe events are moving their way. Expecting to crush the rebellion quickly, they send out a well-equipped army to run down Vieira. Calado notes the soldiers carry advanced rifles, which fire without tinder. This is evidence of the sophistication of Dutch research and manufacturing. The commander of the expedition has a notorious reputation and permits his troops, as they progress toward the enemy encampment, to rob and assault the local residents. Calado claims that he converts Jews to Catholicism, secretly baptizes the infants of Catholics married to heretics, and performs an exorcism. He makes his final plea before the Supreme Council for leniency toward the residents. The councilmembers turn on him.

* * *

On their return to Recife, the Dutch representatives reported that the harbor of Bahia was filled with merchant vessels. However, there was only one warship, which was to accompany a fleet back to Portugal. Everything seemed to be peaceful. The Governor had promised to send an army to capture Vieira.

The members of the Supreme Council were delighted. They of course planned to commit an act of treachery. Since the soldiers the Governor would send from Bahia to capture Vieira were likely to be his best, it would be a simple matter for the Dutch to allow them to penetrate deeply into Pernambuco and then murder them. With this accomplished, they could thereafter seize Bahia and take vengeance on all those who'd sworn to support Vieira.

Impatient for success, the Supreme Council decided to appoint Johann Blar as field commander. He was the most cruel and inhuman Dutchman to be found in Pernambuco. They gave him three hundred soldiers, all armed with modern rifles. These rifles didn't require tinder to fire and therefore produced no telltale smell. They also gave him two hundred blacks and Caboclos. They ordered Blar to depart from Recife at night. He was to head for the mocambos where Vieira and his troops were hiding out. They were ordered to drag Vieira back alive in shackles and to kill everyone else who was with him.

I learned of this cruel plot from a man of Jewish ethnicity who I'd been carefully catechizing. I was doing so in order to bring him into faith in the law of Christ our Lord. I intended to baptize him as I'd already succeeded in doing with other Jews. I'd previously sent two Jews to the Chief Inquisitor in Portugal by way of Bahia, at their request. They wanted to return to live in Portugal, where they could practice the law of Christ in its entirety.

The Jew who revealed the plot to me lacked only baptism to become a Christian. I sent word promptly to Vieira via two trusted men since, due to illness, I couldn't travel. I alerted Vieira that informants were leading the Dutch forces to his camp. He needed to be ready to fight or move quickly.

On receiving my message, Vieira took steps to reorganize his men. He relocated to a more remote location with a small squadron of experienced soldiers. As Blar marched out from Recife, another traitor informed him about Vieira's latest moves. Blar shifted course. Along the way, he permitted his men to rob, kill, and rape as they went. They pillaged churches and destroyed sacred images. The cruelties committed at the hands of this butcher are beyond description.

Vieira got word of the Dutch movements, reorganized, and moved on again. The rivers were full due to the rainy season, which had also turned the roads and paths into thick mud. It was difficult for both sides to maneuver.

While these actions were taking place inland, in Recife the Supreme Council issued another general order. It required all women who had husbands or sons who were accompanying Vieira to go out into the woods to find them. They were given five days to return home with their menfolk. The women were to bring along their small children.

Many of these women had never left their homes except on holy days. They couldn't imagine entering the terrifying forests, filled with wild animals and other dangers. Under the order, if the women were to be found at home without their men after five days had passed, they'd face death and the forfeiture of all family property. The women pleaded to God and the Virgin Mary for assistance.

Knowing how the Dutch respected me, several Portuguese landowners sought me out to help plead before the Supreme Council for the suspension of this terrible order. As an example of how well received I was among the Dutch, when I traveled to Recife, the Dutch children would run after me. They'd call out to me and ask to kiss my hand, which I'd extend to them. However, when they saw other members of the Catholic clergy, the same children would insult them in Dutch, shouting: "Down with the Pope! Scoundrel! Son of a bitch! Devil!"

Truth be told, I'd secretly baptized many of these children. A Catholic father would bring his infant to me, without the Lutheran or Calvinist mother's knowledge, and I'd perform the baptismal rites. I'd do the same for a Catholic mother who was married to a heretic. Many Catholics, especially the Frenchwomen, would come secretly to my home when I conducted Mass on holy days.

One such Frenchwoman once brought to me her ten-year-old son, who'd been possessed by demons. I performed the exorcism of the Holy Roman Church. When he entered the oratory, he was so wild that ten men couldn't restrain him. Many observed the exorcism. At last, I cast out the demon, and the boy became tranquil.

Those who witnessed the event were deeply impressed. When they returned to their homes, they renounced their faith in the false religions of Calvin and Luther. They proclaimed their wish to live within the Roman Catholic Faith. I instructed many people on the path of truth, and as a consequence, my reputation spread by word of mouth.

When we arrived before the Supreme Council, I was treated with courtesy. I was offered a seat, although the landowners had to remain standing. The Councilmembers asked that I speak to them about whatever was on my mind. I spoke as I felt I must:

> Your Lordships would do well to remember the concessions, terms, and conditions under which Prince Johan Maurits, Count of Nassau, and Your Lordships obligated yourselves to protect the residents of this land. You should also recall the acts of the Legislative Council, to which you called the attendance of Pernambuco's leading men, in which all of these undertakings were solemnly adopted. You began to break these undertakings even before the Prince departed. You've violated them in their entirety ever since he left.
>
> You broke all of your pledges and oaths and, on top of this, have harmed the residents beyond all limits. You've failed to take any of the corrective steps that were promised. For these reasons the residents, driven to desperation, are rebelling and taking up arms in self-defense. They're resolved to die if necessary.
>
> I'm now certain that, in light of everything, Your Lordships have no grounds to order your soldiers to commit such cruel acts as are now being perpetrated against the residents. That is, Your Lordships asked the Governor of Brazil to order the cessation of this uprising, which he promised to do within a matter of days. Further, the local residents haven't committed any other offenses against you or challenged your authority in any way, other than by retreating to the forests.
>
> These residents have stayed in their houses, under your passports, which when purchased came with Your Lordships' promise, to the extent possible, of protecting and defending them against enemies. The entire world can now see that this protection and defense amounts to nothing more than theft,

murder, and unjustified compulsion to trek into the forests. They must return by your deadline or never come back.

With no alternatives, they've decided to burn all the cane fields and sugar mills, and head for Bahia. They'll leave the land so devastated that it will take years before the Dutch Lords can obtain any commercial crops or provisions from it. Out of pure necessity and due to excessive costs, without opportunity for any profit, Your Lordships will be forced to abandon this land and return home.

The Governor of Brazil won't delay long in putting down this uprising and capturing those who lead it. He'll do so because Your Lordships requested it and have given him authorization to send experienced officers here to pacify the local residents.

All monarchies throughout the world, as we know from both ancient and modern history, survive through the love and benevolence shown by kings and monarchs to their vassals. When they begin to employ cruelty, oppression, and force, no matter how ordered and stable the situation seems to them to be at the time, they soon begin to lose territory. The most exalted of their glories turn into the deepest pit of misery.

The Portuguese are by nature and character very different from the people of many other nations. That is, they'll endure suffering with patience and an unyielding spirit. They'll put up with any injury, and with the loss of their goods and even their lives. However, they won't tolerate their wives and daughters being treated with disrespect. They'll seek revenge against Your Lordships because you seem to have no compunction about harming and mistreating their women.

These women have no fault for what their fathers and husbands are doing. By acting against the women, you're putting yourselves at risk of being at war with the Portuguese for as long as the memory of what you're now doing endures.

How could these women possibly find their menfolk in the span of five days? They don't know where they are.

Even if they did know, they'd be incapable of making their way along the trails and through the forests, which are crawling with Dutch soldiers and Caboclos. These men rape Portuguese women even when they're at home, surrounded by their families. What will these men do when they find the women isolated and unaccompanied in the woods? Five days simply isn't enough time. Your Lordships need to suspend this decree, or at the very least extend its duration. What you're doing will be rejected by all Christian rulers as an act of barbarism against innocent women.

If the husbands, fathers, and brothers of these women have committed some fault, Your Lordships have soldiers and weapons. You can give orders to hunt the men down and kill them. Even doing this doesn't hold up to reason because you've already requested help from the Governor of Brazil to put down the rebellion. He's promised to do so as quickly as possible.

Having made my arguments, the members of the Supreme Council addressed me with rage and invective. They asserted they had no obligation to retract the decree. If the women failed to go find their husbands and fathers, then they'd all have to die, as was mandated. I told them, with God as my witness, that they'd been warned not to do this.

I prepared to leave with the Portuguese landowners but was ordered by Balestrate, the presiding Councilmember, to sit down. He showed me a letter from Vieira, full of insults and threats, warning the Supreme Council not to rest in pursuing him because otherwise he was going to get all of them within a few days. Vieira responded in the letter to various threats and insults directed toward him. He wrote that he'd been belittled, disrespected, and dishonored, and could not allow such treatment to stand.

The Councilmembers spoke abusively of Vieira. Then Balestrate disclosed: "João Fernandes Vieira lacks caution, thinking that all who are accompanying him are his friends and are loyal to him. Some of those with him are good friends of ours, who will surrender him to us, dead or alive." I replied that there couldn't be a single Portuguese who would commit such an act of treachery. Only a heretic would do such a thing, someone who had forgotten God and his ultimate accounting, perhaps someone who had already surrendered his soul to the devil.

Upon hearing my comments, Balestrate reached into his pocket and handed me a letter from a Portuguese landowner. It had a cryptic introduction, which I recognized immediately as a scriptural reference. It signified that Vieira would soon be dead, by means of a bullet or poisoning. The uprising for liberty would be extinguished.

However, I told the Councilmembers that I didn't understand the riddle. Balestrate took back the letter. He said I didn't need to read any further. At that, we took our leave of the Council and departed.

22 WAR AT HAND

Editor's Note: Calado realizes he will soon be exposed as a supporter of rebellion. He discretely packs up his writings[5] and departs. The landowners accompanying Vieira are in disarray and prepare to abandon him. He finds the right strategy and message to allay their despair and unite them in proclaiming his leadership in the fight for liberty. Vieira is at risk of being assassinated. The Dutch are in pursuit. The rebels are emboldened when news of the pending arrival of Camarão and Dias finally reaches them.

* * *

I promptly sent notice to Vieira to be careful. I disguised my warning in case the Dutch intercepted the messenger. I told him to stay alert as though his life depended on it because "his plot of land was at the mercy of fate." Had I spoken in plain language, the Council would have been able to figure out I was the source. I knew my role would probably soon be exposed. I was afraid that I'd be arrested and killed. Therefore, as soon as I arrived at my house in Mauritsstad I ordered two of my slaves to take my private papers and carry them to safety in a canoe.

I closed up my house, leaving behind all of the furnishings, so as not to arouse suspicion. I then snuck off. As soon as the Dutch and Caboclos were aware I'd disappeared, they pilfered everything from my house, leaving it bare. However, I managed to escape with my life and manuscripts. The leaders of the Dutch community thereafter spoke of me as the greatest of all traitors in Pernambuco. They swore they'd capture me eventually.

Meanwhile, Vieira arrived at a house in the remote backcountry of Pernambuco. One of the landowners—who'd taken the oath to

---

[5] Without this precaution, his book *The Valiant Portuguese and Liberty's Triumph* might not have reached us.

fight for liberty—and his associates confronted Vieira. They asserted that everyone needed to disperse. The enemy was converging on them in a pincer movement. They'd be defeated without a doubt. All would end up being decapitated.

According Vieira's opponents, even those who wanted to fight against the Dutch were lacking the means to do so. They had no place to retreat, no surgeons, no medicine or medical supplies for the wounded, no gunpowder, and insufficient weapons. The Dutch, in contrast, were numerous and well-armed. The rain and mud were intolerable. It was hopeless to look to Bahia for aid.

The Dutch claimed Vieira's plan was to flee to Bahia with the other landowners. They said this plan would fail because they'd intercept Vieira and kill everyone. In the end, the Dutch said the best course of action would be for all of the Portuguese to return to their homes and ask the Supreme Council for passports.

These sentiments began to bubble over into a general mutiny. The majority wanted to return home. The men began breaking up into small groups and getting ready to depart. Faced with this movement to disperse, Vieira spoke harshly to its partisans. The opposing camps nearly came to blows with swords. The Dutch in Recife soon learned of the conflict—and how the Portuguese were dispersing—because spies were sending daily updates from Vieira's camp.

A landowner who was one of Vieira's opponents began ridiculing Vieira. He claimed Vieira had ordered the killing of the landowner's brother and others because they'd spoken the truth. He said Vieira treated them like imbeciles. Vieira pushed people around and tricked them into believing his promises of help from Bahia. Liberation from the Dutch couldn't possibly be achieved. The landowner said his friends and relatives, who were the best and most honorable men in Pernambuco, must avenge his brother's death. Vieira needed to be killed soon.

With nearly everyone in mutiny, some of the leading men advised Vieira to send a false alarm that the enemy was coming. This he did. One of the officers ordered the setting of ambushes. Others gave orders to take up fighting positions. The sentinels soon reported back that everything was quiet. Vieira then called for his captains, one by one, to appear with their companies of troops. He'd walk into the middle of the assembled soldiers, making more or less the same appeal to each company as it appeared:

You gentlemen can see clearly the harsh treatment we've received at the hands of the Dutch, the cruelty and oppression they've applied to us, our wives, and children. You've seen the impunity with which they've been robbing our farms, killing our relatives, raping our daughters, disrespecting our wives, and above all, how they've profaned our holy churches. They've crushed the images of Christ our Lord, and the Virgin Mary, and the Saints, wishing to extinguish the Roman Catholic Faith with a single blow in this miserable Captaincy of Pernambuco.

It is for this reason, carried on by my zeal as a Christian, and by my obligation to come to the defense of the honor of the Faith of Jesus Christ our Savior, that I'm shouldering this undertaking of liberating our homeland. I'm the wealthiest among all of you. I could have lived a splendid life, here in Brazil or in Portugal, selling off my sugar mills, and putting my money into estates in Portugal.

Despite everything, I've chosen to take on this fight. I've already expended most of my wealth and will continue doing so with pleasure. I've put behind me my wife, my mills, everything I have. I will here sacrifice my life to the sharp edges of our enemy's swords only for the sake of liberating all of you from the tyrannical subjugation under which you live.

I can't do this by myself. I need you to join me and help me. I also want each of you to understand no one will be forced to join me. For those who wish to fight with me, pass to the right side and be certain that I'm not going to lead you to Bahia. God's mercy is great. He won't fail His Christian people.

Those who don't wish to join me, go to the left side, and hurry back to your homes. Surrender your lives to the enemy. Stay with the enemy who has already robbed your houses. See if the Dutch will honor the passports they gave you, since they've failed to honor those given to anyone else.

One of the accompanying priests rode after the various groups that had already dispersed. He called them back, appealing to their sense of religious duty. All of the men assembled. In one voice, they began to shout: "We want Lord João Fernandes Vieira to be our Governor and the leader of the fight to liberate our homeland! With him we pledge and vow to fight the Dutch until we win or else die fighting!"

On such a formidable display of resolution, those who were dispersing became disoriented. Governor Vieira was energized and deeply satisfied by the spectacle. He also launched new steps to ensure his personal safety, having been informed by reliable sources that his enemies were all set to poison him. They'd already acquired the dose. He kept himself surrounded by reliable guards. He allowed only his personal slave to enter the kitchen where his meals were prepared. Vieira trusted this slave and gave him his freedom as a reward for his loyalty. He treated the former slave as a friend from that point forward.

Good news arrived at long last. Fourteen indigenous Brazilians under the command of Camarão showed up in camp. They were well armed and even had a trumpet, which was sounded to call all the men. Once assembled, they were given the news that Camarão and his troops, as well as Henrique Dias and his black soldiers, would all arrive within five or six days. The men, who had been as timid as sheep, became so animated that they were like ferocious lions. The Dutch also heard the news. They sent more men, ammunition, and provisions, in preparation for battle.

Vieira called a council of his chief advisors to consider their position. It was clear the present location left them vulnerable to enemy attack. Another farm was identified that would provide significant advantages.

A French surgeon also showed up in camp. The soldiers who seized him wanted to kill him. However, he said to them: "Gentlemen, I'm a Roman Catholic Christian and always treat the Portuguese with great care and affection. If you're going to take me to the woods to kill me, please kill me promptly right here. We're close to a church where some good Christian might bury me out of love of God. Otherwise, let me treat the wounded Portuguese." He was led to the infirmary. His appearance was a great relief to those who were injured.

The entire camp packed up and moved to the new farm, which was in an isolated location on top of a high hill. It was surrounded by thick stands of native bamboo that provided a natural defense. The rebellion had been launched. War was at hand.

23 GOD FAVORED US

Editor's Note: The miraculous victory at Guararapes is the first indication that the Portuguese have a chance against the Dutch. Calado notes that the bulk of his compatriots are armed with nothing more than spears or sharpened sticks. The Dutch fight with the most sophisticated tactics, discipline, and weapons of the era. Although Calado makes much of the religious fervor of the Portuguese, the valor of slaves who were promised freedom turns the tide of the battle at the most perilous moment.

* * *

Governor Vieira, setting up his new camp in early August 1645, knew that it was essential to exercise extreme precaution. He'd been advised by reliable sources that one of his confederates had acquired the poison to be used to kill him. He had a thatched hut set up for himself that was protected by his most trusted guards. They had orders to kill anyone unauthorized who approached at night. He reconnoitered the farm with an experienced officer, determining the routes of access and attack, and where to set ambushes.

The Dutch forces descended on the camp Vieira and his men had recently abandoned. They burned down all of the houses in the vicinity, including slave quarters. They picked up the trail and started their advance toward Vieira's new location. They had fifteen hundred well-armed men—the best of the Dutch officers and soldiers—plus hundreds of Caboclos.

Seeing the smoke in the distance, our scouts went to investigate. They soon reported back about the impending attack. Our men prepared for battle. When the Dutch reached the river crossing close to Vieira's camp, they suspected an ambush on the other side. They discharged their full firepower at the trees on our side. The Caboclos were so excited by this show of force that it seemed they thought they'd already won. However, we hadn't taken up this position. Instead, we'd laid several ambushes along the way. One of our captains then launched a frontal attack as the Dutch crossed the river. The battle raged for over an hour.

The Dutch took heavy losses as they crossed. They began to assemble in a field on our side of the river. Vieira, who had held back with the bulk of our soldiers, was ready to attack. He began to shout: "At them, at them, with swords, with swords!"

However, both a priest and an officer restrained Vieira with pleas that he not risk his life. His leadership was essential to the battle for liberty. After regrouping, the Dutch prepared to launch an attack in the direction of our main position. They kept falling into our ambushes, which impeded their progress. Many were killed.

One of our priests cried out: "Noble Portuguese, here we are with death before our eyes! Should there be any among us who hate one another, now is the time to reconcile and be friends. And if anyone has a guilty conscience, make your confession. Put yourself right with God, so that in His mercy He'll rescue us at this time of great peril." The priests began receiving confessions from those who asked, with as much solemnity as our dire circumstances allowed. Another priest went out into the woods to receive confessions from the men who were hidden in ambushes.

Vieira was at terrible risk of being murdered by those who hated him. Both priests and officers had to restrain him from riding out to fight. The lead officer kept him surrounded by loyal guards. The Dutch reached the entryway to our main position. Our men fought valiantly, again for over an hour. The Dutch pulled back some. Our men began yelling "victory, victory." The enemy, though, sent out several squads and regrouped.

Showing how God favored us, in one case thirty of our men— armed only with spears and sharpened sticks, who in terror had run off into the woods—suddenly came face-to-face with a Dutch squad. Fearing an ambush, the Dutch broke ranks and ran. In this way, even cowards fleeing the battle served a useful purpose in the fight.

The Dutch sergeants encouraged and threatened their soldiers to press on with their attack. They turned the tide of the battle. They began gaining ground against our position, putting us at risk of defeat. Vieira began sending those with him to lend support where necessary. He acted with such enthusiasm, even joy, that it seemed impossible he was engaged in mortal combat.

After more than two hours of fighting without pause, we at last began to push back the enemy. Before long, though, due to exhaustion, we began losing ground again. We had no reserves, while the Dutch could keep calling up fresh troops. They had blistering firepower.

We were at grave risk of total defeat. Only Heaven's intervention on behalf of the faithful could save us. A priest accompanying Governor Vieira held aloft an image of Christ on the cross. He called on Christ in our hour of need. By the merit of His sacrifice and death, and by the pain and suffering endured by the Virgin at the foot of the cross, the priest asked that Christ overlook our sins, which but for the gift of His love and mercy, merit eternal punishment.

The priest beseeched Christ not to allow the enemies of His Holy Faith, who injured it in so many ways, who profaned its temples, who crushed the sacred images of the Saints, to enjoy victory over His Catholic subjects. Since we were fighting for Christ's honor and carrying out His task, the priest asked that Christ give us victory over the tyrannical heretics. From this, the whole world would come to know that those who do battle for the honor of God will never lack for divine favor and assistance.

After calling out in this way, the priest asked all to fight with manly courage for the honor of their God and Lord. He implored all to make their vows to Christ our Savior, that He rescue us, and to the most Holy Virgin, His mother, that she intercede on our behalf. Each man made his pledge, whether of penance, pilgrimage, or offerings. Governor Vieira, as good a Christian as he was a soldier, promised to build two churches.

Vieira then pledged to his many slaves to emancipate them if they would fight courageously where our battle lines were collapsing. He sent them into the thick of the worst fighting. The blacks descended the hilltop in two groups, armed with bows and arrows, spears, and machetes. They wore decorative feathers of their own choosing. They played flutes, rattles, and horns, shouting so loudly and angrily that it created a roar as they came down. Hearing them, our men began to shout, "victory, victory." They began to gain ground against the Dutch. Those with firearms fought in the forefront. Those with spears backed them up.

The enemy's methods of fighting were sophisticated. They'd train fire on us from raised platforms, using split and poisoned bullets. Since night was approaching, they decided to make one last assault on us. They'd either defeat us or else create an opportunity to retreat under cover of darkness.

Their counterattack was ferocious and we lost much ground. We were in fact at the greatest risk we'd been in that day. Governor Vieira shouted out, "Courageous Portuguese, long live the Faith of Christ, at them, at them!" A priest again lifted Christ's statue and acclaimed, "Lord God have mercy!" The men looked to each other and said: "Brothers, let's all say together, Praise the Queen Virgin mother of God." And all shouted, "Praise the Queen, Mother of Mercy!"

The Mother of God showed her favor because, before our eyes, the enemy soon began to fall back in disarray. Our men began to shout, "victory, victory," as they drove the enemy from the field of battle. We achieved glorious victory thanks to the Most Sacred Virgin Mary Mother of God on 3 August 1645.

24 A PRICE TO PAY

Editor's Note: Calado discloses that the Portuguese were outnumbered and had few firearms. In the battle's aftermath, the victors salvage the excellent weapons, gunpowder, shot, and other supplies abandoned by the fleeing Dutch. The African men obtain clothes, which they'd lacked, as well as guns. The Dutch reach a town and seek revenge by robbing and raping the residents.

* * *

This victory was our great honor. It was an enormous disgrace for the enemy, who'd been so dominant beforehand. The Dutch lost their reputation as well as many of their officers and their best soldiers. We had to stop fighting due to nightfall but remained alert. We were ready to attack again in the morning, to kill them off once and for all.

For their part, the Dutch experienced such fear that they spent the entire night in flight down treacherous paths through the forests. There were many signs that our victory was a gift from Heaven. First of all, we had few firearms. Those we possessed were of poor quality, whereas the Dutch and Caboclos were well armed with modern weapons.

They had fifteen hundred soldiers plus Caboclos, while we had twelve hundred whites, of whom only two hundred had guns. The rest fought with spears, swords, machetes, and sharpened sticks. Our gunflints didn't break. Our limited supply of ammunition held up, even though we fought for five hours straight, firing continuously. The Dutch had almost unlimited supplies of gunpowder and shot.

Yet the true miracle occurred during the most furious fusillade, as was testified to by many of the Dutch survivors. The enemy soldiers saw a woman dressed in white and blue appearing in the midst of the Portuguese. She carried a babe in her arms. A venerable old man in a religious habit accompanied her. The Dutch saw them distributing ammunition and weapons to our soldiers.

The figures were resplendent, with eyes so dazzling that it was impossible to gaze into them. Their appearance filled the Dutch with fear. It was for this reason the enemy soldiers fell into disarray and began to flee. The apparition was, of course, of the Virgin Mother and her blessed Son, together with Saint Anthony, who had a nearby pilgrimage site. The Saint had long protected the local residents.

The next morning, we first ascertained that the Dutch had fled and hadn't set ambushes. We killed off some of their stragglers. Our men were joyful and high-spirited, since they now had excellent weapons courtesy of the Dutch. The blacks too were delighted, since they now had clothes to wear and had armed themselves. They'd become like fearless lions.

Governor Vieira ordered the men to give thanks to God and His Holy Mother. They shouted three times in unison, "Long Live the Faith of Christ, and liberty! Victory, victory, victory!" With his hat in hand as a sign of respect, Vieira gave warm hugs to all of his officers and soldiers, thanking and praising them for the courage they'd shown. In order for everyone to share in the happiness of the occasion, Vieira emancipated fifty of his slaves who'd demonstrated courage. The emancipation was subject to the provision that it would take effect only if they continued to fight alongside him until the end of the war.

Elsewhere, that same day after the battle, the surviving Dutch arrived in the small town where I'd taken up residence. They set about caring for their numerous wounded. The commander sent word to Recife, requesting supplies and reinforcements, which were sent immediately. Aid arrived so quickly that the wounded were transported back to Recife on the returning vessels. Once the men had rested and eaten, the commander ordered his soldiers and the Caboclos to take everything of value they could from the local residents. This was done despite the fact that the residents all had Dutch passports.

The men obeyed with zealous cruelty, destroying what they couldn't carry. They stripped naked the women they found, ripping their earrings from their earlobes. They beat women who resisted being raped. The men hung a priest from a tree and hit him until he agreed to show them where he'd hidden some money. When they arrived at my house, they seized what they could haul off, and destroyed everything else.

After devastating the town, the commander took his men to the nearby sugar plantation of Ana Pais, the dishonorable woman who had married three times and consorted with heretics. She had a large, strongly built house with numerous outbuildings. The commander then went to Recife to confer with the Supreme Council about how to proceed.

When the commander returned to Ana Pais' house, he ordered his men to rob another nearby village. They did so with gusto, despite the fact the residents also had passports. The men physically assaulted the residents to make them cough up any hidden valuables. Looking for hidden loot, they broke open walls and dug holes in the backyards of the houses. They managed to find quite a bit. They then robbed the church and destroyed all the images. They committed rape and other unspeakable acts, seizing several women as hostages.

On the following day, 15 August, the men were once again set loose on the town where I was staying, looking for additional booty. They rounded up the livestock of a Frenchman who lived there, including his sheep, goats, and pigs, and some cattle and horses, along with female slaves. They took everything back to Ana Pais' house.

The Frenchman went to the Supreme Council and protested vehemently, claiming the residents all had passports. He said this cruelty would drive them all into rebellion. The Councilmembers responded that this was simply how it was with soldiers, who sought revenge for the deaths of their friends and comrades. By rebelling, the Portuguese caused so much harm to the Dutch that there'd be a price to pay. What had happened was nothing compared to what was going to happen.

Hearing about the Council's response, the local residents were filled with terror. They couldn't flee because the Caboclos were prowling the forests at night and would kill them. God would soon answer their prayers for relief. However, there were a few other developments elsewhere that should be recounted before I describe how the town where I resided was saved.

After Governor Vieira's victory, he received petitions for help from the residents of other Captaincies. He also received sad news about a nearby town where Dutch troops and Caboclos had shown up and wreaked havoc. The Dutch had ordered everyone in the local district to come to the church, where important information was to be shared that would be of great advantage to them. Fortunately, it rained heavily the night before, so many of the residents couldn't make it. However, thirty-nine men showed up. The Dutch and Caboclos butchered them with swords and mutilated their bodies.

In light of this outrage, Governor Vieira thought carefully about how to respond to the petitions for help from the other Captaincies. The landowner who Vieira suspected of plotting to kill him made a strange request: he asked to be placed in charge of a rescue operation. He did so because he had word that Field Commander Andre Vidal de Negreiros and the men accompanying him—who'd been sent from Bahia to put down the rebellion and capture Vieira—had landed in a nearby port. The landowner knew that these men hated him due to various insults he'd given them in the past. By heading up the rescue party, the landowner thought he could get away before Negreiros and his men arrived.

Even though Vieira knew the man was unreliable and probably murderous, he saw this as an opportunity to be rid of him. Vieira sent the landowner on the mission with three hundred well-armed men. Vieira also gave the man orders from Bahia to arrest a traitor along the way. The landowner warned the traitor and avoided taking any other action whatsoever. He always looked out for his own interests. For whatever reason, after months of delay, the landowner eventually fell ill and died later that year.

Once he'd sent the landowner on the rescue mission, Governor Vieira ordered all of his other men to move on to another sugar plantation. There, he finally met up with Governor Camarão and his indigenous Brazilians, and Governor Dias and his black troops. The residents of Pernambuco were delighted to learn that the promised aid had finally arrived.

The men all had good weapons and were ready to fight. After a short rest, the united troops attempted to take a position held by the Dutch. However, a traitor warned the Dutch. They managed to escape through the woods to one of their forts before our troops arrived. The next morning, Field Commander Negreiros and one of his two regiments arrived at the new camp. They'd worked their way inland from the coast. It's important to understand the events that led up to the arrival of Negreiros and his men.

25 IN PURSUIT OF LIBERTY

Editor's Note: Calado recounts events that transpired in Recife and along the coast in the days leading up to the battle of Guararapes. Negreiros lands with his men at a nearby port ostensibly to stop the rebellion and arrest Vieira. Negreiros and the Portuguese soldiers march inland. The Dutch brutally attack the sailors manning the anchored ships. The treachery enrages the Governor of Brazil when word reaches him.

Negreiros, Camarão, and Dias and their troops all arrive at Vieira's new camp as he prepares to attack the Dutch position near the town where Calado now resides. Negreiros carries both his official orders and a secret annex with additional orders. It's clear he isn't there to arrest Vieira. Prompted by a vision, Vieira awakens his resting men and marches until daybreak. The combined Portuguese forces catch the Dutch as they prepare to retreat to Recife. Governors Vieira, Camarão, and Dias proclaim liberty as they ready the attack.

* * *

The Dutch first learned that Field Commander Andre Vidal de Negreiros and his regiments had landed when a separate Portuguese fleet of thirty-seven ships arrived in Recife on 12 August 1645. The Dutch were stunned because they had no warships in port and their most able military men were away chasing down Vieira. The Portuguese, however, anchored out of range of Dutch artillery and therefore didn't present an imminent threat of attack. They sent a small boat to shore under a white flag of peace, carrying representatives who were to meet with the Supreme Council. They created a spectacle and attracted much attention as they strode to the Council's chambers. Once admitted, they addressed the Council as follows:

The Admiral of our fleet, which is anchored offshore, sends greetings to Your Lordships, and wishes you to know that you have nothing to fear from our ships. He hasn't come here to start a war or to fight because the orders of His Majesty King João IV, his Lord, prohibit him from warring against the Dutch in Pernambuco. Rather, he's commanded that we deal with the Dutch in peace and show them courtesy while our armistice remains in effect.

In order placate any fears there might be, please be informed that the large battleship is en route from Rio de Janeiro and Bahia to Portugal, to accompany the sugar fleet. Those who wish to confirm this fact are welcome to take the launch back to the ship, while we remain here as hostages. You can see for yourselves that the Admiral has on board his wife and children for the return trip to Portugal. Anyone who wants to bring fresh produce to sell on the ship will be paid a fair price.

In conclusion, the Admiral wants all to know how the Governor of Bahia is prompt in fulfilling his word. That is, the Dutch requested he put down the rebellion taking place in Pernambuco, under the leadership of João Fernandes Vieira. Toward this end, the Governor has ordered Field Commander Negreiros and two regiments not only to put down the rebellion but, also, to capture those who are at fault. They've already landed at another port and are marching inland. Their ships are at anchor. As soon as they've accomplished their mission, they'll return to Bahia.

The Councilmembers ordered that the representatives be given a place to rest. In the meantime, they were able to confirm that the fleet was one of peace. All of the Dutch felt relieved, after the fright they'd experienced when the fleet first appeared. On visiting the main battleship, Dutch merchants brought cheese, butter, and rum. These products were sold at reasonable prices. The Admiral gave the Dutch representatives a tour, presented his wife and children to them, and allowed them to visit other ships as well. Under the disguise of selling merchandise, the Dutch made note of all that was being carried by the fleet. Later, once the Dutch representatives returned to Recife, the Portuguese who'd remained as hostages were allowed to sail back to their ships. They carried with them oranges, limes, and citrons that they'd purchased in the town plaza.

The next day an enormous storm came up, worse than anyone could recall. The pilots weighed anchor out of fear the ships would be broken to pieces but were trapped in the lagoon for six days. Since the wind came from the south, they feared it would carry the ships in a weakened state to the Spanish West Indies, where they'd be vulnerable to attack. The commanders decided to risk everything and sail out into the Atlantic, directly to Portugal. A couple of smaller Dutch ships followed them. As soon as it was clear the Portuguese fleet was on its way, the Dutch ships returned to Recife with word that they were now safe from Portuguese attack. The Dutch quickly brought in several warships, loaded them with men, arms, and provisions, and set off toward the port where Negreiros and his regiments had landed.

Finding our ships at anchor, guarded by two hundred well-equipped men and a valiant commanding officer, the Dutch commenced what became a vicious, bloody battle. One of our ships got away and sailed for Bahia. Several of our captains intentionally ran their ships aground so that the men could abandon them and make landfall. Under heavy fire from the Dutch, they fought back courageously. Most were saved. In other cases experienced seamen jumped overboard and swam to shore. The Dutch burned several of the ships. They finally managed to overpower the commanding officer's ship and captured him, wounded. They took him and the damaged ship back to Recife.

About half of the Portuguese fighters died in this treacherous encounter. Some drowned, not knowing how to swim. Others died fighting courageously. The wounded captured by the Dutch were tortured and allowed to die slowly. Others had their hands and feet bound and were tossed into the sea. Word of these outrages reached

Governor Vieira and Field Commander Negreiros, who by this time had linked up, as I'll be describing.

When word reached Bahia, the Governor became so enraged that he asked the mothers of the dead men not to go into mourning. Rather, he vowed to seek vengeance. He swore that he'd support the rebellion with men and materiel, expending all necessary efforts to punish the enemy.

On 16 August, Negreiros and one of his regiments arrived at Vieira's new camp. Camarão, Dias, and their men had just joined up with Vieira the day before. When Negreiros saw Vieira, he called out: "Does your Grace know I've arrived here from Bahia?" Vieira replied, "Your Grace so tells me." Negreiros shot back, "I'm here on the orders of the Governor of Bahia to arrest you, to arrest all who are leaders of this insurrection and uprising, and to haul you all back as prisoners to Bahia. I'm also here to calm down the residents, so that they might live in peace and friendship with the Dutch, so long as His Majesty doesn't order us to do otherwise."

Vieira spoke with both warmth and firmness:

> Then your Grace must also know that I and this multitude of men here with me are all going to capture you, and those who follow, and all of your soldiers. We'll bind you up with shackles of love, and fetters of duty, so that you'll help us gain vengeance for the injuries, cruelty, treachery, perfidious disrespect of sacred temples, and violations of divine and human law, which have been committed against us by these disreputable Dutch heretics.
>
> If it's sufficient reason to help even foreigners being oppressed in this way when they plead for it, then it's all the more the case that Your Graces should help us escape our captivity. We're all Portuguese, of the same blood, and vassals of the same King and Lord, who we've begged for help in our trials and tribulations.
>
> I'm going to imprison Your Graces on behalf of God, His Holy Roman Catholic Church, and this troubled

Province. So long as Your Graces refuse to help us seek vengeance for these countless offenses against God and his faithful servants, we're determined to fight on. We'll fight not only the Dutch but also our own relatives and friends, even at the cost of our lives, until our goal is reached.

To this, Negreiros replied: "On this brief trip I've made to get here, after disembarking on the coast, I've already picked up sufficient information about what this Province is going through. Let's find some lodging for these soldiers and let them rest. Then we can deal with whatever will be best for us to do in the service of God, and His Majesty, and for the sake of this Captaincy." The regiment with Negreiros then mixed in with the other men. Everyone had their mid-day meal.

That afternoon, Vieira got word about the robberies and rapes committed by the Dutch, how they'd taken some wives of landowners as hostages, including his own mother-in-law, and were now holed up at the sugar plantation of Ana Pais. He stood up and shouted: "For the sake of our honor, and our women, and children, let's die fighting, because one honorable death is worth more than a thousand undignified lives. Is it possible we're not Portuguese, the sons and grandsons of our fathers and grandfathers, who in other times overshadowed the whole world? What are we doing? Why aren't we on the march?"

Hearing these words, the men began to make an uproar. They began to shout, "Let's go! Let's go!" Vieira took the lead. Negreiros couldn't stop him, so followed behind with his regiment.

The men marched for hours through overflowing rivers and thick mud, then over the hillocks of Guararapes. An hour before sunset, they reached a river, where they found Dutch sentinels. Both were killed. One, however, before his death was forced to reveal the Dutch position at the plantation of Ana Pais. He also yielded details about the Dutch plan to flee the next morning. They continued marching in the dark. Finally, around midnight, they reached a sugar mill where they could rest.

There was so much mud the soldiers had no good resting places, except for those who could find room in the mill or slave quarters. There was no food other than what they still had in their knapsacks. Vieira laid down on a straw mat and Negreiros in a bed, in order to rest a bit after such heavy exertion.

Vieira dozed off and, in a dream, saw Saint Anthony. The Saint chastised Vieira for his carelessness and lack of zeal in his service to God, and in his efforts to lessen the suffering of his companions. Saint Anthony, in the dream, ordered Vieira to arise immediately and go attack the enemy. In doing so, he was promised the Saint's favor and assistance. If he were to fail to arise, then God would hold him accountable for all of the misery the local people would soon be suffering.

Vieira awoke with a start, deeply troubled by the dream. He asked himself, was it an illusion sent by the devil, or was it a vision from heaven? He descended the stairs, murmuring: "Saint Anthony ordered me, I must obey him." Standing in the mill yard, knee deep in mud, he had the lead officer gather the men. Vieira called out, rousing them to action: "It's time, it's time, my good Portuguese, it's time for us to rush to uphold the honor of the Faith of Christ our Redeemer, and our own lives and honor."

He put them all in order and gave the command to march on to the main house of Ana Pais. Vieira and his men were in the vanguard, followed by Negreiros and his regiment. From this position, Negreiros could observe how strongly Vieira and his men were determined to fight. He could also step in to support them if necessary, in whatever manner would best serve God and His Majesty that could benefit and bring peace to the residents of Pernambuco. This was in accord with the orders he'd been given by the Governor of Bahia. On top of these official orders, he carried a secret annex, with additional orders.

At daybreak, the men reached the final river on the way to Ana Pais' house. It had overflowed and was dangerous to cross. There were no boats around. Seeing this, Vieira ordered one of his former slaves, a strong swimmer, to test the current by crossing at the ford.

Vieira then entered on horseback. The water reached the saddleback but he made it across.

Seeing his example, the soldiers all entered the river, guns held high, and crossed over. Scouts were sent ahead. They found two Dutch sentinels, who before being killed revealed that the house was very close. The Dutch soldiers were still there. Rushing forward, the men reached the field next to the house, killing two more sentinels, one by gunshot. One got off a signal before being killed.

At this moment, the Dutch commander was eating lunch, drinking and offering cheerful toasts to his officers and men. The horses were already bridled and saddled. The oxen were yoked to their carts, ready for the four-mile trip to Recife. When the commander heard the shots, he listened closely. However, since the full signal hadn't been given, he assumed it was nothing.

He went on offering toasts and joking, as the Dutch are accustomed to do when they drink. As our men started filling the entry point to the field, the Dutch soldiers standing by the windows saw them. They became so alarmed that they dropped their flasks of beer, rum, and wine on the floor. They scrambled to grab their guns. Those who were quickest ran off toward Recife by themselves.

The Dutch sounded their trumpets and drums. They quickly pulled together in battle formation. Our men also lined up, ready to attack. Vieira urged the men on in a powerful voice:

> My dear brothers and friends, at the cost of our wealth, honor, and lives, we've all suffered the treachery and cruelty that these inhuman traitors from hell have used against us. Now they hold some of our women as prisoners. The crimes they've committed against our Lord God are obvious, profaning His temples and crushing the Holy Crosses and images of the Saints, as well as threatening to kill everyone in this Captaincy.
>
> Here we have the enemy before our very eyes. We fight for God's justice. Our duty is to win in His name. If we are Portuguese, and if we're worthy to display the honored and

illustrious emblem of being Portuguese, then attack them! To liberty's triumph!

The officers made final adjustments to their troops' formations. Governor Camarão blew a whistle to signal to the indigenous Brazilians to encircle the property, thereby preventing any escape. Governor Dias encouraged his black soldiers, telling them: "Able men, we have here the Dutch, enemies of Christ's Faith. We have the chance for all to see what we can do and what each of us is worth. Don't let the whites think they're better than us. I want one squad to go fight from behind the brick kiln. The rest are to come with me. As soon as we've fired twice, we'll all charge in together."

The three Governors, Vieira of the Portuguese, Camarão of the indigenous Brazilians, and Dias of the blacks, lifted their swords together. Vieira shouted, "Long live the Faith of Christ! To liberty's triumph!" The trumpets and horns sounded. Our men attacked from all sides with such fury that the Dutch were stunned to see it.

26 BOUNDLESS COURAGE

Editor's Note: The Dutch are outmatched and retreat into the house. They commit treachery during a parley so the Portuguese start fires to smoke them out. Vieira wants to kill them all but Negreiros insists on allowing the Dutch to surrender honorably. The captives are sent to Bahia. However, Vieira's men demand that the Caboclos, who are traitors in the eyes of the Portuguese, be beheaded. The townspeople join in the celebration as the victors make their way to the town.

* * *

After the first volley, Negreiros and his men started to arrive. They'd struggled to get across the river. Once assembled, they charged into the thick of the battle, attacking ferociously. The Dutch began to fall out of formation. Our men shouted, "to swords, to swords," as they charged in to get them. The Dutch quickly pulled back into the house and barricaded themselves inside, firing from the windows. The Caboclos did the same from some of the outbuildings.

Our men had taken the storehouse where firewood for the mill was stockpiled. They began hauling it out and stacking it around the house, under cover of our musket fire. They also broke holes in the walls and shot through them into the house.

The Dutch, in desperation, pulled the three women hostages they held, one with a babe in arms, up to a window. They shouted they'd kill all of them if the firing didn't stop. Our Governors issued the order to cease firing. Under a white flag, Negreiros sent a trusted man up to the house to discuss terms. He told them if they'd surrender they'd be treated well. He said our intent wasn't to fight but to calm down the residents, and to secure peace and friendship with the Dutch.

However, the Dutch, treacherous as always, took the break in fighting to regroup. In an instant, they were on the verandas and leaning out of the windows with guns ablaze, shooting many of our men. They killed the trusted man bearing the flag of truce. Many tried to hit Negreiros. A split bullet killed his horse out from under him. Another split bullet hit and shattered a box holding two pistols that he kept hidden in his shirt, which saved his life.

In the face of such an outrage, Vieira called out: "Treachery, treachery, these dogs want to kill us all, through blatant deceit. Knowing how vile they are, there's no need to wait. At them, at them, kill them all with steel and fire. Shoot, soldiers, shoot! Put firewood under the house! Burn them all alive!"

With the women pulled back from the windows, our men blasted away with terrifying furor. Others stacked the wood as fast as they could, carrying more than humanly possible, and set it on fire. The accompanying priests entered into the thick of the action, offering confession to the soldiers. Smoke began filling the house, although the Dutch continued fighting back bravely. They decided to abandon the house and die honorably in battle but couldn't get out because we had men stationed at every exit.

A local man appeared, holding up a broken image of the Virgin Mary, crying out that she was sweating. It was a miracle. The men went up and dipped bits of cloth in the drops on the statue to keep as holy relics. Miraculously, new drops would appear. As soon as the image of the Virgin appeared, the Dutch lost heart. They began to wave the white flags of surrender.

When the firing stopped, the Dutch commander came out with his two pistols pointed to the ground. He then removed his hat in a sign of submission. Our men started putting out the fire. Several officers went into the house to negotiate terms.

Although Vieira wanted to kill them all, Negreiros insisted that quarter be offered. Terms were reached, under which the officers would be allowed to leave the house bearing their weapons and military insignia. They'd present themselves to our commanders. The other soldiers would be disarmed upon exiting the house. There were to be no shots fired or all would be killed. All, though, were promised their lives and fair treatment in return. The agreement was carried out.

Seeing how the Dutch were dealt with, the Caboclos asked for the same treatment. However, our Governors decreed that all were to be executed by decapitation. The Governors were attentive to the great uproar among our troops, who asked God to deliver justice against this wild breed of men. After all, the Caboclos were vassals of the King, born in the Captaincy of Pernambuco, cared for in the loving embrace of the Holy Mother Roman Church, and indoctrinated in the Faith of Jesus Christ our Savior.

The Caboclos had mixed themselves up with the enemy, showing the Dutch how to take control of the land, and helping them succeed. In this war, the Caboclos had been the worst traitors and most violent butchers. They'd robbed the residents, profaned the churches, raped the young women, violated the married women, and killed innocent people. They did so in order to please the Dutch, and out of their insatiable thirst for Portuguese blood.

Vieira, eying the captive Dutch, who were formerly so arrogant and were now so submissive, faced the Dutch commander and said to him:

> What's this, Mister Heinrich Hus? Your grace is the one who told me I'd find myself in your stables with shackles on my feet, where I could think of myself as one of your horses. But how is it that your grace is now here under my feet, with your life in my hands? Now you'll know that cruelty and oppression can't prevail.
>
> You'll see that fifteen minutes of service to God, receiving His favor, is worth more than many lifetimes mixed up in the schemes of the devil. Of this, I have no fear, because I'm devoted more to piety than I am to vengeance and cruelty.

The Dutch commander Hus didn't reply to Vieira directly. He instead offered these words: "Since Your Lordship defeated me and holds me as your prisoner you'd do well to go seize Recife. You'd succeed because I have here with me the cream and flower of our soldiery." Negreiros then addressed Vieira, putting on a display for the Dutch captives and for any spies who might be listening:

> Your Grace has done something despicable, which you should not have engaged in. It seems that I've come here from Bahia on the orders of its Governor, in order to pacify the residents, and leave them enjoying peace and friendship with the Dutch. Your Grace told me to come here where my soldiers could be lodged and enjoy some rest.
>
> Without telling me what you were up to, you break with me, and start a war, fighting with the Dutch? Your Grace should have no doubt that you must now come with me to Bahia as my prisoner, where the Governor will send Your Grace to Portugal. There, His Majesty will of necessity punish Your Grace severely.

Vieira responded:

> Being that Your Grace tells me that you have to take me as a prisoner to Bahia, I must respond that I have many courageous soldiers. They'll defend me with the same strength and courage by which they're determined to defend the Faith of Christ. In the same way, they're determined, together with me, to free our homeland of the tyrannical subjugation it now suffers at the hands of depraved Dutch heretics.
>
> As regards His Majesty punishing me for what I've done and am doing, I respond that I'm a vassal, and very loyal. When His Majesty orders me to cut off my head, I will have the most meaningful of deaths.

However, I'm also certain that His Majesty is a righteous Lord and King, just in His acts, and will need to judge my case, and the cases of all these men, with the uniformity and justice of a Christian and Catholic King. I've achieved my intent and am content that I've fulfilled a portion of what I wish. For now, all that's left to us is to give thanks to God for the mercy He's shown us.

May all of us live in the Faith of Christ! May all tyranny be extinguished! Long live liberty! Victory, victory!

Overflowing with joy, everyone began to yell. Three times they shouted "victory." Sounding every instrument they had, woodwinds, drums, and trumpets, and the horns, flutes, and wooden drums of the blacks, the noise was deafening beyond anything ever heard. Many local residents came when they heard the roar. They and the soldiers began to pillage the supplies and stolen goods the Dutch had been carrying with them.

Our men amassed large quantities of gunpowder, bullets, and foodstuffs, as well as many horses already equipped with saddles and bridles. Between this battle and the prior one, we obtained around fifteen hundred firearms, which were essential for the ongoing war effort.

We took two hundred five Dutch prisoners that day. We executed two hundred Caboclos. The original Dutch force of fifteen hundred men had been decimated in two battles, counting the dead, wounded, deserters, and prisoners. As they departed the plantation of Ana Pais, Vieira gave the Dutch commander a horse to ride. He also gave horses to the women who had been rescued.

The noisy, cheering crowd, soldiers and residents alike, made its way back to town. The soldiers moved on to a sugar mill that belonged to Vieira, where they could rest and eat, with the prisoners in train. We achieved victory that day through the boundless courage displayed by our men.

27 FILLED WITH FERVOR

Editor's Note: Vieira learns of the Dutch treachery on the coast. He confronts Negreiros, who concedes that Vieira is acting correctly in the circumstances, even though both of them could be punished. The Supreme Council alleges through a negotiator that Negreiros violated the code of conduct and requests a prisoner exchange, which Negreiros declines.

Back on the coast, Portuguese troops surround the fort under the command of Estrate. He feigns that he's defending the fort while secretly plotting with the Portuguese to surrender it with honor. Once Negreiros returns to the coast the final terms are reached. Without firing a shot the Portuguese acquire one of the best forts in Pernambuco, plus heavy artillery, other weapons, and supplies. Estrate and some of his officers request to be admitted into Portugal's service. His deep experience radically upgrades the military capabilities of the Portuguese.

Calado, now ill, conducts a celebratory mass in which he exhorts the soldiers and residents to carry on the battle for liberty. The commanders decide to disperse troops in smaller camps to surround Recife and cut it off from access to the interior of Pernambuco.

* * *

At the time of the battle at Ana Pais' plantation, neither Negreiros nor Vieira knew of the Dutch treachery committed against the Portuguese down on the coast. Eyewitnesses arrived at our camp, who reported the extraordinary cruelty of the Dutch, who tortured dying men. Vieira seized on the news to justify to Negreiros and his aide the recent battles:

> Now Your Graces know what good cause the residents of
> Pernambuco had for their uprising and rebellion. They were

obligated to defend their homeland by force, at the risk of their lives, to escape their shameful subjugation. You can now confirm with your own eyes the honesty and integrity of these heretic dogs, how they treat people of all types, without fear of God and without shame before the world.

Many times I advised the Governor of Bahia to put no faith in these damnable Lutherans and Calvinists. Now you know the truth of my words. Although you came to put down the rebellion, at their request, at the first opportunity they burned your ships. They hoped you'd imprison me.

You'd then be stuck here in a civil war with my followers, without support from Bahia. You'd unable to return to Bahia for want of ships. You'd be killed by hunger and deprivation. Bahia would lose its best soldiers. The Dutch would become absolute masters of the land. They'd decapitate all the leading men. Their next step would be to mount an invasion. Bahia would fall without its defenders. With Bahia taken all of Brazil would be theirs.

You saw what just happened during the battle at Ana Pais' main house. When you arrived, they waived a white flag. You ordered us to stop fighting and sounded drums to signal we'd negotiate terms of peace. Our negotiator approached under a white flag, told them that you hadn't come to make war but only to pacify the residents, and assured them of proper treatment. Monsters and traitors that they are, they shot and killed the negotiator, and tried to kill you, taking out your horse instead.

This is why they called you here to Pernambuco, so they could kill everyone by deception and tricks. I know their hearts well. I'll never desist in leading this undertaking until they've abandoned our lands or else I'm killed in the effort. Your Grace, according to the law of Christ and as a Portuguese, you have a compulsory obligation to help me defend Christ's Faith and to free this land, which after all is your land as well as mine.

Negreiros responded: "I swear to Your Grace by the holy Christian garment that I wear, with honor, that I must join and support this undertaking until the end. In doing so there can be no wrong even though I know His Majesty could order me to submit to decapitation. I'll act because betrayals of this magnitude can't be tolerated."

Not long after this exchange, a Dutch representative showed up under a flag of truce. He'd been sent by the Supreme Council to find Negreiros, to whom he handed a letter. In it, the Councilmembers expressed shock that Negreiros had violated the code of conduct in such matters. They were dismayed that he'd made war on the Dutch rather than pacifying the residents as he'd been ordered to do. He'd disobeyed orders to arrest the treasonous leaders of the uprising and rebellion. The Councilmembers asked that he might be so kind as to return the Dutch commander and other officers who were his prisoners. In return, they offered to free one of the Portuguese prisoners they held in Recife.

In reply, Negreiros recounted many of the betrayals and offenses committed by the Dutch. He wrote, in part: "Your Graces must imagine that we Portuguese are as dumb as cattle and don't know a crooked scheme when we see it. We uncovered long ago your depraved intentions, which were fully demonstrated when you burned our ships." After describing the recent battle and his commitment to support the rebellion even at the cost of his life, he turned down the prisoner exchange, even though the Portuguese officer involved was his personal friend. He concluded:

> I must inform Your Graces, that your commander Heinrich Hus, along with the other prisoners we had here, have all been sent to Bahia, where the Governor will repatriate them. You should write to the Governor to see if he'd be kind enough to send you Heinrich Hus, assuming he hasn't already been shipped off.

Among the prisoners, we only executed Johann Blar along the way, by a firing squad made up of the accompanying soldiers. We did so in revenge for the acts of cruelty committed by this heartless tyrant against the residents, their wives, and children.

As a final note, I should let Your Graces know that some of your French and Flemish soldiers requested that they be allowed to stay with us and integrate into our forces. They wish to take up arms against the Dutch in Recife. We were delighted to let them serve, although if they want to leave we'll let them. We have no shortage of men whose hearts are aflame with the desire for revenge against you for all of the wrongs you've committed.

Meanwhile, on the coast, we had a regiment under an officer who'd arrived with Negreiros. His men had encircled the best fort the Dutch had, which was located on the Cape of Saint Augustine. It had a deep port suitable for large ships. The officer, Paulo da Cunha, sent a representative to the fort, demanding its surrender. The fort was under the command of Teodosio de Estrate.

Estrate had previously promised the Governor of Bahia that he'd surrender the fort. He'd pledged loyalty to His Majesty King João IV. However, he refused to surrender it, and threatened the Portuguese. This was all for show. Privately, he said to send for Negreiros, and to send representatives for a second parley when Negreiros arrived. This was agreed upon. However, another Portuguese officer, who didn't know about Estrate's secret commitment, demanded his surrender, speaking in highhanded terms. Estrate refused to speak with him and demanded that da Cunha return.

Estrate received da Cunha with dignity and invited him to dine in the presence of his officers and soldiers. He claimed to have always been on good terms with the Portuguese. However, he said that, due to his commitments to his Dutch superiors, he couldn't possibly surrender the fort without fighting and dying an honorable death. To do otherwise would be to commit treason. He then dismissed da Cunha but accompanied him to the gate.

On the way, he shared privately with da Cunha that Negreiros should seize a small fort at the entrance to the harbor. It was poorly equipped and would be unable to resist. Once taken, Negreiros should position men and artillery there so that it could block any attempts by the Dutch to send in reinforcements.

By taking the small fort the Portuguese would also control the supply of fresh water because the main fort lacked an adequate source. Estrate also asked that they delay sending another parley for eight days in order to preserve his honor and that of his men. He assured da Cunha that the fort would be handed over to His Majesty King João IV at such time.

Once Negreiros had returned from the fighting inland he attacked the small fort as indicated by Estrate. He took it easily. Many local residents began showing up to support the fight. The main fort ran out of water. A number of Dutch civilians, including a local official who had been hiding out in the fort, attempted to escape by boat. They were captured and their valuables were seized. The Portuguese soldiers executed the men although they let the women go free.

On 1 September 1645, Negreiros sent da Cunha and other representatives on a final parley to the fort. They demanded its immediate surrender under threat of a merciless attack without quarter. Estrate said, in front of his men, that he couldn't reply the same day without taking the counsel of his officers. Privately, he told da Cunha to have Negreiros make a final threat so that he could overcome any resistance by those who wanted to fight.

Estrate met with his officers. He argued that Recife had no capacity to assist them. Heinrich Hus and the best soldiers had been captured. Many had been killed. The Portuguese offered good terms and kept their word. He said the fort by rights belonged to King João IV. They were fighting for a bunch of merchants who'd failed to pay their salaries or provide necessary food and clothing. The Dutch rulers only thought of their own interests. Estrate promised to make sure the terms agreed to would be honorable and would serve the interests of his men.

In the meantime, da Cunha reported Estrate's words to Negreiros. Negreiros demanded the fort's surrender within three hours or else it would face an all-out attack. On hearing this, one of Estrate's officers continued to argue that they must defend the fort at all costs. The others, however, had been won over by Estrate. He therefore sent one of his men to negotiate surrender terms.

The men were allowed to march out of the fort to the sound of their own drums, with loaded weapons, and flags unfurled. Those who wished to join the Portuguese would be admitted into their service. Those who had farms would be allowed to return to them. The Portuguese would pay all of the back wages owed to them by the Dutch.

On 3 September Estrate delivered the fort to Negreiros. It was a great victory: 275 men surrendered without a shot being fired. We acquired many firearms, large amounts of ammunition, ten pieces of heavy artillery, other war materiel, and a stockpile of provisions.

A Dutch supply ship arrived. Estrate knew the signal, which was given. The ship entered the port. When it was already too late the Dutch could see by way of a spy glass that the fort was in Portuguese hands. They tried to escape but one of our captains seized the ship and its supplies.

After a few days of setting things in order, Negreiros went back to Vieira's camp. He took along with him Estrate and his senior officers, who asked to be allowed into our service.

On 8 September Vieira held a solemn religious festival in honor of the birth of Our Lady the Virgin Mary and to give thanks for our victory. I conducted the ceremony, even though I was quite ill and couldn't get out of bed. With men on either side holding me up at the pulpit, I offered praise to the Virgin Mother of God. I exhorted the soldiers and residents to carry forward the fight for liberty.

Many suffered anguish and repented their sins. Others shed tears of joy. All were filled with fervor and determination for the cause. They left the church overflowing with confidence, ready to attack

Recife, to seize it and its eight fortresses. The commanders, however, recognized that it would have been premature to attempt such an assault. The idea was shelved for the time being.

Although everyone had assembled at the large camp for the ceremony, the commanders determined that it would be better not to be based at one location. They felt there was too much risk of the troops being encircled. Instead, they thought it would be best to set up smaller camps in the countryside surrounding Recife and Mauritsstad. A captain would be posted at each camp together with troops and supplies.

With that strategy, we'd always be able to detect the Dutch when they headed out to attack us, or went to forage for food or water. We'd be ready to set ambushes. Nearby camps could rush in extra men quickly to support those coming under assault. The strategy was quickly implemented. We soon had soldiers posted throughout the countryside near Recife.

28 APOSTACY IS PUNISHED

Editor's Note: A Portuguese camp captures several Jews from Recife. One escapes. Two were baptized Catholic in Portugal as infants and later fled to Holland, where they openly embraced Judaism. They're sentenced to death as traitors to both Christianity and Portugal. Calado proves to them the errors of their beliefs. The audience is impressed with Calado's erudition. The two men joyfully reconvert to Catholicism even though they must die for their sins. Calado leaves them with some Jesuits for their final confessions and execution. Portuguese intolerance is manifest.

* * *

Once established in our new positions, one of the first incidents involved an open boat loaded with provisions. It was sailing to Recife from an enemy-held island. There were several Dutch on board along with three Jewish merchants. It so happened that one of the merchants was born into Judaism but the other two were originally from Lisbon. This made them Roman Catholic by birth; both had been baptized. The two men later fled to Holland where they were circumcised.

Abandoning the Law of Christ, the two apostates embraced the Law of Moses, in which they lived in shameless impudence. In addition, they uttered many blasphemies against Christ our Lord with the intent of causing some ignorant New Christians with whom they interacted to adopt their blind and erroneous beliefs.

Fortunately, the pilot was Portuguese. Sailing by a small bay near one of our camps, he entered it and beached the boat. Some of our soldiers rushed up. They seized the boat and its passengers, who were taken as prisoners. They were later presented to Vieira and Negreiros, who sent the Dutch captives to Bahia. The Jew born into Judaism claimed that he wanted to convert to Christianity. He was turned over to several of the priests who offered to indoctrinate him into the Law of Christ. However, at the first opportunity he escaped. He ran back to Recife.

A magistrate sentenced the other two Jews to death by hanging. Since they would need to be made to suffer prior to hanging, they were sent to the church. Guards were stationed at the doorway. I sat between them both in front of the priests on the steps of the altar. Many local residents came to watch the proceedings. I said the following words of truth:

> My brothers, you're sentenced to death for having taken up arms against the Portuguese—even though you're Portuguese by birth—and for being traitors to Jesus Christ. For even though you were born into the loving arms of the Holy Mother Roman Church, and were sprinkled with the water of Holy Baptism, you became apostates to the Catholic Faith. You went over to the Law of Moses. You had yourselves circumcised and since then have lived openly as Jews, speaking blasphemously against Jesus Christ our Savior, as has been demonstrated.

> In addition, you and those of your kind are the ones who incited the Dutch to use oppression and cruelty against the local residents. You incited them to commit many other offenses, which our magistrates have found to be sufficient justification for condemning you to death.

> Since you already know that you must soon die, I would like to confirm whether before your execution you'd like to be informed of the blindness into which you've fallen. I can explain to you completely how Jesus Christ our Savior is the true Messiah promised in the law, as preached by the Prophets. Those who wish for salvation must believe in His Holy Catholic Faith, without which there is no other way to enter Heaven.

> Enter into discussion with me, put to me all of the objections Jews lodge against Christians, and cite every

214

passage of sacred Scripture you can muster in support of your obstinacy. I will quickly resolve all of your doubts. I will declare to you many passages of Scripture with clarity and truthfulness, so that in the end you'll be deeply satisfied. Yet at the same time, you'll be deeply troubled by the mistaken path you've been following.

The two Jews said they were pleased with the terms for discourse. They began to state their objections, quoting from Holy Scripture. They asserted various arguments upon which they based their denial that Christ was the true Messiah. They explained why they must await another who would deliver them to Jerusalem, where they would prosper and enjoy great wealth.

I listened attentively to their words and then—to the great joy of the Christians in attendance—I began my response from the beginning of the Book of Genesis. In the space of about an hour and a half, I commented on the entire Old Testament. I clarified their mistakes, explaining all of the key passages. I spoke with great erudition, offering proofs of various passages by citing other passages from the Prophets. I referred to the original Hebrew text, quoted from both the Babylonian and Jerusalem versions of the Talmud, and drew from the books they venerate and the explanations offered by their own rabbis.

I explained things so well and so vigorously, with such ease and accuracy, that I fully addressed all of the arguments made by the two Jews. Their arguments happened to be the same shopworn mistakes Jews typically make. I made abundantly clear their blindness to the truth and the great errors by which they were imprisoned.

Those in attendance—including Jesuits, other priests, and the local residents—all marveled at the great show I put on in out-arguing the Jews. They were impressed with how well versed I was in the Holy Scripture. I provided to them a great lesson and erudite explanations. However, from my perspective there wasn't all that much to admire in what I'd done because I regularly went about disputing with the Jews of Recife. I'd already converted seven of them to the Faith of Christ. I baptized them and catechized others. I was always engaged in studying so that I could better overcome their errors.

Just when the two Jews acknowledged they were convinced by what I'd said, I told them that the hour of death had arrived. I said they mustn't lose their souls, the salvation of which had cost the life of God's Son Incarnate. Christ not only shed His precious blood but also, as he underwent the cruelest of torments, gave His life generously while impaled on the Cross. He died with His arms wide open, signifying how even the most depraved sinner in the world— so long as he repented for his sins and believed in Him—would be received into the loving and merciful embrace of a faithful Father.

Therefore, I asked, do you wish to become Christians and beg God's forgiveness, with the certainty of being saved and having your sins forgiven through the mercy of Jesus Christ, Savior of the world? The Jews responded yes, they wished to return to the Law of Christ, and to die as believers in the Holy Catholic Faith.

I then declared to the two Jews, with great fervor and vitality, and with complete sincerity, all of the mysteries of the Holy Catholic Faith. I asked them again, for a second time, did they wish to return to the Faith of Christ of their free will, without compulsion? They said yes. I made them renounce the blindness of Judaism and all of the heresies by which they'd been defiled. They proclaimed their faith holding fast to a prayer book, in the fashion typical of the Holy Inquisition's *auto-da-fé*.

At this point they began to cry. I asked them why they cried. Did they regret returning to the fold of Christ? One of them replied: "Father, these tears we shed aren't out of regret for what we just did or out of fear of death. We admit death is completely deserved because of our sins. Rather, these are tears of joy and the happiness we feel in our souls because until now we were on the verge of falling into hell. Out of His mercy Jesus Christ—the true Messiah—has rescued us, even though we don't deserve it. May He be praised forever."

I turned to face the two Jesuits and said to them: "Reverend Fathers, I don't wish to be the only one acknowledged for our good work. Rather, your Reverences also participated in this worthy act. Therefore, I hand over to you these two Christians that you might receive their confessions, exhort them in their faith, and offer them consolation. I'll go rest a bit since I'm feeling quite ill and weak."

I went out to have some porridge. The Jesuits carried out their duties until the time came to cause the two Jews to suffer the necessary torments. All of the priests stayed with them until they died. Afterwards, they were buried as good Catholics, accompanied by the soldiers in military formation, with the priests reciting the prayers ordained by the Holy Church. Blessed and praised be our Lord Jesus Christ, who out of His great mercy freed these two souls from the mouth of hell when they least expected it.

29 TRAITORS AMONG US

Editor's Note: The Portuguese are emboldened by their string of successes. Estrate is put in command of the foreign soldiers now in Portugal's service. Vieira and Negreiros are eager to capitalize on their momentum and want to attack a fort in Mauritsstad.

Estrate has vast experience and counsels against the proposed action. He recommends an alternate plan of attack on Recife's water supply. The Dutch defenders nearly surrender but the Portuguese soldiers get sidetracked with looting and drinking. They soon lose the advantage. Caboclos fear execution and decide to fight to the death. Dutch reinforcements arrive and the Portuguese flee. Vieira, Negreiros, Camarão, and Estrate all narrowly escape serious injury.

The Portuguese execute a number of their soldiers for dereliction of duty. This is the first indication of the rebels enforcing rigorous military discipline. The former Dutch officer Estrate apparently brings this higher standard of conduct to bear on the Portuguese forces.

After their setback, Vieira and the other commanders decide to establish a principal fort, which Estrate lays out and slaves construct. The Africans under Dias are placed in the most dangerous locations in the camps ringing Recife. The foreigners under Estrate conspire with the Supreme Council and almost expose the rebellion to utter defeat. A long period of stalemate begins.

* * *

Preparing for the onset of war, Governor Vieira thought carefully about what would be needed. He set up an infirmary—for the soldiers who would be wounded—with doctors and surgeons. He also set about gathering foodstuffs from the locals to the extent they could contribute to the war effort.

The Dutch had a small fort nearby, which posed a risk. Vieira put Estrate in charge of the foreign soldiers and had them besiege the fort. It held seventy of the enemy, who surrendered. We thereby acquired more weapons and ammunition. Two hundred fifty Dutch, English, and French soldiers entered our service. We paid them regularly. Estrate, to his credit, refused to accept payment. He stated that his service was out of loyalty to His Majesty King João IV. His only hope was that someday his service might be rewarded.

Vieira and Negreiros, seeing that we had a string of successes, thought we should press on with the attack. They didn't want to give the Dutch a chance to regroup. They plotted a brazen assault on a fort that protected the entrance to Mauritsstad. We'd captured a man of mixed race who served Ana Pais. The rope broke while we were hanging him. Taking this as a sign, we decided to spare his life. He ran back to Recife and alerted the Dutch about our plans.

Estrate had vast military experience. He counseled against the attack, especially since it would now be anticipated. We didn't have enough men or ammunition for a sustained assault. Vieira and Negreiros challenged his assessment, arguing that an audacious attack would keep up the pressure on the Dutch. Estrate argued back:

> Your Lordships need to know that we've already won this campaign. The enemy no longer holds anything other than the fortresses of Recife, Mauritsstad, and a few other locations. They have no place to go for provisions. They don't even have drinking water except what they can get on a nearby island.
>
> If we seize that island, within a few days they'll have to surrender out of necessity. To me, it looks like the best option—God willing—is to attack the island and take it. This will guarantee our success in the war for liberty.

Vieira and Negreiros recognized this was solid advice. They acted on it at once. The two organized a force of eight hundred well-armed men. These men, together with reinforcements and stocks of supplies, were deployed to the nearest camps, where they could be engaged as needed. Dias and his black troops were sent to the most dangerous position.

Unfortunately, a traitor revealed what we were doing. The Dutch rushed to resist our attack, sending two ships, followed by two smaller vessels, with men and supplies. For our part, we took every canoe and small boat available to reach the island.

Our forces landed successfully. We fought our way to the village, where the fortifications were located. Our men seized the first fort, which held all of the enemy's stockpiles of weapons, ammunition, and food. The Dutch fled to a second fort with our men in pursuit. We pounded on the front door and began to scale the walls.

Seeing they were surrounded, the Dutch began blasting away with artillery. However, with our men coming over the walls, the enemy began to signal a willingness to surrender with quarter. The commanders decided to grant this. They had the horns sounded to proclaim victory. Regrettably, thinking the battle already won, many soldiers, especially those from Bahia, began to focus on pillaging nearby houses. They became blinded by greed.

The Caboclos trapped inside the fort feared for their lives. They knew how we'd decapitated those captured at Ana Pais' plantation. All four hundred fifty of them decided to die fighting with their weapons in their hands. They fought bravely, in a cruel, bloody battle. We killed many but also lost some men.

Camarão was wounded. Vieira took a bullet to the chest. Miraculously, it didn't penetrate his skin, and fell to the ground. Another bullet clipped a chunk of hair off his head. Negreiros had a pistol shot out of his hand. Estrate was also wounded.

Many of our soldiers got drunk as they gathered booty. We had to punish them. Twenty-five of our men were shot for dereliction of duty, as were a dozen of Camarão's indigenous Brazilians and thirty foreigners serving under Estrate. Accursed avarice ripped what should have been a landmark victory from our hands.

At this point the Dutch ships began to arrive. Our position was dire. Our men, having fought all day, were exhausted. They'd gone without food or water for nearly twenty-four hours. Vieira decided there was no choice but to retreat. With great effort, we got to the boats and sailed to a small island. Once there, we confirmed who was missing.

Estrate found seven of his Dutch soldiers disarmed. They were so used to pillaging the Portuguese residents that all they thought about was breaking into houses. Intoxicated, they didn't realize what was happening until it was almost too late. They tossed aside their weapons but not their bags stuffed with booty. Estrate ordered that they be shot. Many pleaded for the men to be spared, so Estrate allowed them toss dice. The one getting the lowest score was to be shot as an example to the others. A firing squad then executed the loser.

In the aftermath of this difficult struggle, Vieira and the other commanders determined it would be best to establish a principal fort. We could retreat to it if needed and stockpile ammunition there. Estrate, with his foreign expertise, laid out the fort. Vieira and the other landowners brought in their slaves to carry out the construction.

While the fort was being built, during the latter part of 1645, Dutch patrols would frequently leave Recife. They'd be on the lookout for our camps or go out to get water and firewood. With our men in position, we almost always managed to kill or wound some of the Dutch, who were forced to retreat back to their forts. The Dutch foraging patrols always went out with slaves to carry the water or wood back to Recife. We captured many of them.

The black soldiers under Dias were often on the front lines of these skirmishes. They were placed in the most dangerous location, near one of the main Dutch forts. They took most of the slaves we captured, who were the ones accompanying the Dutch patrols. Other slaves began to flee Recife due to lack of food. Dias' men seized many of them, too.

The slaves were turned over to our commanders, who would distribute some of them among our camps. For other slaves, we could tell by the brands burned into their skin that they belonged to

Portuguese landowners. In these cases, we'd return the slaves to their rightful owners. In exchange, the landowners paid a monthly stipend as a reward, which was then distributed to the men. Slaves who hadn't been stolen from Portuguese landowners but had originally been acquired by the Dutch or Jews were sold off. These funds were distributed to those who merited rewards.

After a series of encounters with the enemy, some of the officers and their soldiers returned to Vieira's camp with twenty-six blacks they'd captured. The commanders kept thirteen to offset the costs of the war and distributed the other thirteen to the officers and soldiers who had captured them. Vieira knew that the landowners, who served in his regiment, had other blacks they'd captured but hadn't brought back to camp.

These landowners, for their own profit, had hidden fifty blacks in the woods. They thought what they'd done was justified because they'd risked their lives in the struggle. Vieira feigned ignorance, knowing how much the Dutch had stolen from these men. They'd lost almost everything in the fight for liberty. Well aware of how much money they could make by stealing blacks from the Dutch, the men took all the more risks in their attacks. They tried to outdo each other in this regard.

The Supreme Council, faced with our successes, hatched a diabolical plot. They noted how we'd managed to block all of the routes out of Recife. They knew that we had two hundred eighty foreign soldiers in our service, including Flemish, Germans, English, and French. The foreigners were in a single regiment under Estrate and his French lieutenant.

The Councilmembers wrote letters in the foreigners' languages. At night, they had men in disguise leave the letters along paths where the men serving under Estrate would find them. In the letters, the Supreme Council promised the men that all of their offenses against Holland would be forgiven. This offer even applied to the Dutch, who were fighting against their compatriots. The foreigners were promised higher pay and promotions upon returning to Recife. They were also offered rewards for any actions they might take that would benefit the Dutch or harm us.

Our sentinels also found these letters. They exposed the scheme to our commanders, who decided that, in future battles with the Dutch, the foreign soldiers would be split up and placed at the front of our formations. In this way, if they committed any treason, we'd be in position behind them and would kill them first.

The Dutch soldiers in our service also got their hands on these letters. They began scheming. Committing treason is a Dutch characteristic. Some of them began sneaking off at night to meet with the Supreme Council in order to help plot how to betray us. By daybreak, they'd return to their posts. They began to insert small pieces of white paper into their hatbands as a signal to the Dutch. With this insignia they were allowed to enter Recife. In skirmishes they'd fail to load bullets into their guns so as to fire only blanks at the enemy. They watched constantly for any mistakes we might make.

Every couple of days the Dutch sent out patrols, knowing that there were traitors among us. They were looking for openings to launch an attack. Strangely, the Portuguese soldiers, noticing the white pieces of paper on the hatbands of the Dutch, began to imitate them. The Portuguese in general are fascinated by novelty. They'll copy whatever seems to be the fashion. This confused the Dutch, who thought the Portuguese must have caught on to their plot. This wasn't the case. However, from the time the letters were distributed, Vieira made sure that the Dutch soldiers were never positioned together in large numbers.

On 16 November 1645, the Dutch soldiers approached Vieira and Negreiros with a proposal. They were nervous and fearful that their treason had been discovered. It was payday. The soldiers claimed they wanted to show their appreciation to the Portuguese for how they were always paid promptly. Their proposed plan was to set an ambush for the Dutch in the place where they went for fresh water. They requested three days of rations for the undertaking.

Vieira and Negreiros agreed to the plan. Estrate, who knew the traitorous nature of the Dutch better than anyone and who was experienced in military matters, wouldn't allow the leaders of the ambush to take the men they wanted. He split them up and added other men. Once they got past all of our camps and into the brush where the ambush was to be set, they sounded their drums and marched straight into Recife.

A black who fled from Recife that day reported that a contingent of Dutch soldiers had marched into the city. The Dutch and Jews were delighted. On hearing this news, Vieira ordered experienced men to locate the place where the ambush was to have been set. They were to take up positions there without leaving behind any traces that they'd done so.

Vieira and Negreiros then consulted with Estrate about the situation. They asked what should be done in light of this betrayal. Although a foreigner, he was a loyal man. He gave this advice:

> Lord Governors, I couldn't believe that these men were headed for Recife because many of them left behind in camp with us their wives, children, and slaves. However, once they left there was no doubt that all were involved in the conspiracy to commit treason. I know this because, as Your Lordships are aware, I moved around the soldiers first presented by the leaders, removing some and substituting others.
>
> My thought was that if they were reshuffled like this and yet even so went to Recife, then it would be clear that all of them, not just a few, are traitors. Under military justice, in which I was trained, all are at fault, and deserve death, without remission. I deserve death most of all because I accepted the position of commander of such a vile lot, despite my vast experience in dealing with the Dutch, who are all traitors.

Estrate withdrew to his house, along with his lieutenant. He refused to speak with anyone. He was weighed down by remorse and shed many tears. Our commanders acted at once, disarming all of the foreign soldiers still among us. They put our troops on high alert.

The commanders had the Dutch barracks searched. In them, they found cheeses from Holland, biscuits, butter, herring, and smoked fish, none of which were available to the Portuguese. These foodstuffs served as irrefutable evidence that the Dutch soldiers had been sneaking off to Recife, where they plotted treason with the Supreme Council. Without doubt, they'd revealed everything about our locations and movements.

Uncovering this plot was the greatest miracle granted by God in our fight for liberty. Had it not been uncovered by the order of Heaven, the slightest mistake on our part would have led to the death of every Portuguese in Pernambuco.

We rounded up all the Dutch under our control, including soldiers, women, and children. We sent a total of four hundred of them in small groups, under guard, to Bahia. Vieira ordered the officers in other locations, who had Dutch serving under them, to disarm the Dutch soldiers and send them to Bahia. The Portuguese residents along the way wanted to kill the Dutch prisoners because of the great harm they'd caused. Vieira had to threaten the Portuguese with capital punishment to prevent them from taking things into their own hands.

One of our officers came up with the idea of arousing suspicion against the seventy-five Dutch soldiers who had betrayed us. He left a letter at one of the forts in Recife, where it was found. The letter informed the Supreme Council that the men who led these soldiers were actually agents of Vieira. Their job, according to the letter, was to offer large sums of money to the military officials in Recife in exchange for surrendering the city.

This news greatly agitated the Councilmembers. They ordered that word of the letter be suppressed. Their spies went into the city to verify whether there might be any truth to it. Two of the soldiers were found drinking in a tavern. They spoke very highly of the

Portuguese and how well they'd been paid. They bought rounds of beer and rum for everyone. The two men were arrested and tortured. After three days they were hung since they admitted nothing. The leaders of the soldiers were then locked up. However, before they were tortured, a spy revealed the trick and they were released.

In November, a ship from Bahia got past the Dutch blockade. It delivered needed supplies, especially ammunition. It carried some letters, including a request from the Dutch commander Heinrich Hus, who was being held in Bahia, for a prisoner swap. We sent a representative to Recife, but nothing came of it. However, our representative returned with some Dutch magazines carrying news of the outside world, which we hadn't received in some time. He also picked up a letter for Estrate. Our commanders asked Estrate to read the magazines and comment on their truthfulness. One article read:

> In Brazil there was an uprising by the residents of the Captaincy of Pernambuco. Although under our rule, they rebelled against the States General and against the illustrious Company. Taking up arms, they withdrew into the forests. However, these rebels are pathetic beasts, who will soon be punished, as they deserve.
>
> None of them have sufficient resources to defend themselves against our power. None have the courage to make war against us, although they are capable of causing us some damage. We would have been left unprepared had we not been advised of the treason by various landowners, who are our faithful friends.

Estrate became animated when he read the letter addressed to him. He sent a reply to the Supreme Council, in which he stated his delight to be among the Portuguese and to be fighting for their liberty against the Dutch. The letter to Estrate read:

> You are an infamous dog, a traitor to the States General and the Company. With such little shame, having been made

commander of the fort at the Cape of Saint Augustine, which was the best we had on this coast, you surrendered it to the Portuguese. Now, to your dishonor, you're serving in the war as a scoundrel and wretch.

For this reason, the Lords of the Supreme Council will soon condemn you to death, along with your lieutenant, who although French is likewise a traitor. We'll slit your throat from behind while you're tied to a post, as befits a traitor, and burn you in front of everyone. We'll hang your lieutenant, and quarter him, and hang his body parts from the gallows. For us, your life and honor will amount to nothing.

While these events were taking place, Pernambuco was in its dry season, and it was terrible. Several communicable diseases started to spread, killing people throughout the Captaincy. The diseases were extremely virulent. Death came within twenty-four hours of the outbreak of symptoms. In one house nine people died within two days. Many of the Dutch in Recife also died.

Vieira saw how the infirmary overflowed with sick soldiers. Many passed away. We had limited supplies for treating or comforting them. Vieira ordered that images of the Saints be set up. Hymns were sung; prayers were offered.

I preached that day at our church in the main camp, where the people shed many tears. I led a devotional procession in which all who were able to join participated, including our commanders. Everyone proceeded without shoes, with some mortifying themselves in acts of physical penitence, as is done in the procession of the Holy Footsteps. God being served, within a few days, by the blessings of the Saints, the submission and tears of the residents, and primarily by the death and suffering of Jesus Christ our Savior, the diseases ended.

Despite the outbreak of disease, we raised our new fort with incredible speed. We completed it during the months of October to December and outfitted it with artillery. On 1 January 1646, we discharged the cannons for the first time, in honor of the

Circumcision of Our Lord Jesus Christ, and to celebrate the New Year.

The Dutch were startled when they heard the report of heavy artillery, so close to Recife, that hadn't been fired from their own guns. We got word that two ships from Bahia had arrived at the Cape of Saint Augustine, one bringing basic necessities that Vieira had purchased with a shipment of sugar and the other with weapons and ammunition, sent by the Governor of Bahia. Vieira and Negreiros went there to oversee the offloading of supplies.

A traitor in our midst alerted the Dutch that the two had departed our main fort. The Dutch sent out a squadron to take up a position where they could erect defenses and launch future operations. Dias and his black soldiers, as well as other troops, attacked the Dutch position from multiple directions. The Dutch quickly abandoned the effort and retreated to their forts. Vieira and Negreiros got word of this success. They raced back to the main fort as quickly as possible, arriving on 13 January.

On 26 January the Dutch tossed a disabled Portuguese man out of Recife. He got about using crutches. Back when Recife was filled with Portuguese, he lived by begging for donations at the doorways of faithful Christians. Since the uprising began and the Portuguese left, there was no one to help him out. The Dutch wouldn't sustain the man because they only care for themselves. They think more about robbery than charity. Therefore, they left him at a way station outside the city walls.

Our sentinels found the disabled man. They brought him back to our main fort. We learned from him that the Dutch were running out of food. Prices were astronomical. Even fresh water was unaffordable for most. People were drinking water out of wells contaminated with salt water, which was making them sick. Many had died as a result.

The people were suffering and downcast, hoping only that Holland would send relief. Many of the Dutch were ready to stop fighting the Portuguese. However, the Jews continued to give money to the Supreme Council to carry on the war. They even paid the soldiers' salaries. Many Jews pleaded with the Council for passage on ships to return to Holland. These requests weren't granted except in a few cases where large sums of money were paid to the Council.

Over the next couple of days we captured several Caboclos. They told us that many of their fellows wanted to come over to our side. They said there was no food except for those who could pay the high prices. The reason they hesitated to come over to us was that the Dutch kept a close eye on them. They split up family members and friends. The Dutch had also convinced them that the Portuguese would kill all Caboclos as traitors.

We asked where they'd like to be and they said with us, with the Portuguese. We forgave them and provided them with clothes, which they lacked. We sent them back to Recife, so that they could inform all of the Caboclos there that they'd be forgiven and treated well. Without the assistance of the Caboclos the Dutch would be helpless.

During the last few days of January several groups of blacks escaped from Recife. Our men captured the blacks and brought them to our main fort. The first group of five told us three ships full of wounded soldiers had just arrived. They'd barely escaped with their lives from a major battle with Camarão and our indigenous Brazilian allies further up the coast. Many Dutch and Caboclos had been killed.

The Supreme Council had sent reinforcements and munitions in support, leaving Recife poorly defended. The blacks said that all of the other blacks in Recife wanted to get out and come over to us. However, the Dutch had convinced them the Portuguese would hand them over to the indigenous Brazilians, to be killed, roasted, boiled, and eaten. Another couple of blacks reported that many of the Dutch and Jews in Recife were dying because some Senegalese blacks had poisoned the water in one of the cisterns the Dutch used. The blacks in Recife all knew what was going on and avoided the cistern, so none had been poisoned.

In February, we captured a Frenchman, who told us that all of the French and English soldiers serving the Dutch wanted to escape from Recife to join us. They were also afraid of being killed by us as punishment. Our commanders decided to draw up letters in Dutch and French, in which we offered to forgive their offenses and treat them well.

These letters were posted around the Dutch forts in Recife. The Frenchman, in his own hand, wrote letters to several of his friends, informing them of how well he was being treated. He did so to help convince them our offer was genuine. We decided not to allow him to stay with us in the main fort, since we'd had such a bad experience with treacherous foreigners. He was sent further inland but was very happy to be out of Recife.

30 EXITING BRAZIL

Editor's Note: Calado is now in his early sixties and frail. Rumors of massive fleets, be they Dutch, Spanish, or Portuguese, keep everyone on edge. Food shortages plague both sides. Calado acknowledges that the Dutch are expert merchants but finds them untutored in the ways of kings and their vassals. He grabs the opportunity to flee Brazil. The rebellion has shown some successes. It now needs the king's open support. When final victory is achieved the servants of God and the king will enjoy freedom as loyal subjects.

* * *

Throughout this period, Camarão continued to battle the Dutch in the north. As mentioned, he had a major victory, killing and wounding many Dutch and Caboclos. He was supported by reinforcements commanded by Negreiros. We had constant skirmishes with the Dutch around Recife.

At the beginning of March, we received encouraging news. Our sentinels found an enemy soldier asleep outside one of the Dutch forts. He had a rope tied to his leg, which was attached to the horse of the fort's captain. As the horse grazed, our men cut the rope without waking the man, freeing the animal.

When the soldier awoke and realized his predicament, he came to our camp and surrendered. He was afraid the captain would hang him for losing the horse. He reported to us that a Dutch supply ship had arrived in Recife. It brought news that a massive fleet of over fifty ships had been spotted near Cape Verde. The ships weren't displaying their flags. It was unclear whether they were Portuguese or Castilian. We obtained the same information from an Englishman captured by Dias' soldiers.

Although we didn't know whether the reported fleet was coming our way, possibly bringing the help we so desperately needed, the

Dutch clearly suspected something. We knew this because they called in the dozen ships they usually had patrolling the coast and had them take up positions in the deep water outside of Recife's harbor. We prayed to God that He might turn everything into blessings for His Church and for His Catholic people.

The Holy Week fell in late March that year. We celebrated the most elaborate Easter ceremonies ever held in Pernambuco at the head church in our main camp. Governor Vieira paid the entire cost of the celebration out of his own pocket. On Easter Sunday we discharged all of our artillery, even at our camps that ringed Recife and Mauritsstad. The Dutch were terrified, not having realized how much heavy artillery we possessed, positioned so close to them.

We took another two Dutch prisoners in early April, who told us the residents of Recife were facing starvation. Many wanted to abandon the city to join us. However, they were cowed by the Supreme Council's threats. They claimed we would kill anyone who surrendered, or worse, would hand them over to be eaten by the indigenous Brazilians. Our commanders had the Dutch write letters to their friends, telling them how well they'd been treated, and that the Portuguese pledged similar treatment to all who surrendered. Over the next few days others came to us, including people from Flanders, England, and Ireland, and they were also asked to write letters to their friends.

In one case, three Flemings tried to escape from one of the Dutch forts. A squad of Dutch soldiers pursued them and captured two of the men. One screamed out for help to Dias' men, who were hiding nearby. Dias' men fired on the Dutch, who ran off. They captured the man who requested assistance. Back at our main fort, the man confirmed the absence of food in Recife. He also brought additional news.

The captive said a ship had arrived bringing only a few men and limited supplies. However, the Supreme Council claimed the ship brought news of a massive rescue mission that would arrive from Holland by the end of the month. They asserted two thousand soldiers would arrive in Recife. They also claimed four thousand were headed to Bahia in order to seize Brazil's capital. However, the captive said everyone in Recife thought the story was a lie. They believed it was being told simply to deceive the soldiers so that they wouldn't desert to the side of the Portuguese.

The man also described the chaos into which Recife was falling. The Dutch were ready to give up but the Jews continued to insist on sustaining the war effort. The Supreme Council ordered all food supplies in Recife to be brought to a central storehouse protected by armed guards. They knew that Jews had stockpiled food and drink in their homes, including manioc and wheat flour, salted meat, fish, vegetables, wine, olive oil, vinegar, rum, and beer.

The Supreme Council sent in soldiers to seize the Jews' supplies. The Jews thereafter received food rations just like any soldier. It irritated them to be dependent on rations handed out by others. In response, they instigated a popular protest. However, this backfired because the Dutch in turn responded with armed soldiers. Seven Jews were killed.

With soldiers and slaves escaping from Recife every day to join us, the Supreme Council, as recommended by its Jewish advisors, issued two forged letters in the name of King João IV. Copies of the first letter were placed prominently throughout Recife for the purpose of discouraging further defections. It read:

> To Francisco de Sousa Coutinho, Portuguese Ambassador to the Netherlands: I the King send you greetings. I've just received news from Brazil, which is detailed in the enclosed document. I'll send the original notice separately to the esteemed and powerful States General and to Their Supreme Highnesses so that they'll see the manner in which Governor Antonio Teles da Silva has conducted himself in this matter.
>
> At this very moment I'm dispatching two ships carrying this message, whereby I expressly decree that no one outside of the limits of my jurisdiction is acting under my command. Only those who govern Pernambuco are to be obeyed.

Without delay, the troops that were sent to Pernambuco to pacify the Portuguese residents are to be recalled to Bahia.

Further, I order severe punishment for Henrique Dias, Camarão, and their soldiers. I do so because, although they were sent to assist the Dutch, as was the intention of Governor Teles da Silva, and as is demonstrated in the documents I'm sending, they must be severely castigated to remove all suspicion that I, or my governing officers, condone what they've done.

Based on information I've received from various sources, I find no evidence that Governor Teles da Silva has stepped outside the bounds of his obligation, which was to maintain excellent relations with his Dutch neighbors.

Lisbon, 4 October 1645, under seal of His Royal Majesty

The second forged letter was written in Portuguese. Copies were posted on sticks outside the forts on the trails where our men would be likely to find them. Many read the postings, including our commanders. The letter stated:

The States General of the United Provinces of the Netherlands, having received the written statement and supporting evidence presented by the Ambassador of the King of Portugal, Lord Francisco de Sousa Coutinho, to Their Supreme Highnesses, on 28 October 1645, have no doubts about the good faith and honesty of His Majesty in all of his undertakings.

The States General do not doubt that those actions which have been prejudicial to these States, in particular the damages to the West India Company that have been inflicted in Brazil, will be rectified in good faith with the restoration to the Company of all territory seized in Brazil.

The subjects of these States are to be freed from the prisons in which they're held and returned to their former liberty. His Majesty will show his Royal authority, punishing severely those who provided arms to His rebellious subjects in this Province or who in some unauthorized manner aided or advised the rebels.

Finally, it is required that Teodosio de Estrate and his accomplices, who surrendered for money the fort at the Cape of Saint Augustine, be handed over to the Company.

In all of these matters, Their Supreme Highnesses have acted with decorum in regard to the dignity of the Ambassador, properly ordering matters according to custom, as is the case in dealing with a King's Ambassador ordered to serve in these States. We request that Your Excellency might wish to send this response to His Majesty as quickly as possible by various means to ensure prompt delivery.

By act of the Supreme Council of the most powerful States General, The Hague, 5 November 1645.

In examining these two letters, our commanders quickly realized that they had to be forgeries carried out with the assistance of clever Jews in Recife. It would have been impossible for the information contained in these letters to have reached Holland by the dates indicated. In addition, some of the language employed was completely inappropriate for communications from a King to his vassals and ambassadors. The Dutch might be expert merchants but they know little about the manner of expression employed by Kings.

These letters had limited effect. Defectors continued to trickle out of Recife. We made some gains but were also suffering from a lack of food, due to the damage to crops caused by torrential rains. Governor Vieira had to visit landowners in person to make pleas for continued support in terms of both money and food.

In June, a French sergeant surrendered to us. Under questioning, he revealed that three ships had arrived from Holland, loaded with supplies and carrying four hundred soldiers. He confirmed that the Dutch anticipated the arrival of two fleets carrying a total of six thousand men.

Our officers became suspicious, thinking the Frenchman might be a spy. They asked him why, if a large supply of food had just arrived, he claimed that hunger motivated him to leave Recife. He said that a group of men had sworn to leave Recife before the ships docked. Afterward, someone informed on them and two of the men were hung. He expected, as the leader of the group, to be sentenced to death shortly. Therefore, he decided to get away while he could. The commanders were satisfied with his explanation and allowed him to join our forces, maintaining his rank.

At the end of June we captured a small supply boat that was stocked with wine, rum, beer, biscuits, salted beef and pork, fish, bread, butter, cheese, and vegetables. We killed most of the men from the boat but brought back two wounded men, one Dutch and the other Portuguese. The latter had been a captive and was being used as an oarsman. They confirmed the arrival of the three large supply ships and four hundred or so soldiers.

The Dutchman affirmed that two fleets would soon arrive, one to restore Pernambuco and the other to seize Bahia. However, the Portuguese said most of the men who had arrived were sick. He also said that the information about the fleets was uncertain because the men from the Dutch ships had been making contradictory statements.

On 13 July another Frenchman escaped from Recife and surrendered to us. The day before, the Dutch had been discharging artillery and gunfire from morning until night. We didn't know why. The Frenchman told us that one of the Nineteen Directors of the Company had arrived, together with Admiral Lichtart. The Admiral had been previously stationed in Brazil. The blasts were set off each time they offered toasts as a celebration and also to intimidate the Portuguese.

Word had it that a fleet carrying eighteen hundred men had left Holland for Pernambuco. Pirates based in Dunkirk attacked the fleet as it sailed the English Channel. The fleet was then becalmed and stuck at sea for four months, with insufficient water, resulting in widespread sickness and many deaths. Not all of the ships had arrived. The fleet that was supposed to attack Bahia was still being assembled and hadn't yet sailed.

In light of the likelihood of a major Dutch attack our commanders had previously decided to pull in all available men who were positioned in other Captaincies. However, with the knowledge that there were no more than eight hundred enemy soldiers currently in Recife they decided to rescind the order for the time being. We were able to continue to pressure the Dutch everywhere except in Recife itself.

It was time for me to leave Brazil. I wished to petition His Majesty on behalf of the suffering people of Pernambuco, with a request that such loyal vassals might be aided. I secretly got on board a ship that was to sail to Portugal, carrying letters and my manuscripts. I was afraid the local residents wouldn't let me depart if they knew about it since they'd be lacking in spiritual care in my absence. I dressed in the ordinary attire of a layman. I let my beard grow so that I wouldn't be easily recognized in the event the Dutch captured the ship en route to Portugal. The Dutch hated me. One of their ships pursued us as we sailed not far from Recife but we escaped.

May God give me the grace that I might be able to present to His Majesty, in a fitting manner, the weight of the obligation that exists to come to the aid of his subjects, who are fully resolved to give their lives in his service. With this, the first part of our battle for liberty must end.

May God grant that the second part of our battle shall be more pleasing. With the full restoration of Pernambuco everyone will feel delight in being free. Each one will be able to serve without impediment our Lord God, and the Saints, and His Royal Majesty, as good and loyal vassals. All of this I have written subject to the correction of the Holy Mother Roman Church, as befits Her obedient son that I am.

Part Three

The Idea of Liberty

We've reached the end of Friar Calado's account. His narrative, according to a Brazilian historian, brims with venom. He attacks by name Brazil's bishop, prominent clerics, and other powerful individuals. He takes liberties that were unusual for his day. Far stranger was the permission granted by the Roman Church to publish such vitriol. The Church back then rarely—if ever—tolerated criticism. Even now it tends to protect its servants.

From today's perspective, Calado's book is both disturbing and bizarre. Consider Calado himself: a well-educated, Latin loving, slave owning priest, who engaged in espionage and was complicit in murder. He cast out demons and converted heretics. What about his stories? The Virgin Mother and her babe distribute ammunition; statues spout drops of water; a saint appears in a dream and orders a commander into battle; apparitions on horseback deliver news of a restored king; a scheming merchant employs sorceresses to control the Dutch governor; and so on.

Where does liberty fit into this account? The idea of liberty spread as a current through meandering channels. I'd like to illustrate the process by focusing on one stream that had cascading effects. The example relates closely to the nascent freedoms found in the Dutch Republic. First, though, let's bring to a close the events of Friar Calado's story. He passed away in 1654, the year in which Recife was retaken and Dutch Brazil vanished forever. Despite its victory, Portugal's tribulations didn't end. Dutch claims loomed over Brazil for years. They were extinguished only after Portugal agreed to pay massive indemnities to the Netherlands. Brazil was but one of the Dutch Golden Age's many glories and heartaches.

Dutch Brazil's Twilight. Following Calado's departure in 1646, both Portuguese loyalists and Dutch occupiers endured unabated suffering. The Dutch navy controlled the coast; Portuguese guerillas dominated the interior. In theory the Dutch West India Company could have continued to supply Recife and a few other outposts indefinitely. However, Dutch Brazil in its final stages failed as a commercial enterprise. The losses, human and financial, had become unbearable. In Europe and elsewhere, the Dutch Republic faced a resurgent France and an increasingly bellicose England.

Opportunities to produce sugar—without the need to fight deeply entrenched opponents—were cropping up elsewhere. Over the span of twenty-odd years the Dutch established sugar plantations and refineries in Suriname and the Caribbean, using the know-how gained in Brazil. Dutch farms and mills in these new lands were often owned and operated by Jews and New Christians. Brazil lost its importance for the Netherlands. In contrast, Brazil remained crucial for Portugal, which would likely have ended up as a Spanish province without its prize colony.

In the end, Dutch officials in Recife conspired to negotiate an unauthorized capitulation. The desperate residents had come to detest the West India Company and its board of directors. In this, they echoed Calado's contempt for government by merchants. No one was willing to die or suffer another day for the ignoble cause of a bankrupt corporation.

The Dutch surrender wasn't strategic. It was prompted by the unmitigated misery of disease, treachery, thirst, starvation, incessant fighting, unpaid wages, and despair. The Portuguese forces weren't much better off than those on the Dutch side but, crucially, they believed in the ends for which they fought. As noted in Book One, Portuguese conduct following the Dutch handover was exemplary. Military discipline was rigorously enforced. Civilians—including Jews—and disarmed troops who chose to depart exited unmolested. Many of Dutch Brazil's Jewish refugees went to the Caribbean or Suriname. Some founded the first synagogue in what was to become the United States in New Amsterdam, which is now New York City. Gentiles who embraced Catholicism and wished to remain in Brazil were allowed to do so.

The Aftermath. Modern Brazil's military claims that the country's national identity was first forged during the battle of Guararapes. It could be compared to Valley Forge in the founding of the United States. According to Calado, three mounted Governors converged on the fleeing Dutch and raised their swords in unison to proclaim liberty. The soldiers under Vieira, a Portuguese landowner whose Madeiran mother was African, together with those under the Native Brazilian Camarão and the African-Brazilian Dias, were of the same three ethnicities as their commanders. The majority of present-day Brazilians are mostly descended from some blend of these three ethnic groups.

The freedom promised to enslaved Africans at Guararapes spurred their fearless counterattack on the Dutch. Their valor turned the battle's tide. It was a crucial moment in which a poorly armed ragtag outfit proved it could scatter the most advanced army in the world. Can we call this a victory for liberty? At the very least, we can say that liberty triumphed briefly for those who were emancipated thereafter.

Unfortunately, nascent African-Brazilian liberation didn't run very far. Apart from those who fought and survived until the fall of Recife, Brazil remained a hellish prison for Africans and African-Brazilians. Escaped slaves would flee to quilombos. Even Dias' soldiers suffered abuse; many of the promises made to them were broken. Native Brazilians who battled on the Portuguese side likewise ended up restricted and marginalized post-rebellion. They tasted freedom only when unleashed on the Dutch. Their descendants for the most part merged into Brazil's ethnic potpourri. Brazil's present-day indigenous bands must often scrape by on society's fringes.

We can finish up Calado's story by tracing the fate of its main protagonists and examining a few key events. Calado, as noted, passed away in Portugal in 1654, the year Recife fell. Governors Vieira and Dias, to whom we'll return, marched into the city with their soldiers. Camarão, Governor of the Native Brazilians, passed away in 1648, before the moment of triumph.

Gaspar Dias Ferreira had a colorful career after he arrived in Holland with Prince Maurits in 1644. Under the Prince's sponsorship, in 1645 Ferreira became a naturalized citizen of the Netherlands. True to his character, he engaged in treasonous secret correspondence with both Spain and Portugal. A packet of his letters was taken by pirates. It ended up with a Jewish merchant in Algiers. He recognized the importance of the correspondence and forwarded the batch to the West India Company's board of directors. Ferreira was arrested, tried, and convicted of high treason. His citizenship was revoked; he was lucky not to have been executed. He made a spectacular escape from prison in 1649, leaving behind a letter written in excellent Latin justifying his conduct. Somehow he made it to Portugal, where he was well received by King João IV. Ferreira and his son were knighted. He received other honors and appears to have died in Portugal in 1656 or so. João IV also passed away in 1656 and was succeeded by his three-year-old heir under a regency.

Back in Brazil, the black, indigenous, and mixed race soldiers who bore the brunt of the fighting were on the verge of rebellion. Their post-war mistreatment triggered justifiable outrage. Members of the Pitiguares tribe and other Dutch allies among the Native Brazilians sought to take advantage of the soldiers' discontent. They tried to enlist Henrique Dias and his troops for a Dutch reconquest of Brazil. The realignment never quite came together. Dias passed away in 1662.

Seeking to exploit Portugal's weaknesses and Brazil's turmoil, the Dutch issued an ultimatum in 1657. They threatened hostilities unless all lands reconquered by Portugal in Brazil and Africa were returned. The Portuguese rejected the ultimatum but offered to pay an indemnity instead. At the same time, the Portuguese quietly sought French and British support. Neither the French nor British wanted to see Portugal seized by their mutual opponent Spain. They also didn't want to allow the upstart Netherlands to gain any further advantages. The British had their own commercial interests at stake. The Dutch were pressured into a negotiated settlement with Portugal.

An additional factor arose for England. King Charles II was restored to the throne in 1660, following the English civil war, and became engaged to the Portuguese noblewoman Catherine of Bragança. Their marriage further intertwined the interests of England and Portugal. Territory in India encompassing the city of Mumbai, formerly Bombay—*Bom Bahia* or "Good Bay" in ungrammatical

Portuguese—was handed over to England as part of Catherine's dowry. Great Britain took on the role of Portugal's protector.

Under a 1662 treaty the Dutch gave up their territorial claims in Brazil in exchange for an indemnity. Portugal levied a special tax to finance both the indemnity and Catherine of Bragança's dowry. Brazilians were still paying this tax as late as 1830. In a final act, the Dutch made new threats in 1667. Under additional Anglo-French pressure, the Netherlands released all claims in 1669 upon the award of a final indemnity that was secured by Portugal's salt revenues.

Vieira passed away in 1681 while in his late seventies. He was a poor man when the Dutch first arrived in Recife. By the time of the rebellion he was wealthy but also heavily in debt to the Dutch. His critics said he instigated the revolt for that reason. Most contemporary observers considered Vieira to have been indispensable to the restoration of Pernambuco. After the recapture of Recife, he became the governor of the Captaincy of Paraiba. He was transferred to Africa to serve as governor of Angola from 1658–1661. In that capacity, Vieira had a violent quarrel with the Jesuits, who were busy running plantations reportedly worked by 10,000 slaves. His final decades were spent in Brazil. He received numerous awards and other bestowals of royal favor. Vieira was acknowledged to be Brazil's richest man and largest landowner, with many estates and sugar mills. He helped large numbers of settlers from Madeira and the Azores immigrate to Brazil, supporting them while they became established in their new land.

After the fall of Recife, escaped slaves living in a large complex of quilombos known as Palmares—as well as the indigenous allies of the Dutch who were ensconced in remote areas—temporarily managed to avoid Portuguese wrath. Authorities at the time had to deal with a major uprising by Native Brazilians elsewhere, in Bahia and Pernambuco. The outburst was triggered by Portuguese cattle ranchers encroaching on indigenous lands. Unfortunately, as the Portuguese administration gained power, it brought in ferocious frontiersmen known as Bandeirantes from the Captaincy of São Paulo.

Following years of fighting, severe drought, and decimation by disease, in 1692 the Pitiguares and other tribes reached a negotiated settlement with the Portuguese. The Native Brazilians were awarded reservations, which was the first time that indigenous land rights had been recognized. The Bandeirantes thereafter destroyed the quilombos of Palmares. Captives, both African and indigenous, were enslaved. By the 1720s the lands set aside for the Pitiguares were overrun by cattle ranchers. Encroachment of other Native Brazilian reservations by ranchers, loggers, and miners has never stopped.

Prince Maurits continued to serve the Netherlands in various capacities. He nearly agreed to return to Brazil in 1647 as governor and commander to quell the rebellion. However, he and the West India Company couldn't reach mutually agreeable terms. His new city, Mauritsstad, was destroyed by the time Recife fell. Later in life he was quoted as stating that, had the land been at peace, he would have preferred to remain in Pernambuco until his death. Instead, he entertained nobles and officials at his magnificent Mauritshuis in The Hague. The structure is now a museum that houses several of Vermeer's masterpieces, including *Girl with a Pearl Earring*, along with other notable works. The Mauritshuis was famous for its magnificent staircase and beautiful paneling made of Brazilian wood. Charles II received word of his restoration to the English throne while lodging there. The Prince was the first noble to congratulate him.

At an advanced age Prince Maurits played an important role in the defense of the Netherlands during the difficult years—to be described subsequently—of 1672–1674. He regularly frequented his estates in Germany. Later in life, the Prince took up residence at one of his German estates, where he passed away peacefully in 1679, physically decrepit but still sharp mentally.

The curtain has now closed on the story of Dutch Brazil. Apart from the history of events, it's time to shift gears. Let's turn to the history of ideas.

Liberty's Advance. As noted in Book One, Calado's story illustrates a transition in notions about liberty that continues to reverberate globally. Space somehow opened up within the European cultural sphere for expanded individual liberties, greater equality of rights, and the freedoms of association and commerce. The Low Countries were at the heart of such developments. Much of the attitudinal change among the Dutch was spurred by movements such as Modern Devotion and Christian Humanism. These movements in turn were stimulated by the recovery of ancient Greek and Roman science and philosophy—by way of Byzantine Greek and Muslim scholars—that gave birth to the Renaissance.

Calado was a man of certainty. God, Christ, Saint Paul, the Pope, the Church councils, Saint Augustine, Aristotle, Plato, the King and his vassals: Calado's world was filled with absolute authorities who went unquestioned. Every unspeakable act imaginable was justified by their words or carried out in their names. What broke the back of such self-righteousness?

The ancient version of liberty—the right and power of a select class to dominate others—is what Judge Hand refers to as the "ruthless and unbridled will" in his *The Spirit of Liberty* speech, cited in Book One. Hand tells us that liberty isn't grounded in institutions but, rather, must derive from widespread acceptance of innate fallibility. We lack access to absolutes. The views of others might be justifiable in some way, at least for them or in some set of circumstances. Such a perspective goes beyond mere tolerance by civic authorities. It is liberty bounded only by the legitimate requirements of citizens to constrain violence, criminality, or excessive strife.

The doubting of absolutes is often called "mitigated skepticism." It differs from classical or Academic skepticism, in which no claim of knowledge is accepted. Mitigated skepticism allows for working, practical, evidentiary, or probabilistic knowledge: not Truth with a "T" but lower-case truths of a commonsense variety; those that enable us to get on with the business of life. This is the type of truth associated with the sciences. A scientific theory might be the best available explanation of a phenomenon that we have. However, it's always subject to revision, correction, or replacement based on new data or discoveries. No scientific theory is absolute.

It's difficult to imagine a time in which asking the wrong question might cost our lives. Yet that was Calado's world, despite the influence of the Renaissance. When the Renaissance began, the doctrines of the world's major religions were for the most part firmly set. Church dogma was rigidly enforced in Europe. The introduction of skeptical views turned the pages of history. The process can be partially traced through some of the events described in Book One.

Florence in northern Italy is a good place to start. It was one of the epicenters of the Renaissance. The surviving works of an ancient Greek skeptical philosopher, Sextus Empiricus, made their way into the libraries of the dominant Medici clan—as well as those of the Vatican—during the fifteenth century. Knowledge of classical Greek was limited in most of Europe at the time. However, associates of the Dominican friar Savanarola (1452–1498) provided him with information from the Greek texts. He ordered several of them to prepare Latin translations of Sextus' works. It's unknown whether they did. Savanarola was the first to suggest that such materials in Latin could be used in the defense of true religion.

Savanarola is often caricatured because of his "bonfire of the vanities" and florid prophesizing. His supporters aided a French invasion of northern Italy and forced the Medicis to abandon Florence in 1494. Savanarola claimed that Florence would become the center of world Christianity. The Pope excommunicated him in 1497. He was condemned, hung, and burned in 1498. Despite this turn of events, the Medicis were unable to return to Florence until 1512. Regardless of his bizarre claims and repugnant acts, many people—including Martin Luther—have viewed Savanarola as a precursor to the Protestant Reformation.

Why did a fanatic like Savanarola seek the tools of skepticism to defend what he called true religion? His issues with the Papacy were similar to those of Luther and Erasmus. One tool he found in Sextus was the Problem of the Criterion. The problem is, in summary: how do we establish a valid standard for judging a claim made about things outside of our direct experience? In order to evaluate the claim, we require a standard or criterion for evaluation. We also need experts who can apply the standard. However, any such standards and experts must also be evaluated by appropriate standards and experts. This process can go on forever. Therefore, such claims are unprovable in any ultimate sense. The Problem of the Criterion can be used to contest each link in the logical chain of almost any argument.

By what criterion could the Pope defend the dogma of his authority? How does one have true and certain religious knowledge? Savanarola claimed that he had special prophetic knowledge by which he could discern the precepts of true religion. He used Sextus' arguments to attack the Church's religious and philosophical dogmas. He thereby dethroned what had been the accepted criteria for absolute knowledge of God and true religion. Savanarola asserted that only knowledge given directly by God, such as through prophecy, could be used to judge truth and falsehood in matters of religion.

Disciples of Savanarola—and others stimulated by his views—disseminated Sextus' ideas and Greek manuscripts of his works. Erasmus, a proponent of Christian Humanism, was one of those influenced by Sextus. A generation after Savanarola's death Luther asked the same question about the criterion of faith. His answer differed from that of Savanarola; yet both men agreed on the inadequacy of the Church's standard.

Before examining the spread of skeptical thinking in the sixteenth and seventeenth centuries, let's look a bit more closely at Sextus and his work. As mentioned, he was a Greek, who is thought to have lived in Egyptian Alexandria around 200 CE. It appears that he practiced medicine in what's known as the Empirical tradition; hence his name. He might not have been a notable philosopher but, because his works survived, his texts became the leading example of Pyrrhonism, or more properly of its later version, which is known as Neo-Pyrrhonism.

One might question how the writings of a single author could have had any significant impact. For a sense of perspective, imagine living during an era in which no authority figure or sacred doctrine could be questioned. Here's an analogy. Think of the first commercial computers from the 1950s and 1960s. International Business Machines—IBM—dominated the industry. The head of IBM at the time predicted a long-term global market of no more than a couple of thousand computers. Computers were packed with tubes and laced with miles of cables. They sat in cavernous, air-conditioned, hermetically sealed facilities. The devices were designed by brilliant PhDs—Doctors of Philosophy—and operated by highly skilled technicians dressed in spotless white lab coats. The whole setup resembled the holiest inner sanctum of a shrine, with otherworldly theologians spinning their mysteries, and clerics in their vestments performing the rites. Ordinary people, in regard to the computer facility—or the shrine for that matter—could only marvel at its wonders from a distance.

Imagine further that IBM's chieftains had maintained a stranglehold on computer technology for the next thousand years. That's about where the intellectual elites of Europe were circa 1500 CE. As everyone knows, the world of computers began shifting dramatically from the 1970s onward. Knowledge was disseminated and revolutions took place in laboratories and garages. Today, there are billions of devices that fit more computing power into a pocket or purse than was contained in a 1960s computer. Fortunately, IBM couldn't maintain its hammerlock on computers the way the Church and its appendages did in the realm of knowledge and beliefs.

Sextus' texts fell like an alien object from outer space that landed in late Renaissance Europe. No one in the universities, the Church, or among the nobility could imagine questioning Aristotle, Plato, Thomas Aquinas, Augustine, the Pope, scripture, the Church councils, the King, or any other source of absolute truth. Yet Sextus' works began to open eyes to the possibility that received authorities might not be sacrosanct.

The Pyrrhonist approach, as mentioned, differs from pure skepticism. The reality of lived experience is accepted as such. However, attempts to speculate beyond the quotidian are to be resisted. Something deemed to be a disputable matter, in which different views could be argued over without any conclusion, calls for nothing more than the suspension of judgment. The matter can't be decided. If you can't know through sense experience the subject under dispute, then in most cases arguments about it will fail in some way. They fail because certainty must be presumed in the premises of structured arguments.

Absolute certainty about most things can't be established. Challenges can be raised on one grounds or another. This method of refutation is known as the dialectic; it calls assertions into question but makes no assertions of its own. One method is to show that something both is and is not what the proponent claims. In a dialectic critique, the things presumed to be certain—even those left unstated—are what's targeted.

Syllogistic logic, of the type associated with Aristotle, depends on definitions and premises, from which conclusions inevitably flow. A textbook example is: (a) Socrates is a man; (b) all men are mortal; (c) therefore, Socrates is mortal. A no-brainer, right? The objective of a Pyrrhonist philosopher isn't to construct arguments but, rather, to take them apart. With key definitions or premises dismembered, a syllogistic argument will fail. The Problem of the Criterion is one such tool. By questioning the standards and experts relied upon to establish premises, a Pyrrhonist might show that a syllogistic argument runs to infinity—that is, *ad infinitum*—and thereby can never prove anything.

Pyrrho of Elis is credited with founding the Pyrrhonist philosophical school. He traveled to India in 326 BCE in the entourage of Alexander the Great. Some scholars believe that he absorbed Buddhist perspectives while there. There are elements in his thought that resemble early Buddhist themes. Pyrrho sought a state of *ataraxia* or quietude that seems to resemble Buddhist nirvana. He summarized his negation of dogmatic assertions in a form known as a *tetralemma*.

In outline, a tetralemma runs like this: in regard to an ethical or disputable matter, it no more is than is not, or both is and is not, or neither is nor is not. The tetralemma form is found in early Buddhist texts as well as in the works of the Buddhist saint Nagarjuna, who was Sextus' contemporary. It is therefore an element of both Greek and Indian philosophy. Sextus deployed it in a manner highly reminiscent of that of the Buddha and Nagarjuna. Because the Pyrrhonist use of dialectic and the tetralemma can seem foreign to us, I provide an example in the Appendix. It might not be persuasive but, at the least, it offers a taste of how the dialectic can be applied.

Late Renaissance dabblers such as Savanarola didn't use Sextus' techniques to reach a state of spiritual calm. They also didn't question the existence of God. God was taken as a given. They found within Sextus' works a clear path for bypassing religious skepticism. Sextus wrote that one should simply go along with the religious customs of the country in which one resides. This for Sextus was a way to avoid needless disputes. Since quietude was his objective, he didn't actively seek gratuitous conflict.

Considering that prior to the Reformation all of Central and Western Europe adhered to the same Roman Catholic religion, one could embrace the faith while employing Sextus to question rational arguments. For instance, some theologians used syllogistic logic to prove God's existence. For people like Savanarola such proofs are unnecessary. They might even be harmful. Why emphasize logic when simple faith will suffice?

Sextus noted that the religious practices of Athenians, Egyptians, Babylonians, and other peoples differ markedly. One couldn't conclude that any of their religions were better than the others. They were simply customary. This little detail found in Sextus' texts about religious relativity was for the most part ignored.

What the early European adopters of Sextus' methods, including Luther and Erasmus, failed to acknowledge was that religion in the ancient world wasn't the same affair that it had become in medieval Europe. In prior times religion was more of a package of communal rites. No belief was required. The absolute belief in dogmas demanded by Catholic and Protestant clerics in the sixteenth century was nearly unheard of in antiquity.

An example of this distinction appears in European religious interactions with the Chinese. Europeans found it difficult to define the nature of Confucianism. The first Catholic missionaries to China were Jesuits. They held that Confucianism was nothing more than an assortment of civic rituals. One could therefore be a Catholic in belief but remain a good Chinese subject who joined in the local rites. Later missionaries, though—of the Dominican and Franciscan orders—convinced the Pope that Confucianism is in fact an idolatrous religion. The Catholic faithful in China were required to abandon their local customs, which caused them to be branded as deviants in Chinese society.

The first non-religious impact of Sextus' methods occurred in the field of astronomy. One of his texts is a criticism of astrology. Copernicus, Brahe, Keppler and others picked up Sextus' arguments and began to challenge astrological assumptions. They also questioned the Ptolemaic system of celestial spheres rotating about the earth, which was Church dogma. Through careful observation—and by posing alternative models—early astronomers demonstrated the flaws in Ptolemy's earth-centered system. Galileo Galilei (1564–1642), who employed telescopes to expand on his predecessors' work, fell afoul of Church authorities. Galileo's methods, however, inspired a generation of early scientists in a range of disciplines.

Martin Luther adopted the Pyrrhonist line of questioning in regard to the criterion of true and certain religious knowledge. He walked down the same path as Savanarola. He denied the authority of the Pope, Church tradition, councils, and decrees. In place of Savanarola's reliance on prophecy as the standard to be applied, though, Luther claimed in 1520 that only the conscience—guided by scripture—could serve as the true criterion of faith. Like Erasmus, Luther favored widespread literacy. He also sponsored biblical translation to make scripture accessible to the masses.

In response, Catholics came to argue that Luther had asserted an unreliable criterion. Scripture isn't always clear even in translation. Individuals might reach different conclusions about matters of faith. Most lack proper theological training or philosophical understanding.

Catholics claimed that only the orthodox traditions of the Church could provide any certainty in the weighty matter of eternal salvation. Both sides proclaimed that intellectual, moral, and spiritual catastrophe would ensue should the other sides' criterion for certain religious knowledge be accepted.

For nearly two centuries the European intellectual world became embroiled in what was known as the Pyrrhonist crisis. Disputants would use Sextus' dialectical techniques and examples to tear apart their opponents' assertions. With the translation of Sextus' works from Greek into Latin and their publication in Switzerland in the 1560s, Europe's educated elite gained full access to the rhetorical weapons that could destroy opposing arguments. Unfortunately for the combatants, their own positions were just as susceptible to attack.

As described in Book One, by the 1560s the populace in what became the United Provinces of the Netherlands had largely abandoned Catholicism. Nurtured by the literacy promoted through the Modern Devotion movement, imbued with the nondogmatic spirit of Christian Humanism exemplified by Erasmus, and appalled by the homicidal fanaticism of their Austrian and Spanish overlords, the Dutch between 1579 and 1585 revolted and established a republic. It had an extraordinary degree of tolerance for the time period. The relative freedom to conduct scientific inquiry, publish, speak out, and believe as one wished provided an oasis in the midst of a continent still mired in feudalism. Although France and England were also intellectual centers, with Paris in particular serving as a hotbed for radical thought, the power of king and clergy in both nations remained an ongoing threat to liberty's expansion.

Montaigne. The Frenchman Michele Montaigne (1533–1592) was a transitional figure active at the end of the Renaissance and in the early stages of the Reformation. His father was Catholic; his mother was Protestant, from a prominent Spanish New Christian family. Her Jewish great-grandfather had been burned at the stake for his role in the assassination of the first Grand Inquisitor of Spain. Montaigne's father had him raised by Latin-speaking attendants so that Latin would be his native tongue. His father had associates in

Bordeaux from a Portuguese New Christian family which had fled Lisbon following the 1506 massacre mentioned in Book One. Montaigne trained as a lawyer. He later moved in court circles and among the educated elite. He was instrumental in formulating the Edict of Nantes, by which Henri IV guaranteed toleration to Protestants.

Montaigne more than anyone of his time absorbed and popularized the Pyrrhonist perspective, which he gained from the Latin editions of Sextus' works. He wrote a series of learned essays on a range of topics that were infused with humanism, doubt, and the suspension of judgment regarding propositions. He pointed to the Native Brazilians as an example of people who led noble lives without the aid of laws, kings, or religions. Through examples from the New World and classical Greece and Rome, he emphasized the relativity of beliefs and culture. Montaigne remained Catholic but in the manner of a Pyrrhonist, simply adhering to the laws and customs of his country. Some of his ideas were adopted by Catholics as part of the Counter-Reformation, in which simple faith served as the basis of belief; proponents used Sextus' methods to attack the intellectual arguments of the Protestant leaders Luther and Calvin.

Castellio. Luther and Calvin were once advocates of religious tolerance, back when they and their followers were being persecuted by Catholics. Later, as they gained influence and the support of secular authorities, they became as intolerant of heresy—whether Catholic or Protestant—as was any Roman Pope. One of Calvin's close associates, Sebastian Castellio (1515–1563), turned against him following Calvin's role in the execution of a Protestant heretic. Castellio was a humanist scholar and conversant in Greek. He relocated to Basel, Switzerland, from Calvin's Geneva. In Basel, possibly in collaboration with other exiled dissidents, he wrote a number of tracts in opposition to Calvin, including the anonymous *Concerning Heretics and Whether They Should Be Persecuted* of 1553.

Although Castellio used arguments against persecution drawn from the Christian tradition—especially those of Erasmus—he also employed skepticism to attack the very notion of heresy. He claimed there is much uncertainty in matters of religious doctrine. If violent oppression is to be employed against heretics, then every sect is obligated to attempt to murder the adherents of every other sect of every religion worldwide. Such an outcome seems to be the antithesis of the entire purpose of religion. Given his reliance on doubt and skepticism, the environment in which he wrote, and his knowledge of Greek, it seems likely that Castellio had at least a passing acquaintance with Sextus' work. Castellio's writings were widely disseminated in the Netherlands by Dirck Coornhert (1522–1590), a Dutch patriot in the fight against the Spanish, who strongly advocated religious toleration.

Sanches. A distant cousin of Montaigne named Francisco Sanches (1550–1623) pioneered the use of doubt as a tool in scientific inquiry. He was a Spanish-Portuguese New Christian whose family fled to Bordeaux to escape the Portuguese Inquisition. He eventually became a professor of philosophy in France. At the time, philosophy included natural philosophy, which is what we now call science. In his groundbreaking work *That Nothing Is Known* (published in 1581) he negates the syllogistic logic of Aristotelianism. He claims that causes as defined by Aristotle can't be known; arguments based on causality of this type descend into infinite regress. As was noted, demonstrating the *ad infinitum* outcome of a proposition is a common form of Pyrrhonist negation.

Sanches concludes that achieving perfect knowledge is impossible. He allows that faith can be relied on in matters of religion. Beyond that, though, all we have access to is limited imperfect knowledge. Nothing is known absolutely. Through careful observation, experience, and judgment we can draw workable inferences about things but nothing more. Sanches was the first to use the term "scientific method" to describe this mode of inquiry. It has also come to be known as mitigated skepticism. Although Sanches' method isn't purely Pyrrhonist, the philosophy described by Sextus certainly played a powerful role in its development. Sanches' work influenced key figures in the history of science, including Marin Mersenne (1588–1648), Pierre Gassendi (1592–1655), and the luminaries of the

British Royal Society—founded in 1660 for the advancement of science—as well as its French equivalent.

Descartes. René Descartes (1596–1650) was a skilled mathematician who moved within French elite intellectual circles. Both Marsenne and Gassendi knew him well. Much of his work was carried out in the relative freedom of the Netherlands. As the Pyrrhonist crisis continued to spread, Descartes came to believe that an absolute criterion of truth is necessary. Without one, the basis for all knowledge and religion is destroyed.

Rather than lead from a position of naïve faith, Descartes instead chose to doubt everything. He did so in order to find something absolutely true. Prior thinkers had believed that a good God wouldn't have given us unreliable senses. This assumption had been left unchallenged. Descartes took the plunge. In doubting all, he hypothesized that an evil demon could be feeding impressions into our senses. As a result, we might be mistaken about everything. However, even if such were the case, there could be no doubt about the existence of the perceiver. Descartes said famously, "I think, therefore I am." He had found an absolute criterion that couldn't be doubted.[6]

From his foundational criterion, Descartes went on to spin out an entire set of propositions that allowed for the discovery of true knowledge, including in regard to religion and God. He was attacked by theologians for having commenced from a position of doubt, rather than faith. Secular scholars began to poke holes in each of the steps he took in extending his propositions beyond his initial criterion. Descartes' attempt to find an unassailable true criterion ultimately failed. However, his philosophy and mathematical discoveries contributed to further refinements in experimental science. His work helped bring about the eventual overthrow of Aristotle's dominant position in European universities, starting in the

---

[6] It of course can be doubted. Neuroscientific research suggests the function that integrates multiple inputs from our sensory apparatus generates the illusion of a perceiver. The Buddha taught something similar around 2500 years ago.

Netherlands. Descartes' rationalism has had a lasting intellectual impact.

Spinoza. One of Descartes' rationalist successors, Benedict Spinoza (1632–1677), likewise took a step beyond what only a handful of others had dared to consider. His family had been Portuguese New Christians, who openly reverted to Judaism upon arriving in Amsterdam. His father Miguel de Espinoza was a merchant and served as a warden of the Amsterdam Sephardic synagogue and Jewish school. Spinoza's family engaged in trade with Dutch Brazil during its heyday. In his youth he studied at the Jewish school but at the age of seventeen, on the death of his elder brother, he quit school and entered the family business. His father died in 1651. Two years later, Spinoza was expelled from the synagogue because of his unorthodox views. He denied that Moses had authored the Torah; both Jews and Christians found this stance scandalous because it broke the key link to divine authorship of holy scripture.

Spinoza transferred his share of the family business to his younger brother. He thereafter devoted his life to philosophy. He supported himself by working as a lens grinder. This was an exacting profession in his day. Microscopes and telescopes, which require quality optics, were both invented in Holland. These and other new instruments were rapidly expanding the range of phenomena that could be directly apprehended. Spinoza became a student of a radical thinker, from whom he learned the Latin necessary to engage in serious philosophy at the time. In 1663 he published one of the first authoritative works on the philosophy of Descartes. This helped establish his reputation among intellectuals throughout Europe.

However, Spinoza disagreed with Descartes. He found numerous problems in Descartes' reasoning, especially in regard to what's known as the mind-body problem. Descartes had posited a dualistic view in which the substance of mind is separate from the substance of body. Spinoza noted that Descartes provided no basis for mind-body interaction. He also opposed Descartes' foundational method of arguing from the particularistic entity of his own mind. Spinoza claimed that it's impossible to reach an understanding of the infinite by arguing from the finite. His approach was to start with God or the Infinite, and from there to work back to the details of finite existence.

Spinoza's God, being infinite, comprises the totality of nature throughout time. Spinoza used the terms God, the Infinite, and Nature interchangeably. For Spinoza, the universe contains only one substance, not two—mind and body—as posited by Descartes. The sole infinite substance manifests as different attributes through various modes. Thought and extension in space are the two attributes of which we're aware but, as conceived by Spinoza, God has infinite attributes beyond the limits of our perception. Spinoza in his lifetime was branded as an atheist since his God or Nature wasn't the Judeo-Christian God. Later commentators labeled him as a pantheist, that is, one who finds God in everything. For orthodox Christians pantheism is a sin on a par with atheism.

Apart from the Netherlands, could Spinoza have avoided violent persecution anywhere else in Europe? Even so, in 1670 he took the step of publishing his *Theological-Political Treatise* anonymously, with a fictitious publisher and the place of publication falsely identified as Hamburg. Yet he wrote that those who lived in the free republic of the Netherlands—where liberty of thought and religion were accepted—enjoyed rare good fortune. The Dutch, he said, held that nothing is more precious than freedom.

In Spinoza's *Theological-Political Treatise*, he applied the newly emerging scientific method to religion. Based on his knowledge of Hebrew, he deconstructed the Jewish scriptures. The authors were people of varying skill sets. Moses couldn't have authored the Torah. Prophets, he said, were people with active imaginations. Others had only touched on such views. Spinoza stated them explicitly.

Spinoza drew his philosophy in part from the Stoics and Epicureans. He noted that good and evil are relative concepts. At times, along Pyrrhonist lines, he spoke of suspending judgment in regard to unresolvable matters. Ultimately, he advocated for freedom of conscience and belief, and for the state to keep out of matters of religious dogma. Spinoza asserted the superiority of secular, republican, and constitutional government above all other forms. He castigated monarchy.

In his major posthumous work, the *Ethics*, Spinoza laid out a rigorous geometrical presentation of his philosophy, with definitions, propositions, and demonstrations. While this book is widely considered to be his masterwork, some have claimed that the *Theological-Political Treatise* has greater significance. The *Ethics* might have been Spinoza's way to confound his opponents, whether they attacked from a theological, Aristotelian, or Cartesian perspective. Such opponents would have been hard pressed to reject the logical structure of the *Ethics*. They were forced to argue against Spinoza's definitions and propositions. Their arguments became dialectical fodder for those who followed in Spinoza's footsteps because the opponents' positions were equally susceptible to skeptical rebuttal. Although the *Ethics* is generally categorized as a rationalist work, the universe it describes is vastly different from the one offered by Descartes. Spinoza's perspective has been compared to that of Adi Shankara, a prominent Hindu philosopher of the eighth century.

The United Provinces of the Netherlands was in turmoil during Spinoza's productive years. His *Theological-Political Treatise* was intended in part to support the republican Grand Pensionary Jan De Witt against the schemes of the Prince of Orange. De Witt protected Spinoza and went so far as to provide him with a stipend. De Witt and his supporters had been working to limit or even eliminate the role of Stadtholder in the provinces and collectivity of the Netherlands. Holland and several other provinces abolished the position in 1670, the year in which the *Treatise* was published. The same year, England and France entered into a secret compact, wherein they pledged jointly to destroy the Dutch state.

Prince of Orange & King of England. Prince William of Orange (1650–1702) was the son of the Stadtholder William II and Mary Stuart, who was the daughter of King Charles I of England. King Charles II was the Prince's uncle. The Prince wasn't privy to the joint plot of the French and English. It came to fruition in 1672, which is known as the "Disaster Year" in Dutch history.

Pursuant to the secret treaty, France invaded the Netherlands by land. A combined French-British naval operation attacked by sea. The people of the Netherlands turned on De Witt, who they viewed as having been too accommodating to France's aggressive King Louis XIV. Supporters of the Prince of Orange murdered De Witt and his brother. The desperate Dutch installed the Prince as Stadtholder of the Netherlands and commander of the army. The English monarch, Charles II, offered to make his nephew Sovereign Prince of Holland in exchange for his capitulation to England and France. William, however, had been raised in the Netherlands and considered himself to be more Dutch than English. He refused to betray his homeland. The Dutch defenders under his command resorted to flooding huge swaths of territory in order to halt the French advance. The destruction of crops and buildings this caused was extremely unpopular but also generally recognized as necessary.

In 1673 the Dutch defeated the British navy in three major encounters. Charles II withdrew from the conflict. Stalemated, the French finally desisted in 1678. In the meantime, Spinoza, who was deeply troubled by De Witt's murder, was outed by followers of the Prince as the author of the *Theological-Political Treatise*. Spinoza's friends continued to protect him. His book was proscribed everywhere; even the tolerant Netherlands banned it in 1674. The year Spinoza died, 1677, Prince William married his cousin Mary, the daughter of another English uncle who became King James II in 1685.

As a Catholic, James II was deemed to be a threat by many in Anglican England and Presbyterian Scotland. Prince William was afraid that James II would enter into a new alliance with Catholic France. Some of England's nobles began to conspire with the Stadtholder; both he and his wife were in the line of succession to the English throne.

Once he received firm assurances of support, William organized a Dutch invasion of England. He used state resources to advance his personal political agenda. The fleet he launched in 1688 was larger than the Spanish Armada of 1588. It carried 35,000 men, including cavalry with their horses. It was the massive assault that the Spanish had planned but failed to execute a century beforehand. The winds this time were favorable. James II had little support and eventually fled to France. The Dutch invasion was recast as England's Glorious Revolution.

Through negotiations with Parliament, William consented to a Bill of Rights. England became in effect a constitutional monarchy. The Prince of Orange and his wife were jointly crowned as King William III and Queen Mary II. In 1689 the new King issued the Act of Toleration, assuring religious freedom to all Protestant subjects. Catholic Ireland rebelled. Many Protestant nobles contested Parliament's authority to depose James II, who was after all God's duly appointed sovereign. War and intrigue in support of the deposed king continued for years. Nevertheless, under Dutch military leadership, the rebellions were eventually quashed.

In addition to extending religious toleration, William III brought in Dutch experts in finance, drainage, commerce, and military affairs. In 1694 he chartered the Bank of England, which was modeled on the Bank of Amsterdam. Reforms carried out over generations in the Netherlands were transplanted into England over the span of a single decade. The reforms contributed greatly to the country's prosperity and global dominance during the eighteenth century.

Dutch notions of freedom, tolerance, and republican government took hold in the British colonies of North America. They reached the future United States by way of England following the Glorious Revolution, from the former colony of New Netherlands, and by the relatively free flow of ideas from continental Europe. The city of New Amsterdam retained its charter and many of its customs when it became New York City. Dutch influence is evident from words borrowed into American English such as cookie rather than the British biscuit and boss rather than master for an employer. The British dismissively referred to Americans when they rebelled as Yankees—a name that still sticks—which derives from the Dutch name Janke, or Johnny. It should be noted that those from America's former secessionist southern states tend to associate the Yankee label only with northerners.

Bayle. France throughout the period we're considering was a leading center of scientific and philosophical innovation. However, pressure from its absolute monarchy, the powerful Church, and an entrenched nobility began to snuff out incipient freedoms. A prominent intellectual, Pierre Bayle (1647–1706), abandoned France when the Protestant academy at which he held a chair in philosophy was closed in 1681. The tolerance enshrined in the Edict of Nantes of 1598 was finally revoked in 1685 by Louis XIV. Protestant clergy were given two weeks to convert to Catholicism. Calvinist Protestants known as Huguenots fled from France, even though emigration was prohibited as a capital offense.

Bayle took up residence in Rotterdam in the United Provinces. He became a professor there as well but lost his chair in philosophy in an academic dispute in 1693. Bayle began publishing his most influential work, the *Historical and Critical Dictionary*, beginning in 1697. The series became the touchstone for European Enlightenment philosophers, including the Encyclopedists who sought to codify and expand access to knowledge. Bayle, although Calvinist, was in fact an unabashed Pyrrhonist. As an outspoken proponent of tolerance, "truth" for Bayle was mostly mere opinion. The famous French philosopher and Encyclopedist Voltaire (1694–1778) called Bayle the greatest dialectician to have ever written.

Bayle condemned authoritarianism and violence, especially in matters of religion and philosophy. His skepticism turned him away from rationalists such as Descartes. Even worse for him was Aristotle. Bayle criticized the fact that governments continued to require the use of Aristotle's texts in the universities. Aristotle and his works were treated with the same reverence in academia as the saints and scriptures were in the cathedrals and monasteries. In addition to his powerful critique of Aristotle and his influence on Voltaire and others, Bayle served as the source of the Pyrrhonism taken up by the eminent Scottish philosopher David Hume (1711–1776).

Newton and Locke. Great Britain's rise in the realm of science was cemented during the time of Sir Isaac Newton (1642–1727). The brilliant mathematician and physicist took the astronomical studies of his predecessors and deduced that the forces acting on the moon and other orbiting bodies were in fact the same as those that caused an apple to fall to the earth. At the time, the Ptolemaic system remained official Church dogma. The sky above consisted of concentric spheres rotating about the stable earth. Galileo had been forced by the Inquisition to recant his advocacy of an earth that moves. With Newton, a solid and testable theory emerged that united the heavens and earth in a single cosmos.

Newton's friend the philosopher John Locke (1632–1704) incorporated the new scientific method into a theory of knowledge. We can learn important and useful things by observation, testing, and theorizing. Knowledge, however, is probabilistic; science doesn't deliver absolute truth. Theories might appear to be true, yet they can be revised or rejected based on new data or discoveries. Widely acclaimed as Britain's "father of liberty," Locke lived in exile in Holland for five crucial years before returning to England in the wake of the Glorious Revolution.

A New Paradigm. We can see that in less than two centuries the European intellectual world underwent a dramatic paradigm shift. Dogmatism and belief in absolutes began to break down. Mitigated skepticism, open questioning, tolerance, and expanding liberties changed the tenor of the times. Although we touched on but a few names, they were all part of an interconnected milieu. Eighteenth century writers and thinkers popularized the intellectual framework that emerged during the seventeenth century. Common people began to resist oppression and demand new freedoms. Voltaire in France, David Hume in Great Britain, and countless others carried on the work of the Enlightenment. In the latter part of the century, the American and French Revolutions forged a paradigm shift in the institutions and role of government that continues to echo like a shot around the world.

In the first chapter of Part Two, we considered what is now mostly viewed as the quaint notion of collective punishment for sin. Eighteenth century thinkers sought out natural explanations for various phenomena, rather than relying on divine intervention as being their cause. Deism, the belief in non-personal divine providence, began to spread. Should there actually be a principle of cosmic justice, the Lisbon earthquake, tsunami, and fire of 1755 might stand as its exemplar. Engorged on the riches extracted from Brazil, Africa, and Asia through the relentless toil of the enslaved and oppressed, Lisbon had by then become the wealthiest city in the world. On All Saints Day, 1 November 1755, a massive earthquake occurred off Portugal's coast. It could be felt throughout Europe and the Atlantic region. Buildings collapsed. Candles lit for the holy day fell and began a conflagration. About forty minutes after the main quake, a tsunami rolled up the Tagus River into Lisbon's port. An estimated 50,000 people died that day; Lisbon was leveled.

France's great social critic Voltaire was among those deeply stunned by the Lisbon catastrophe. He had previously embraced the ideas of the German philosopher Liebniz. A brilliant man and coinventor of calculus, Liebniz believed in a benevolent God who had created the best of all possible worlds. The trade-offs God had made led to some things being not quite so good as others. Yet the overall combination was the best one possible. Lisbon and other horrors finally convinced Voltaire that no such resolution to the problem of evil was viable. He discussed the earthquake in one of his most popular books, *Candide, or Optimism*. The work was a biting attack on the abuses of power and religious authority common in his day. In it, Voltaire ridiculed Liebniz through the figure of the philosopher Pangloss, who claimed the world to be the best among those possible, regardless of the repeated disasters faced by the story's protagonists. *Candide* was but one of the bricks tossed in the run-up to the French Revolution. Despite Voltaire and others abandoning belief in divine providence, many saw Lisbon's earthquake as punishment of some sort, although for and by what was in dispute.

President Abraham Lincoln (1809–1865) of the United States attributed the calamity of the American Civil War to the sin of slavery. He speculated that the nation was paying in blood and treasure for every last cent painfully squeezed from the lives and labors of slaves. Divine providence ordained certain victory for the Union while castigating the nation as a whole. Lincoln believed that America, a nation "conceived in Liberty," dedicated to the proposition that "all men are created equal," would have a "new birth of freedom" with the Union restored and slavery abolished forever. He didn't live to see it.

The twentieth century gave us the horrors of totalitarians, warmongers, and fascists gaining control of advanced weaponry and technologies. On the positive side, during the latter part of the century new scientific tools unlocked the secrets of our genes, showing conclusively the common origins and oneness of humanity. We now live under a balance of terror, wherein the threat of mutual annihilation has tamped down overt hostilities among the world's major powers. Is there a path forward by which we can accentuate and reinforce that which binds us together?

I'd like to suggest that the views of Pyrrho can serve as an antidote to absolutism. Europe's Pyrrhonists of past centuries borrowed piecemeal from Sextus to formulate new theories of knowledge and mitigated skepticism. For the most part, they neglected the original spiritual aspiration of Pyrrhonism. The purpose of the dialectical technique isn't to engage in debate; it's to overcome one's inner tendencies to accept or cling to mistaken views about reality. Only by steadfastly turning away from rigid beliefs that are unsupported by everyday experience can one calmly enjoy life. The focus isn't to best others. Naturally, we might use dialectical arguments to counter those who insist on asserting positions. We undermine their positions by challenging faulty presumptions, not by making additional dogmatic claims.

Sextus' writings, as mentioned, in a sense fell from the sky. No teachers who actually lived as Pyrrhonists transmitted Pyrrhonism to Renaissance Europe. That isn't to deny that many important and useful developments came from the work of those inspired by Sextus. What we can note is that there might be an untapped spiritual vein lying within Pyrrhonism. A dose of Pyrrho's philosophy could help us mitigate the corrosive effects of absolutist viewpoints, such as those being messaged so intensely across today's media platforms. Vehement postings have instigated inhumane bullying and, in some countries, even murderous rampages. Totalitarian or absolutist propaganda in particular deserves to be trounced.

By now it's likely you've acquired some sense of the reasons why Dutch and Portuguese attitudes differed in the days of Dutch Brazil. In many respects, the Dutch Republic served as the incubator or testing ground for the ideas and institutions that shape much of today's world. Liberty has in a sense triumphed. Yet the work is incomplete; the quest for liberty begins anew in each generation.

To what extent should liberty be limited in the interests of fairness or communal peace? Full equality of outcomes is appealing but would necessitate draconian restrictions on individuals and their choices in life. At what point is liberty so curtailed that priceless freedoms have been surrendered to the thug, party boss, surveillance state, mobster, intelligence agency, zealot, or despot? Freedom for a privileged few tramples equality underfoot. The Dutch started taking steps down a blended path. Liberty mitigated by equality—as with skepticism mitigated by ordinary knowledge—could well be the most humane path for all of us to tread.

Appendix

A Dialectical Encounter

The following fictitious dialectical encounter took place in February 2020 at an undisclosed location in California, between Cosmo, a cosmologist, and Dia, a dialectician (with apologies to D. Hume).

Cosmo: The universe is 13.8 billion years old.

Dia: Relative to what?

Cosmo: What do you mean, relative to what? It began 13.8 billion years ago, relative to today.

Dia: You didn't understand my question. To which years do you refer?

Cosmo: Very well, these are Earth years, 13.8 billion Earth years.

Dia: And did the Earth exist 13.8 billion years ago?

Cosmo: Of course not. The Earth is around 4.6 billion years old.

Dia: So you're projecting back the years relative to something that didn't exist at the time.

Cosmo: What of it?

Dia: Well, correct me if I'm wrong, isn't time relative to velocity?

Cosmo: Certainly, Einstein's General Theory of Relativity tells us that.

Dia: What was the length of a year or the velocity of the Earth 4.6 billion years ago?

Cosmo: We don't know exactly. We have estimates.

DIA: But we can't say with precision that the universe was 9.2 billion years old using the length of a year at the time our planet first formed.

COSMO: That's true. However, we have to apply a standard, which is current Earth years.

DIA: You're applying a localized standard to the entire universe. Isn't that arrogant?

COSMO: Not at all. Without baseline assumptions we can't engage in the work of science. We rely on General Relativity, for instance, because the predictive power of Einstein's theory has held up in observations.

DIA: I grant you that science is based on testable theories and assumptions.

COSMO: You seem to accept General Relativity. By running its equations in reverse we end up at a starting point 13.8 billion years ago.

DIA: A theory is useful if it explains things. As you noted, General Relativity has been very successful. It predicts black holes, for example, which were later validated through observations. So based on accepted theories and observations, one could claim the universe is 13.8 billion current Earth years old.

COSMO: Quite so.

DIA: Yet I'm troubled by other aspects of your assertion. May I continue?

COSMO: Yes, of course.

DIA: Your claim is questionable even for the incipient Earth. What about other frames of reference?

COSMO: Such as?

DIA: Einstein imagined time as experienced at the speed of light. How about that?

COSMO: Well, at the speed of light, per Einstein time freezes due to time dilation.

DIA: So from the perspective of a photon, the universe isn't 13.8 billion years old. It's timeless.

COSMO: But you can't possibly assert such a thing. The universe has a fixed beginning.

DIA: It might have one, but I'm not making any assertions. We don't really know, do we?

COSMO: You're extrapolating from a single phenomenon to make a trivial point.

DIA: How so? Light isn't really singular, it's everywhere. Don't other phenomena travel at its speed?

COSMO: All massless particles in a vacuum travel at the speed of light.

DIA: That would include electromagnetic radiation, correct? What about massless particles not in a vacuum or particles that have an infinitesimal mass? Wouldn't all such particles experience time much differently than we do?

COSMO: Let's just acknowledge that the science is settled: the universe is 13.8 billion years old from the perspective of today's Earth.

DIA: You didn't originally qualify your statement. You've recast it as relative to a particular timeframe of one planet, which makes it parochial, not universal.

COSMO: Isn't the perspective from where we stand today the only one that matters?

DIA: No. It's only one very limited view. We can't claim a universal starting point based on this.

COSMO: The equations of General Relativity, as I described, when run in reverse give us a starting point 13.8 billion years ago. Observations support this. The universe began as a singularity of infinite density and temperature. There were no other initial frames of reference. Einstein's theory is beyond questioning.

DIA: Can General Relativity be extended to the conditions of the singularity?

COSMO: The equations of General Relativity do not apply in the singularity.

DIA: If General Relativity doesn't apply, then how can we assume its equations in reverse lead to something it can't explain? How do we get from the singularity to the early universe?

COSMO: The theory of cosmic inflation describes how the universe emerged from the singularity.

DIA: Isn't that theory disputed? Doesn't it assume without a causal explanation that during a miniscule fraction of the first second after the Big Bang, which also lacks a causal explanation, the universe expanded exponentially at an inconceivable rate?

COSMO: Of course we have alternative theories. Those accepted by contemporary cosmologists point in the direction of the Big Bang and cosmic inflation.

DIA: Are all of these alternative theories supported by everything in the cosmos?

COSMO: We only have access to the causally linked events within our cosmological horizon, which is limited by the speed of light and the age of the universe. Beyond that boundary we must make assumptions. The detectable parts of the cosmos are consistent with the main theories. Since the cosmos appears to be uniform, we can extrapolate that the undetectable parts are the same as those within our cosmological horizon.

DIA: You seem to privilege the isolated perspective of present-day Earth. You make claims about the entire universe based solely on observations from the part within our cosmological horizon. Does anyone know whether our part is half of the whole universe, or one percent of the whole, or just one instance within an infinite cosmos?

Cosmo: I need to emphasize that cosmology, like all of the natural sciences, relies on well tested theories and assumptions. If you go beyond such theories and assumptions, then you're dealing with nothing more than unfruitful speculation.

Dia: There's nothing wrong with admitting that something isn't known with certainty. We dialecticians suspend judgment in such cases.

Cosmo: Dialecticians are not scientists. Scientists must stake out positions on important matters.

Dia: I acknowledge that science progresses through principled debate. However, there's a difference between arguing a position and claiming it represents an ultimate truth. There clearly isn't certainty about what lies beyond event horizons. Even in our galactic neighborhood, experts disagree about what exists beyond the event horizons of black holes. Isn't there an equivalence between the event horizons of black holes and the cosmological horizon?

Cosmo: I must reiterate what I said about unfruitful speculation. The same can be said of whatever exists beyond event horizons. Our assumption is that uniformity prevails.

Dia: Regardless, you've affirmed that theories and assumptions, not obvious facts, underlie your claim that the universe is 13.8 billion years old. Isn't it possible that time was meaningless during and immediately after the hypothetical Big Bang?

Cosmo: The Big Bang has been solidly established both theoretically and through observations. It is reasonable to apply measurements based on our current frame of reference. To assert otherwise borders on sheer ignorance. Half of the 2019 Nobel Prize in Physics was awarded to James Peebles precisely for his work in describing the evolution of the early universe. Do you seriously contend that the most prestigious of all awards was granted by mistake?

DIA: I'm not making assertions and wouldn't be so presumptuous as to contend such a thing. We need only consider the words of Dr. Peebles himself. Even though his theoretical work focused on the first few seconds of the universe, he disapproves of the term "Big Bang" and is skeptical about what we can actually know about the very beginning of things. He was recently quoted as stating that we have no good theory about something like a beginning and shouldn't even be thinking in those terms. His humility in the face of uncertainty is exemplary. Given his comments, how can you continue to claim a known age for the universe?

COSMO: The current model is widely accepted and remains our best estimate. I'm sticking with it in the absence of a more convincing theory.

DIA: My understanding is that there are physicists who have postulated nonlinear models, such as multiverses, for the ongoing evolution of the cosmos. Other theorists engaged with quantum mechanics and the hard problem of consciousness are questioning assumptions about the reality of spacetime and perceived or detectable objects within it. We don't know which—if any—of the various cosmological theories will remain viable over time. How can you assert the universe's age when it depends so heavily on disputed theories and assumptions?

COSMO: We must be able to assert an age! What's the alternative? If we as experts don't proclaim a fixed beginning for the universe, then people will fall back into superstition. They'll believe in fables about creation. Uncertainty leads to chaos.

DIA: People deal with uncertainty all the time. You underestimate our species. You concur, based on current theories and evidence, which I'm not questioning here, that for photons and other massless particles in a vacuum time is frozen. Therefore, for an array of phenomena it seems the universe has no beginning, or is constantly beginning, or else the entire concept of a beginning is meaningless. Our access to the cosmos is limited by event horizons; we don't know with certainty what lies beyond them. Much about the hypothetical beginning is described by theories which are in dispute.

If there's no coherent way to speak of a common beginning for the full array of cosmic phenomena, then we can't truly discern the universe's age, or whether or not it even has an age.

COSMO: I won't concede that, because it isn't the current consensus among cosmologists. I'd be ridiculed.

DIA: You don't need to concede. This isn't a debate. But in regard to your claim that the universe is 13.8 billion years old: it no more is than is not, or both is and is not, or neither is nor is not.

Suggested Readings and References

PORTUGUESE SOURCES

Calado, Frei Manuel. *O Valeroso Lucideno e Triunfo da Liberdade*. 1648. Reprint, São Paulo, Brazil: Edições Cultura, 1943.

Mello, José Antonio Gonsalves de. *Frei Manuel Calado do Salvador: Religioso da Ordem de São Paulo, pregador apostólico por Sua Santidade, cronista da Restauração*. Recife, Brazil: Universidade do Recife, 1954.

----------------. *Tempo dos Flamengos: Influência da ocupação holandesa na vida e na cultura do norte do Brasil*. 4th edition. Rio de Janeiro, Brazil: Topbooks Universidade Editora, 2001.

IN ENGLISH

Beckwith, Christopher. *Greek Buddha: Pyrrho's Encounter with Early Buddhism in Central Asia*. Princeton, NJ: Princeton University Press, 2015.

Boxer, C.R. *Four Centuries of Portuguese Expansion, 1415-1825: A Succinct Survey*. Berkeley, CA: University of California Press, 1972.

----------------. *The Dutch in Brazil 1624-1654*. Oxford, UK: Clarendon Press, 1957.

Crowley, Roger. *Conquerors: How Portugal Forged the First Global Empire*. New York: Random House, 2015.

Brookhiser, Richard. *Give Me Liberty: A History of America's Exceptional Idea*. New York: Basic Books, 2019.

Empiricus, Sextus. *Outlines of Scepticism*. Edited by Julia Annas and J. Barnes. Cambridge, UK: Cambridge University Press, 2000.

Floridi, Luciano. *Sextus Empiricus: The Transmission and Recovery of Pyrrhonism*. New York: Oxford University Press, 2002.

Groessen, Michiel van, ed. *The Legacy of Dutch Brazil*. New York: Cambridge University Press, 2014.

Hendrix, Scott. *Martin Luther: Visionary Reformer*. London: Yale University Press, 2015.

Hoffman, Donald. *The Case Against Reality: How Evolution Hid the Truth from Our Eyes*. London: Penguin Random House, 2019.

Israel, Jonathan. *Enlightenment Contested: Philosophy, Modernity, and the Emancipation of Man 1670–1752*. 2006. Reprint, Oxford UK, Oxford University Press, 2013.

----------------. *The Dutch Republic: Its Rise, Greatness, and Fall 1477-1806*. Oxford, UK: Oxford University Press, 1995.

Jardine, Lisa. *Going Dutch: How England Plundered Holland's Glory*. London: Harper Press, 2008.

Kagan, Richard, and P. Morgan, eds. *Atlantic Diasporas: Jews, Conversos, and Crypto-Jews in the Age of Mercantilism, 1500-1800*. Baltimore, MD: The Johns Hopkins University Press, 2009.

Kuzminski, Adrian. *Pyrrhonism: How the Ancient Greeks Reinvented Buddhism*. Lanham, MD: Rowman & Littlefield Publishers, Inc., 2008.

Lery, Jean de. *History of a Voyage to the Land of Brazil*. Translated by Janet Whatley. Berkeley, CA: University of California Press, 1990.

Mattoso, Katia M. de Queiros. *To Be a Slave in Brazil, 1550-1888*. Translated by Arthur Goldhammer. New Brunswick, NJ: Rutgers University Press, 1986.

McEvilley, Thomas. *The Shape of Ancient Thought: Comparative Studies in Greek and Indian Philosophies*. New York: Allworth Press, 2002.

Polasky, Janet. *Revolutions Without Borders: The Call to Liberty in the Atlantic World*. New Haven, CT: Yale University Press, 2015.

Popkin, Richard. *The History of Scepticism from Savonarola to Bayle*. New York: Oxford University Press, 2003.

Spinoza, Benedict de. *Theological-Political Treatise.* Translated by Michael Silverthorne and J. Israel. Cambridge, UK: Cambridge University Press, 2007.

----------------. *A Spinoza Reader: The Ethics and Other Works.* Edited and translated by Edwin Curley. Princeton, NJ: Princeton University Press, 1994.

Zagorin, Perez. *How the Idea of Religious Toleration Came to the West.* Princeton, NJ: Princeton University Press, 2003.

www.ingramcontent.com/pod-product-compliance
Lightning Source LLC
LaVergne TN
LVHW041152080426
835511LV00006B/560